Spoken Burmese

BOOK TWO

by WILLIAM S. CORNYN

Identical with the edition prepared for

THE UNITED STATES ARMED FORCES INSTITUTE

HENRY HOLT AND COMPANY

The Armed Forces edition of this book was published by the Linguistic Society of America and the Intensive Language Program of the American Council of Learned Societies.

CONTENTS

PART III

PART IV

PART V

PART THREE

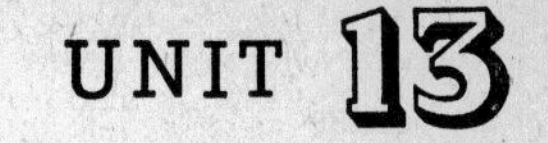

RAILROAD

SECTION A—BASIC SENTENCES

To the Group Leader: If you have been working only with the phonograph records, without any Guide, you will be on your own from now on. When the group goes through the *Basic Sentences* and the *Listening In* sections, choose someone with good pronunciation to do the reading. From now on all the group members will have to be particularly on the watch to detect and correct faulty pronunciation.

ENGLISH EQUIVALENTS	AIDS TO LISTENING
	kóu sán yà
straight ahead	*šèi tèdè*
That big building you see up ahead is the railroad station, my friend	*θaŋéjîn, šèi tèdègà myín-yàdè yóunjîhá mîyathâ búdáyóumbê*
	máun kalaʔ
Where are the tickets sold?	*lephmaʔ béhmá yâunðalê*
	kóu sán yà
opening, aperture, hole	*ʔapauʔ*
They're sold right at this window.	*dí ʔapauphmábê yâundé*
Prome [city of Prome]	*pyéi myòu*
How much is one ticket [to go] to Prome?	*pyéi myòugóu θwâbòu mîyathâ lephmaʔ tazáun bélauʔ yâunðalê*

sayêi (clerk)

class	*ʔatân*
What class do you want to go?	*bé ʔatânnè θwâjínðalê*

kóu sán yà

first class	*pathamàdân*
How much is one first class ticket?	*pathamàdân lephmaʔ tazáun bélaullê*

sayêi

It comes to Rs. 15 8 As. 9 pies.	*shè ŋâjaʔ šippê kôubáin càdè*
second	*dùtìyà*
second class	*dùtìyàdân*
Second class is Rs 10, 7 as, 3 pies.	*dùtìyàdân shéjaʔ khúnnapê θôumbáin*
third	*tatìyà*
third class	*tatìyàdân*
Third class is Rs 5, 5 as, 6 pies.	*tatìyàdân ŋâjaʔ ŋâbê chauppáin*

kóu sán yà

Very well, here's 35 rupees.	*kâumbábí, díhmá ŋwéi θôunzè ŋâjaʔ*
Give us two first class tickets.	*pathamàdân lephmaʔ hnasáun pêibá*
What time does the Prome train leave?	*pyéi mîyathâ bé ʔachéin thwemmalê*

sayêi

8:45	*kôunáyí mattîn*
It'll leave at 8:45 P.M.	*nyà kôunáyí mattîn thwellèimmé*

máun kala?

thrusts at, strikes	*thôudé*
What time is it now?	*?akhù bé hnanáyí thôubalê*

sayêi

minute	*mani?*
It's 8:20.	*šinnáyí mani? hnashé šìbí*
There's still twenty-five minutes before the train leaves.	*mîyathâ thweppòu hnashè ŋâmani? lóuðêidé*

máun kala?

I'm hungry. Where can we get dinner?	*cou? shádé, thamîn béhmá yàmalê*

kóu sán yà

We can get it in the station restaurant.	*búdáyóun thamînzáimhmá yàhnáindé*
shop, store	*sháin*
That shop ahead is the station restaurant.	*hóu šèigà sháin, búdáyóun thamînzáimbê*

máun kala?

before it leaves	*mathwekkhín*
I'll be eating (in another place)	*sâlai??ôummé*
I'll go and eat before the train leaves.	*mîyathâ mathwekkhín θwâ sâlai??ôummé*
articles, things	*pyissîdéi*
Wait here a moment with the baggage.	*díhmá pyissîdéinè khanà sàun néibá*

kóu sán yà

car, carriage	*yathâ*
platform	*phalepphâun*
Which platform does the Prome train leave from?	*pyéi yathâ bé phalepphâuŋgà thwemmalê*

sayêi

number	*námba?*
Platform number 5.	*palepphâun námba? ŋâ*

máun kala?

carries from one place to another	*θédé*
coolie	*kúlí*
Where's there a porter?	*θébòu kúlí béhmálê*

kóu sán yà

is hot, is troubled	*púdé*
Don't worry; there are some over there.	*mapúbánè, hóuhmá šìbádé*
Hey, two coolies come here.	*hè, kúlí hnayau? dígóu lábá*
the space behind (a thing)	*nau?*
having fetched, fetching	*yú pî*
Follow us and bring these things.	*dí pyissîdéi yú pî, couttòu naukkóu laikkhèbá*
This is the Prome car; let's get on.	*dá pyéi yathâbê, teccàzòu*

máun kala?

railway car	*twê*
is tight, is crowded	*catté*
It's very crowded in this car.	*dí twêhmá lú θei? catté*

It's crowded in the rear car, too.	*nauttwêhmálê lú catté*
changes place, moves	*pyâundé*
if one rides	*sîyín*
is loose, is not tight, is not crowded	*cháundé*
If we move to a forward car there'll be more room, I think.	*šèidwêgóu pyâun sîyín, lú cháunlèimmé, thíndé*

kóu sán yà

Come on, let's go.	*lá, θwâjàzòu*

máun kala?

porter's fee	*kúlígà*
How much should I pay the porter?	*kúlígà bélau? pêiyàmalê*

kóu sán yà

give (definite)	*pêilaippá*
Give him 12 annas.	*θôumma? pêilaippá*

máun kala?

drinking water	*θauyyéi*
Is there drinking water on the train?	*mîyathâbóhmá θauyyéi šìðalâ*

kóu sán yà

Yes, there is.	*šìdé*
You can get drinking water only in the first and second class.	*pathamàdânnè dùtìyàdâmhmáðá yàhnáindé*
You can't get water in the third class.	*tatìyàdâmhmá yéi mayàhnáimbû*

máun kala?

traveller	*khayîðé*
if he is thirsty	*yéi ŋayyín*
If that's the case, what do third class passengers do when they get thirsty?	*dílóu shóuyín, tatìyàdân sîdè khayîðémyâ yéi ŋayyín, bènè loummalê*

kóu sán yà

There's nothing to worry about.	*sôuyéinzayá mašìbábû*
any station at all	*be búdáyóummashóu*
At any station where the train stops you can get food and drink.	*bé búdáyóummashóu, mîyathâ yattè ?akhá, sâzayá θaussayámyâ yàhnáindé*

máun kala?

place to sleep	*?eipphòu néiyá*
Is there a place to sleep in the third class?	*tatìyàdâmhmá ?eipphòu néiyá šìðalâ*

kóu sán yà

Not in the third class.	*tatìyàdâmhmá ?eipphòu néiyá mašìbû*

máun kala?

arrives	*yautté*
What time in the morning will we get to Prome?	*mane? bé ?achéin pyéi myòugóu yaummalê*

kóu sán yà

I can't say for sure.	*?ahmán mapyôhnáimbû*

once, one time	*takhau?*
not once	*takhaummà*
I myself have never [once] gone to Prome by train.	*cou? kóudáinlê pyéimyòugóu mîyathânè takhaummà maθwâbûbû*
We'll probably get there about 5 or 6 o'clock in the morning, I think.	*mane? ŋânáyí chaunnáyílau? yaullèimmé, thíndé*

máun kala?

is long in time	*cádé*
long (time)	*cájá*
How long will you be in Prome?	*khímbyâ bélau? cájá pyéi myòuhmá néimalê*

kóu sán yà

I won't stay long.	*cájá manéibábû*
day (24 hours)	*ye?*
figures out, plans	*sei? kûdé*
I plan to stay just about a day or two.	*taye? hnayellaupphê néimélòu, sei? kûdé*
wanders, roams about	*lédé*
steamer	*θîmbô*
I want to take a trip by steamer to Mandalay, too.	*mândalêi myòugóulê θîmbônè θwâ léjíndé*

SECTION B—WORD STUDY AND REVIEW OF BASIC SENTENCES

1. Word Study

A. -téi, -twéi

dí pyissîdéigóu θîmbôbógóu θé yé θwâbá	Take these things and carry them aboard the steamer.
díhmá pyissîdéinè khanà sáun néibá	Wait here a moment with the things.
ʔakhândêhmá lúdéi šìdé	There are people in the room.
dí hádéigóu yú θwâ	Take these things away.
dí sáʔouttéigóu wéjíndé	I want to buy these books.

The syllable *-téi* (sometimes pronounced *-twéi*) in noun expressions denotes a sort of collective plural. We pointed out in Unit 10 that the verb *myâdé* modifying a moun was a sign of an indefinite sort of plural. The unmodified noun may also represent the plural. Thus you will hear *pyissî* 'thing, things,' *pyissîdéi* 'things (as a group)', *pyissîmyâ* 'thing, things (indefinite or vague)'.

B. tabáin 'one pie'

shè ŋâjaʔ šippê kôubáin	Rs. 15, 8 as., 9 pies
shéjaʔ khúnnapê θôumbáin	Rs. 10, 7 as., 3 pies
ŋâjaʔ ŋâbê chauppáin	Rs. 5, 5 as., 6 pies

In Unit 9 you learned that three *pies* make one *pice*, four *pice* make one *anna*, sixteen *annas* make one *rupee.* Prices are rarely quoted in *pies*. Only in accounting and as here in quoting prices of railroad tickets are *pies* used. You will notice that the number of *pies* is always such that the amount quoted comes out even in *pice.* In the examples quoted above you see 3 *pies*, 6 *pies*, 9 *pies*, that is, 1 *pice*, 2 *pice*, 3 *pice*. Payment is always made in *pice*, not in *pies* which are no longer in circulation.

C. Time

bé hnanáyí šìbalê	What time is it?
bé hnanáyí thôubalê	What time is it?
tanáyí, hnanáyí, θôunnáyí thôubí	It's 1 o'clock, 2 o'clock, 3 o'clock.
tanáyí, hnanáyí, θôunnáyí šìbí	It's 1 o'clock, etc.
ŋâmaniʔ, shémaniʔ, shè ŋâmaniʔ	5 minutes, 10 minutes, 15 minutes

maniʔ hnashé, maniʔ θôunzé, maniʔ lêizé, maniʔ ŋâzé	20, 30, 40, 50 minutes
θôunnáyí shémaniʔ šìbí	It's 3:10.
lêináyí shè ŋâmaniʔ šìbí	It's 4:15.
ŋânáyí maniʔ hnashé šìbí	It's 5:20.
chaunnáyí hnashè ŋâmaniʔ šìbí	It's 6:25.
khúnnanáyígwê šìbí	It's 7:30.
šinnáyí maniʔ lêizé šìbí	It's 8:40.
nyà kôunáyí mattîn thwellèimmè	It will leave at 8:45 P.M.
maneʔ kôunáyí mattîn thwellèimmé	It will leave at 8:45 A.M.
shénáyí shé manittîn šìbí	It's ten to ten.

Time is told in Burmese in hours *náyí* and minutes *maniʔ*. The question is either *bé hnanáyí šìbalê* 'how many hours exist already?' or *bé hnanáyí thôubalê* 'how many hours have struck already?' The answer is either *šìbí* or *thôubí* for the even hours: *chaunnáyí šìbí*, *chaunnáyí thôubí* 'it's 6 o'clock'. If the answer is in hours and minutes the answer is usually *šìbí: šinnáyí maniʔ hnashé šìbí*.

In counting minutes the number *hnashé*, *θôunzé*, *lêizé* follow. The others precede.

From forty-five minutes to the end of the hour time is reckoned back from the following hour. *kôunáyí mattîn* '9 hours less a quarter' *shénáyí shémanittîn* '10 hours less 10 minutes'.

khwêdé 'cuts in half' is used for the half hour. *tanáyígwê* 'one thirty'.

nyà 'night' and *maneʔ* 'morning' are used respectively for P.M. and A.M.

D. *ma . . . khín* 'before'

mathwekkhín	before one leaves
maʔeikkhín	before one goes to sleep
maθwâgín	before one goes
malágín	before one comes
masâgín	before one eats
mayaukkhín	before one arrives
macágín	before long
khúnnanáyí makhwêgín	before seven-thirty
šinnáyí mathôugín	before eight o'clock
môu maywágín	before it rains

-khín is attached to negated verbs with the meaning 'before'. The whole expression is then treated as a noun expression.

E. Burmese Sentences

1. Narrative sentences

pathamàdâŋgà θeiʔ zêi cìdé	The first class charge is very expensive.
nepphyíŋgá θwâmelòu, seiʔ kûdé	I thought I'd go tomorrow.

tatìyàdâmhmálê lú θei? catté	It's very crowded in the third class.
θîmbô thwettòmè	The steamer is about to leave.
?akhú θwâlaippá?ôummé	Well, I'll be going now.
cúndó šèidwêhmá tháin néimé	I'll be sitting in a forward car.
hô, yauppí	Ah, we've arrived.
dayyathâ ya? néibí	The streetcar is coming (is in sight).
šinnáyí mani? hnashé šibí	It's 8:20.
mábáyè	I'm fine.
houkkè	That's so.

A Burmese sentence which has as its final particle one of the set *-té*, *-mé*, *-pí* we call a *Narrative* sentence. Sometimes the final particle *-té* is replaced by the final particle *-yè*, or *-kè*. The final particle *-té* refers to either present or past time, *-mé* refers to future time; *-pí* refers to an action or a condition which is completed or which has already started.

2. *Imperative sentences*

lá	Come! Come on!
dígóu lábá	Come here (polite).
khanà sàun néibá	Wait a moment.
couttòu naukkóu laikkhèbá	Follow us.
θwâ wélaippá	Go and buy.
pêilaippá	Give (it to him).
shînjàzòu	Let's get off.
teccàzòu	Let's get on.
θwâjàzòu	Let's go.
θwâ θauccàzòu	Let's go and have a drink.

A sentence which ends in a verb expression but which does not have a final particle we call an *Imperative* sentence. An imperative sentence gives an order or makes a request. Usually in polite speech the secondary verb particle *-pá* is present.

Imperative sentences which include the speaker and someone else, like the English 'let's go', end in *-càzòu*.

3. *Equational sentences*

dùtìyàdân shéja? khúnnapê θôumbáin
díhmá ŋwéi θôunzà ŋâja?
hóu šèigà sháin, búdáyóun thamînzáimbê
dá pyéi yathâbê

Sentences which have no verb expression, and which consist of two noun expressions equated we call *Equational* sentences.

4. *Interrogative sentences*

dí ?apauphmábê yâundé	They're sold right at this window.

lephma? tazáun belau? yâunðalê	How much does one ticket sell for?
θìmbônè θwâmé	I'm going by steamer.
mîyathânè θwâmalâ	Will you go by train?
bé ?atânnè θwâmalê	What class will you go?
lêináyí thôubí	It's four o'clock.
bé hnanáyí thôubalê	What time is it?
mábáyè	I'm fine.
máyèlâ	How are you?
houkkè	It is so.
houkkèlâ	Is that so?
houyyèlâ	Is that so?

Interrogative narrative sentences consist of narrative statements followed by one of the interrogative particles *-lâ*, or *-lê*. The particle *-lê* is used when the question contains one of the interrogative nouns *bá*, *bé*, *badú*. Otherwise *-lâ* is used.

Before *-lâ*, *-lê* the final particle *-té* is replaced by *-θá-*
-mé is replaced by *-ma-*
-pí is replaced by *-pa-*
-yè and *-kè* remain unchanged.

hóu šèigà sháin búdáyóun thamînzáin
hóu šèigà sháin búdáyóun thamînzáinlâ
cúndó bamá
khímbyâ bamálâ
cúndó ?améiyìkán pyéiðâ
khímbyâ ?améiyìkán pyéiðâlâ
khímbyâ bé pyéiðâlê
khímbyâ badúlê
hóuhá bálê

Interrogative equational sentences consist of equational statements followed by one of the interrogative particles *-lâ*, or *-lê*. The particle *-lê* is used where the question contains one of the interrogative nouns *bá*, *bé*, *badú*. Otherwise *-lâ* is used.

There are no interrogative forms of imperative sentences.

5. *Minor sentences*

béhmálê	Where is it?
bélaullê	How much?
phalepphâun namba? ŋâ	Platform No. 5.
?akhân námba? ši?	Room No. 8.
?ayíŋgà ?éimhmábê	Right in the same old house.
khímbyâgô	How about you?

Many sentences do not fall into the classes listed above. These are usually fragments. We call such sentences minor sentences.

2. Covering English and Burmese of Word Study

Give the English equivalents of all Burmese expressions in the *Word Study* and the Burmese for all the English.

3. Review of Basic Sentences

Further oral practice with the first part of the *Basic Sentences*.

SECTION C—REVIEW OF BASIC SENTENCES (*Cont.*)

1. Review of Basic Sentences (*Cont.*)

Further oral practice with the second part of the *Basic Sentences*.

2. Covering the English of Basic Sentences

Check your knowledge of the meaning of all words and phrases in the *Basic Sentences*. This is individual study.

3. What Would You Say?

Answer the following questions with full sentences.

1. *šèi tèdèkà myín-yàdè yóunjîhá, bá yóunjîlê*
2. *lephmaʔ béhmá yâunðalê*
3. *lephmaʔ tazáun bélauʔ yâunðalê*
4. *pathamàdân lephmaʔ tazáun bélaullê*
5. *dùtìyàdân lephmaʔ tazáun bélaullê*
6. *tatìyàdân lephmaʔ tazáun bélaullê*
7. *bé ʔatânnè θwâjínðalê*
8. *pyéi mîyathâ bé ʔachéin thwemmalê*
9. *ʔakhù bé hnanáyí thôubalê*
10. *bé hnanáyí šíbalê*
11. *mîyathâ thwepphòu maniʔ hnashé lóuðèiðalâ*
12. *khímbyâ sháðalâ*
13. *thamîn béhmá yàhnáimmalê*
14. *hóu šèigà sháin thamînzáinlâ*
15. *mîyathâ mathwekkhín θwâ sâmalâ*
16. *pyissîdéinè badú sàun néimalê*
17. *pyéi yathâ bé phalepphâuŋgà thwemmalê*
18. *θébòu kúlí béhmálê, hóuhmá šíðalâ*
19. *dá pyéi yathâlâ*
20. *sâjínðalâ*
21. *shînjínðalâ*
22. *hóu twêhmá lú θeiʔ caθθalâ*
23. *nauttwêhmá lú caθθalâ*
24. *šèidwêhmá lú caθθalâ*
25. *šèidwêgóu pyâun sîyín, lú cháunlèimmé, thínðalâ*
26. *nauttwêhmá pyâun sîyín, lú cháunlèimmé, thínðalâ*

27. *kúlìgà bélau? pêiyàmalê*
28. *pathamàdânnè dùtìyàdâmhmá θauyyéi yàhnáinmalâ*
30. *tatìyàdâmhmá yèi yàhnáinðalê*
31. *yéi ŋayyín, bèné loummalê*
32. *thamînzáimhmá sâzayá θaussayámyâ yàhnáinðalâ*
33. *khímbyâ kóudáin yáŋgóun myòugóu θwâbûðalâ*
34. *khímbyâ dí myòuhmá bélau? cájá néimalê*
35. *mândalêi myòugóu θîmbônè θwâ léjínðalâ*
36. *couttòu ?akhân námba? bélaullê*
37. *hóu ?akhândêhmá lúdéi šìðalâ*
38. *thamîn masâgín bíyá takhwellau? θwâ θaucchinðalâ*
39. *khímbyâ ?akhù béhmá néiðalê*
40. *khímbyâ ?éin bé nâhmálê*

SECTION D—LISTENING IN

1. What Did You Say?

With the other members of your group give orally your responses to the previous exercise as the Leader calls for them.

2. Word Study Check-up

Give the Burmese for all the English equivalents in the *Word Study* as the Leader calls for them.

3. Listening In

1. Mr. Clark, Mg. Hla, and Mg. Ba start off on a trip to Prome.

máun bà: *máun hlà, khímbyâ pyéi myòu θwâ lémalâ*

máun hlà: *houppádé, nepphyíŋgá θwâmélòu, sei? kûdé*

máun bà: *mîyathânè θwâmalâ*

máun hlà: *mahoupphû, θîmbônè θwâmé*

máun kala?: *bé ?atânnè θwâmalê*

máun bà: *θîmbônè θwâmé shóuyín, pathamàdâŋgà θei? zêi cîdé tatìyàdâmhmálê lú θei? catté dùtìyàdâmhmá lú cháunlèimmé, thíndé*

máun hlà: *θwâmé shóuyín, pyissîdéi yú pî, mótókânè shînjàzòu*

[They arrived at the dock.]

máun kala?: *hô, yauppí*
máun hlà, hóu ?apauphmá dùtìyàdân lephma? θôunzáun θwâ wélaippá

máun bà: *hèi, kúlí dí pyissîdéigóu θîmbôbógóu θé yú θwâbá kúlí:* *shayájîdòu, cájá manéijàbánè θîmbô thwettòmé*

máun kala?: *couttòu ?akhân námba? bélaullê*

máun bà: *?akhân námba? ši?*

máun hlà: *?akhândêhmá θôun-yau? ?eipphòu néiyá šìðalâ*

máun bà: *šìbádé*

máun kala?: *pyissî θédè ?atwe? kúlígà paisshán bélau? pêiyàmalê*

máun bà: *ŋâmûlau? pêilaippá*

máun kala?: *θîmbôbóhmá bé ?achéin thamîn sâðalê*

máun hlà: *shè tanáyí thôu pîyín, bé ?achéimmashóu sâhnáimbádé*

máun kala?: *cou? yéi ŋatté*
thamîn masâgín bíyá takhwellau? θwâ θauccàzòu

máun bà: *couttò maθaucchímbû*
khímbyâdòu hnayau? θwâ θauppá

2. Two friends meet on the street and make an appointment.

máun bà: *máyèlâ, khímbyá*

máun hlà: *mábáyè*
khímbyâ ?akhù béhmá néiðalê

máun bà: *?ayiŋgà ?éimhmábê*

máun hlà: *kóu thûn séiŋgô, béhmálê*

máun bà: *kéu thûn séin ?éin pyâundé shóudá khímbyâ maθìðêibûlâ*

máun hlà: *maθìðêibû*
pyâundá bélau? cá θwâbalê

máun bà: *θei? macáðêibû*
lêi ŋâyellaupphê šìðêidé

máun hlà: *khímbyâ θù ?éiŋgóu yaupphûðalâ*

máun bà: *takhaummà mayaupphûbû*

máun hlà: *θù ?éin bé nâhmálê*

máun bà: *mawêibábû*
ŋâmanillau? šèi tèdè šau? θwâyín, nyábekkà šìdé taipphyújîbê

máun hlà: *khímbyâ ?akhù bé θwâmalòulê*

máun bà: *mândalêigóu dí nèi nyàyathânè θwâmalòu*

máun hlà: *yathâ bé phalepphâuŋgà thwemmalê*

máun bà: *námba? kôugà šinnáyí mani? lêizé thwemmé*

máun hlà: *kâumbí, cou? búdayóuŋgóu šinnáyí hnashè ŋâmani? ?ayau? lágèmé*

máun bà: *cúndó šèidwêhmá tháin néimé*
?akhù θwâlaippá?ôummé

SECTION E—CONVERSATION

1. Covering the Burmese of Basic Sentences

With the Burmese covered, practice until you can speak the Burmese for each English sentence without hesitation.

2. Vocabulary Check-up

Give the Burmese for all English sentences in the *Basic Sentences* as the Leader calls for it.

3. Conversation

Suggested Topics:

1. In the station: Where's the station? Where do you buy tickets? What class ticket do you want? How much is it? How much are the tickets in the other classes? What time does the train leave? Where from?
2. You have to wait. You're hungry. You want to eat. Where can you get something to eat? Go into the station restaurant and eat.
3. Call a porter and tell him when your train leaves, which train it is, which platform. Ask him to take your baggage onto the train.
4. Discuss Burmese train travel with your friend.
5. Discuss American train travel as if explaining to a Burmese.

SECTION F—CONVERSATION (*Cont.*)

Continue conversation. Additional check-up on the material of the *Basic Sentences* by the Leader if it seems necessary.

Review: Complete check-up on the material of the *Word Study* and *Basic Sentences.*

Finder List

ʔapauʔ (*pautté*)	opening, aperture, hold
ʔatân	class
bé búdáyóummashóu	any station at all

cádé	is long in time
cájá	long time
cháundé	is loose, not tight
dùtìyà	second
dùtìyàdân	second class
ʔeipphòu néiyá	place to sleep
khayîðé	traveller
kôunáyí mattîn	8:45
kúlí	coolie
kúlígà	porter's fee
lédé	wanders, roams; turns around
maniʔ	minute
mathwekkhín	before (it) leaves
námbaʔ	number
nauʔ	space behind a thing
nauttwê	rear car
pathamàdân	first class
pêilaippá	give (definitely)
phaleppháun	platform
púdé	is troubled; is hot
pyâundé	changes place, moves
pyéi myòu	Prome [City of Prome]
pyissîdéi	articles, things
sâlaiʔʔôummé	will be eating (in another place)
seiʔ kûdé	figures out, plans
sháin	shop, store
sîyín	if one rides
šèidwê	forward car
šèi tèdè	straight ahead
tatìyà	third
tatìyàdân	third class
thôudé	thrusts at, strikes
twê	railway car
takhauʔ	once, one time
takhaummà	not once, never
θauyyéi	drinking water
θédé	carries from one place to another
θìmbô	steamer
yathâ	car, carriage
yautté	arrives
yeʔ	24 hour day
yéi ŋayyín	if thirsty
yú pî	fetching, having fetched

UNIT 14

STEAMSHIP

SECTION A—BASIC SENTENCES

ENGLISH EQUIVALENTS	AIDS TO LISTENING
	máun hlà
is about to leave	*thwettòmé*
Mg. Kyaw, the steamer is about to leave.	*máun có, θîmbô thwettòmé*
loosens, unties	*phyoutté*
The rope is being cast off.	*côu phyouˀ néibí*
	máun có
enjoys oneself, is glad, is happy	*pyódé*
rejoices, is joyful	*šwíndé*
happiness, enjoyment	*pyóbyó šwínšwín*
Have a good time, the three of you.	*khímbyâdòu θôun-yauˀ pyóbyó šwínšwín θwâjàbá*
is well, healthy	*májádé*
well-being, state of health	*májâun chájâun*
a writing, something written, a letter	*sá*
writes	*yêidé*
forgets	*mèidé*
When you get to Mandalay don't forget to write [to tell us] how you are.	*mândalêi yauttè ˀakhá, májâun chájâun sá yêibòu mamèibánè*

	máun hlà
feels easy in mind	*sei? chàdé*
Don't worry.	*sei? chàbá*
the true facts	*?acôu ?acâun*
the whole, all	*?akóun*
will write (definitely)	*yêilaippàmé*
We'll write everything about how	*?acôu ?acâun ?akóun yêilaippàmé*
	máun bà
Well, goodbye.	*θwâdòmé nó*
	máun có
Goodbye.	*θwâdò nó*
	máun kala?
is fast	*myándé*
speed	*myámmyán*
old fellow, my friend	*kwé*
Hurry up, old man.	*myámmyán lábá, kwé*
[On the boat.]	
playing cards	*phê*
card game (circle)	*phêwâin*
plays	*kazâdé*
the playing (of a game)	*kazâ néijàdá*
is fun, ('is good for being happy')	*pyózayá kâundé*
It's a lot of fun playing cards in that big game.	*hóu phêwâinjîhmá phê kazâ néijàdá θei? pyózayá kâundé*

a hand at cards, 'house'	*?éin*
a hand each	*ta?éinzí*
let's play	*kazâyà?áun*
Let's get in [too] and each play a hand.	*couttòulê ta?éinzí wín kazâyà?áun*
[Time interval]	
	máun kala?
How goes it, Mg. Ba?	*máun bà, bènélê*
wins	*náindé*
Are you winning?	*náin-yèlâ*
	máun bà
I won a little at first.	*?asàdò nênê náindé*
winnings	*?anáin*
loses	*šôundé*
capital, stock in trade	*?ayîn*
I've lost my winnings and now I'm back where I started.	*?akhùdò ?anáin šôun pî, ?ayîmbê*
How about you?	*khímbyâgô, bènélê*
	máun kala?
As for me, I've won about five rupees.	*couttò ŋâjallau? náin néibí*
	máun hlà
more than we	*couttòude?*
luck	*kán*
is lucky, has good luck	*kán kâundé*
In that case, you're luckier than we are.	*dílóu shóuyín, khímbyâ couttòude? kán kâundé*

máun bà

let's eat	*sâyàˀáun*
Come on, let's go eat.	*lá, thamîn θwâ sâyàˀáun*

máun hlà

school friend, school mate	*câun néibeˀ θaŋéjîn*
Over there's a school friend of mine, Ko Aye Pe	*hóuhmá câun néibeˀ θaŋéjîn kóu ˀêi phéi*

kóu ˀêi phéi

Well, if it isn't Mr. Hla!	*hà, kóu hlàbálâ*
not having the opportunity of meeting	*matwèiyàdá*
it has been a long time	*cá θwâbí*
I haven't seen you for a long time.	*matwèiyàdá, cá θwâbí*
all	*ˀâlôun*
state of being well, healthy	*mámá chájá*
Is everybody all right?	*ˀâlôun mámá chájá šìjàyèlâ*

máun hlà

We're fine.	*májàbáyè*
we	*dòu*
we Burmans	*dòu bamá*
Here are my friends, an American, Mr. Clark, and (one of) us Burmans, Mg. Bà.	*díhmá couˀ θaŋéjîn, ˀaméiyìkán pyéiðâ máun kalannè dòu bamá máun bà*

	kóu ˀêi phéi
much, many	*ˀamyâ (myàdé)*
the opportunity of meeting	*twèiyàdá*
rejoices, is joyful	*wûn θádé*
Very pleased to meet you.	*twèiyàdá, ˀamyâjî wûn θábádé*
Have you had dinner?	*khímbyâdòu thamîn sâ pîjàbalâ*
	máun hlà
Not yet.	*masâyàðêibû*
	kóu ˀêi phéi
accompanies, is with, has along	*pádé*
I have all kinds of food with me.	*couphmá sâzayá θaussayá ˀamyôuzóun pádé*
Come, let's go eat together.	*lá, ˀatúdú θwâ sâjàzòu*
[Time interval]	
	máun bà
because one eats	*sâlòu*
relishes, enjoys	*méindé*
How are things, Clark, my friend.	*bènélê, meisshwéijî máun kalaˀ,*
Did you enjoy the meal?	*thamîn sâlòu méin-yèlâ*
	máun kalaˀ
very (much)	*ˀímmatán*
I liked it very much.	*ˀímmatán sâlòu méimbádé*
one word	*zagâ takhûn*
There's one thing I'd like to say.	*cúndó zagâ takhûnlauˀ pyôjíndé*

is angry	*sei? shôudé*
Don't take offense, please.	*khímbyâdòu sei? mashôubánè*
	kóu ?êi phéi
is deterred by fear of offending	*?â nádé*
There's no reason to be delicate.	*?â názayá mašìbábû*
just say (it)	*pyôðá pyôbá*
If you have something to say, go ahead and say it.	*pyôzayá šìyín, pyôðá pyôbá*
	máun kala?
The meal was good.	*sâlòu kâumbáyè*
although it is good	*kâumbéimè*
is hot tasting, pungent	*satté*
However, the curry was a little hot.	*kâumbéimè, hîn nênê satté*
	máun bà
Don't worry about it.	*dí ?atwe? masôuyéimbánè*
cool	*?êi?êi*
disappears, is lost	*pyautté*
If you drink a glass of cool beer it will probably go away.	*bíyá ?êi?êi takhwe? θauyyín, pyauppálèimmé*
	máun kala?
tries, feels	*sândé*
I'll try it to see.	*sân cìbámé*

	kóu ʔêi phéi
before long	*macágín*
We'll be in Mandalay before long.	*macágín mândalêi myòugóu yauppálèimmé*
We're almost there.	*yauthlùbí*
	máun hlà
changes, exchanges	*lêdé*
puts, places	*thâdé*
Change your clothes	*ʔawummyâ lê thâjàbá*
Don't be very long.	*khimbyadòu θeiʔ cájá manéibánè*
There isn't time.	*ʔachéin mašìbû*
is short	*tóudé*
shorts (short pants)	*bâumbídóu*
shirt	*šaʔ*
short-sleeved shirt	*šallettóu*
When you walk around in the city wear shorts and sport shirts.	*khímbyâ myòudêgóu šauʔ lédè ʔakhá, bâumbídóunè šalettóu wukkhèbá*
	máun kalaʔ
this (that has been mentioned)	*ʔêdí*
is strange, unusual	*thûzândé*
strange, unusual things	*ʔthûdû shânzân*
What is there that's remarkable in this city?	*ʔêdí myòuhmá bámyâ ʔthûdû shânzân šìðalê*
	máun hlà
I can't really say.	*ʔahmán mapyôhnáimbû*
I've never been to Mandalay either.	*coullê mândalêi myòugóu takhaummà mayaupphûbû*

SECTION B—WORD STUDY AND REVIEW OF BASIC SENTENCES

1. Word Study

A. Doublings

cádé	'is long in time'	*cájá*	'long time'
pyódé	'enjoys oneself, is glad'	*pyóbyó*	'happiness'
myándé	'is fast'	*myámmyán*	'speed'
méindé	'relishes, enjoys'	*méimméin*	'relish, enjoyment'
ʔêidé	'is cool'	*ʔêiʔêi*	'cool'
kâundé	'is good'	*kâuŋgâun*	'well'
nêdé	'is small'	*nênê*	'little'
hnêidé	'is slow'	*hnêihnêi*	'slowly'
satté	'is hot tasting'	*sassaʔ*	'hot'

Verbs are often doubled. The doublings which results act like nouns. Often they may be translated in English by means of adverbs, adjectives and so on.

myámmyán lábá	Come quickly.
hnêihnêi pyôbá	Speak slowly.
kâuŋgâun loutté	He did it well.
hîn sassannè thamîn méimméin sâyàyín . . .	If I can eat some spicy curry and tasty rice . . .
bíyá ʔêiʔêi	cool beer
ʔêiʔêi louʔ manéibánè	Don't work so slowly.

májádé 'is well, healthy'	*mámá chájá* 'state of being well, health'

The parts of a dissyllabic verb are also doubled. Each syllable is repeated separately.

thûdé	differs from others
shândé	exceeds others, is extraordinary, unique
thûzândé	is strange, unusual
ʔathû	something different
ʔashân	something unique
ʔathûdû ʔashânzân	something strange, unusual
ʔathûdû shânzân	something strange, unusual
ʔathû ʔashân	something strange, unusual
thûdû shânzân	something strange, unusual
bámyâ ʔathû ʔashân šìðalê	What is there that is unusual or remarkable?
bámyâ ʔathûdû ʔashânzân šìðalê	What is there that is unusual or remarkable?
pôu lóunjí ʔashâmmyâ manèigàbê yauʔ ládé	Only yesterday some new designs in *lóunjis* arrived.
dí ʔashínhá shânlê shândé, pôulê sitté	This design is new, and it's (the *lounjí*) real silk too.

Various types of doublings occur from some verbs. Nouns occur which are derived from the verbs by a prefixed *ʔa-* (Unit 11), *ʔathû*, *ʔashân*. These nouns may then be doubled: *ʔathûdû*, *ʔashânzân*. Finally the dissyllabic verb *thûzândé* may be doubled *thûdû shânzân*.

B. *-tá*

twèidé 'meets, finds'	*twèidá* 'meeting'
twèiyàdé 'has the opportunity of meeting'	*twèiyàdá* 'the opportunity of meeting'
kazâ neijàdé 'are playing'	*kazâ néijàdá* 'the playing'
matwèiyàbû 'has not had the opportunity of meeting'	*matwèiyàdá* 'not having had the opportunity of meeting'
mayaupphû 'did not arrive'	*mayauttá* 'not having arrived'
shóudé 'speaks'	*shóudá* 'the expression, the saying'
khódé 'calls'	*khódá* 'call'

The syllable *-tá* added to a verb makes a noun of it.

C. *-cà-* 'plural'

θwâjâdé	(they, we, you) go, went
θwâjàbá	Go! (to more than one person)
kazâ néijàdé	They are playing.
ʔâlôun mámá chájá šijàyèlâ	Is everybody well?
khímbyâdòu thamîn sâ pîjàbalâ	Have you had dinner?
ʔatúdú θwâ sâjàzòu	Let's go eat together.
ʔawummyâ lê thâjàbá	Change your clothes.
bémyâ pyauʔ néijàðalê	Where have you been (keeping yourself)?

The secondary verb particle *-cà-* (see Unit 7) is used where more than one person is referred to. *θwâdé* may refer to one or more than one person; *θwâjàdé* refers only to more than one person.

D. *shí* 'presence, proximity'

badùzígóu pêibòu sá yêi néiðalê	'to whom are you writing?'
badù shígóu or *badúzígóu*	'to whom'
θù shígóu or *θùzígóu*	'to him'
θaŋéjîn shígóu or *θaŋéjînzígóu*	'to a friend'
khímbyâzíhmá náyí páðalâ	'do you have a watch on you?'

shi is a noun meaning 'presence'. It does not occur by itself. Different speakers use this noun differently Some run it together with the preceding noun: *θùzíhmá* 'on him'; some do not: *θù shíhmá* 'on him'. You will hear it both ways. It is used with persons.

E. -the? 'more than, above'

couttòude?	more than we
khímbyâde?	more than you
?ayíŋgàde?	more than before
?éinde? cîdé	it is bigger than a house
couthe? θú cîdé	he is bigger than I am
di háde? kâundá mašìbûlâ	isn't there something better than this

-the? is a general particle which is added to a noun expression denoting that to which something is compared.

F. dòu 'we'

dòu bamá	we Burmans
cou?	I
couttòu	we
cúndó	I
cúndódòu	we
khímbyâ	you
khímbyâdòu	you (plural)
θú	he
θúdòu	they

dòu by itself means 'we'. You will hear this form but should not try to use it as it would sound rude in most situations. There are several levels of speech in Burmese and we have tried to give you examples of that level which would sound best coming from you. The examples we have given you and will give you are of a level of speech that most Burmans use when they are talking to friends and acquaintances. The difference in levels of speech is most striking in the use of words for 'I, you, we, they'. There are words for these other than the ones you have learned. We shall give you a list so that you may understand them if you hear them, but we warn you against using them yourself.

I	*ŋá, canou?, cou?, cúndó, cúndómyôu*
we	*ŋadòu, dòu, couttòu, cúndódòu*
you (singular)	*nín, mîn, khímbyâ*
you (plural)	*níndòu, mîndòu, khímbyâdòu*
he	*θú*
they	*θúdòu*

ŋá, nín, mîn are not used in polite conversation. You will hear them used to very young people. A Burmese father, for example, will use these forms in talking to his children. You should avoid them.

You should use the forms *cúndó* and *khímbyâ* until you know the people to whom you are talking fairly well. Then, if they are about your age, you may use *cou?* in place of *cúndó*.

A woman speaking will use *cúmmà* instead of *cúndó* or *cou?*, and *šín* instead of *khímbyâ*.

Burmans often address other people or refer to them by their names, their titles, or their professions such as *máun kala?*, *shayájî*, *shayawún*. The word for 'uncle' *?û*, or 'aunt' *adó* is often used in addressing an older person.

You will soon get the hang of it if you listen carefully. Remember that for your purposes *cúndó*, *khímbyâ*, and *θú* with their plurals are the safest and best.

G. Burmese Sentences (Cont.)

1. Negative Sentences

a. Negative narrative statements.

θwâdé; θwâmé; θwâbí	(he) goes, went; will go, has gone
maθwâbû	(he) does not go, did not go, will not go, has not gone
pyôhnáindé	(he) can say
mapyôhnáimbû	(he) can not say
yaupphûdé	(he) has been [there already]
mayaupphûbû	(he) has never been [there].

A negative narrative statement consists of a narrative statement in which the syllable *ma-* is prefixed to the verb, and the final particle is replaced by the negative final particle *-phû*. Notice that there is no distinction in the negative parallel to the distinction of *-té*, *-mé*, *-pí* in the positive statement.

b. Negative imperative sentences.

θwâ, θwâbá	go!
maθwânè, maθwâbánè	don't go!
sei? shôu néibádé	(he) is angry
sei? shôu manéibánè	don't be angry
?êi ?êi lou? manéibánè	don't take it so easy
?êi ?êi lou? néidé	he's working calmly (slowly)
cájá manéibábû	(I) won't stay long.
cájá manéibánè	Don't stay long!

A negative imperative sentence consists of an imperative sentence in which the syllable *ma-* is prefixed to the verb and the negative final particle *-nè* is added at the end. As was pointed out in Unit 4, the secondary verb particle *-pá-* is usually present in polite speech, particularly in a negative command.

c. Negative equational sentences.

θú tayou? pyéiðâ	he is a Chinese
θú tayou? pyéiðâ mahoupphû	he is not a Chinese.

A negative equational sentence consists of an equational statement plus *mahoupphû* 'it is not so.'

d. Negative questions.

θìðêidé	(he) already knows
maθìðêibûlâ	doesn't (he) know yet?
maθwâbû	(he) hasn't gone
maθwâbûlâ	hasn't (he) gone?
θú tayou? pyéiðâ mahoupphû	He is not a Chinese.
θú tayou? pyéiðâ mahoupphûlâ	Isn't he a Chinese?
bá phyillòu myámmyán yau??áun, maláðalê	Why didn't you come so as to get here quickly?

A negative question consists of a negative narrative sentence or of a negative equational sentence plus interrogative particle *-lâ* or *-lê*. Notice that before *-lê*, the negative final particle *-phû* is replaced by *-θa-*. *malábûlâ* 'didn't he come?' but *bá phyillòu maláðalê* 'why didn't he come?'

SECTION C—REVIEW OF BASIC SENTENCES (*Cont.*)

1. Review of Basic Sentences (*Cont.*)

Further oral practice with the second part of the *Basic Sentences*.

2. Covering the English of Basic Sentences

Check your knowledge of the meaning of all words and phrases in the *Basic Sentences*. This is individual study.

3. What Would You Say?

Give full answers for the following questions.

1. *θîmbô thwettòmalâ*
2. *θîmbô bé ?achéin thwemmalê*
3. *côu phyou? néibalâ*
4. *khímbyâ pyóyèlâ*
5. *khímbyà θaŋéjîn khímbyâzígóu májâun chájâun sá yêiðalâ*
6. *?acôu ?acâun ?akóun yêimalâ*
7. *myámmyán lá néiðalâ*
8. *phê kazâdá θei? pyózayá kâunðalâ*
9. *khímbyâ ta?éin wín kazâjínðalâ*
10. *khímbyâ náinðalâ*
11. *khímbyâ šôunðalâ*
12. *bélau? náinðalê*
13. *bélau? šôunðalê*
14. *?ayíŋgàde? khímbyâ kán kâunðalâ*
15. *?akhù khímbyâ thamîn θwâ sâjínðalâ*
16. *máun kala? hóu lú khímbyânè câun néibe? θaŋéjînlâ*

17. *θùgóu matwèiyàdá θei? cá θwâbalâ*
18. *?âlôun mámá chájá šìjàyèlâ*
19. *khímbyâ θùgóu twèiyàdá wûn θáyèlâ*
20. *thamîn sâ pîbalâ*
21. *thamîn masâyàðêibûlâ*
22. *khímbyâzíhmá náyí páðalâ*
23. *θúdòu ?atúdú θwâ sâðalâ*
24. *thamîn sâlòu méin-yèlâ*
25. *khímbyâ θúnè zagá pyôjínðalâ*
26. *khímbyâ sei? shôuðalâ*
27. *khímbyâ ?â náðalâ*
28. *pyôzayá šìyín, pyôhnáimmalâ*
29. *hîn saθθalâ*
30. *yéi takhwe? θauyyín, pyaummalâ*
31. *sân cìjínðalâ*
32. *macágín pyéi myòugóu yaummalâ*
33. *dí pyéihmá bâumbídóunnè šallettóu wuθθalâ*
34. *khímbyâ mândalêi myòugóu yaupphûðalâ*
35. *khímbyâ hóu lúdéigóu myínðalâ*
36. *khímbyâ hóu lúgóu θìðalâ*
37. *khímbyâ wûn θá néiðalâ*
38. *khímbyà θaŋéjîn bá phyillòu lábòu mèi θwâðalê*
39. *cúndó pyôdá nâ léðalâ*
40. *?akhù bé hnanáyí šìbalê*

SECTION D—LISTENING IN

1. What Did You Say?

With the other members of your group give orally your responses to the previous exercise as the Leader calls for them.

2. Word Study Check-Up

Give the Burmese for all English equivalents in the *Word Study* as the Leader calls for it.

3. Listening In

1. A card game.

máun bà: *khímbyâ badùzígóu pêibòu sá yêi néiðalê*

máun kala?: *cúndónè câun néibe? θaŋéjînzígóu mámá chájá májâun chájâun θìyà?áun, pêibòu sá yêinéidé*

máun hlà: *kóu sán yà, khímbyâ bá mêiðalê*

kóu sán yà: *dòu bamá pyéihmá pyózayá kâundè ?acôu ?acâuŋgóu máun kala? yêi néiðalâlòu, mêidá*

máun kala?: *houppádé*
cou? díhmá bâumbídóunè šallettóu wu? pî, pyóbyó šwînšwín néidè ?acâuŋgóu yêi néidé

máun hlà: *lábá, kwé, máun kala?*
hóuhmá phêwâinjîgóu myínðalâ
?êdíhmá couttòu ta?éinzí wín kazâyà?áun

máun kala?: *?ayîn bélaunnè sà kazâmalê*

kóu sán yà: *cou? takhámàlê makazâbûbû*
?ayîn ŋwéi tashélaunnè kazâyín, ?ahmán náinlèimmé, thíndé

máun bà: *cousshíhmá ŋwéi tajammà mapábû*

máun kala?: *máun bà, dí ŋwéi ŋâjannè sà kazâ*

máun bà: *sei? chàbá*
cou? náin?áun, cì kazâbàmé

máun kala?: *kóu sán yà tayautthê couttòude? kán kâunlòu, náindé*

máun bà: *cúndó takhámà manáinðêibû*

máun hlà: *sei? tóu pî, sei? shôu manéibánè macágín, náimbálèimmé*
kazâðá kazâ

máun kala?: *couttòu ?akóunlôun šôundé*
kóu sán yà náinlóu, wûn θá néidé

2. Where shall we eat?

máun hlà: *θaŋéjîn tayau? yauthlùbí*
khanà sàun néibá?ôun

kóu sán yà: *khímbyà θaŋéjîn mayaukkhín cou? ?awı.? θwâ lê?ôummé*

máun hlà, cou? phanaccôu phyou? mayàlòu, phyou? pêibá?ôun

máun bà: *hà, máun cóbálâ*
bá phyillòu myámmyán yau??áun, maláðalê
lábòu mèi θwâðalâ

máun có: *cúndó meisshwéi tayaunnè twèidánè zagâ takhûn hnakhûn pyô néilòu cá θwâdé*
khímbyâdòu sáun néiyàdè ?atwe? ?â nábádé

máun kala?: *bé thamînzáimhmá θwâ sâmalê*

máun bà: *θwâjíndè sháiŋgóu θwâbá*
couttò hîn sassannè thamîn méimméin sâyàyín, tóbí

3. At the market.

máun hlà: *zêigóu mayauttâlê cá θwâbí*
bámyâ ?athû ?ashân šiðalê shóudá, θwâ cìyà?áun

máun bà: *khímbyâ bé zêigóu θwâmalê*

máun hlà: *θêinjî zêigóubê θwâmé*

máun bà: *lánchânè θwâmalòulâ*

máun hlà: *mahouppábû*
lân šau? θwâmé

máun bà: *θwâmé shóuyín, ?êi?êi lou? manéibánè*

shâinšin: *khímbyâdòugóu matwèiyàdá ?ímmatán cá θwâbí*
bémyâ pyau? néijàðalê

máun hlà: *pyéi myòuhmá šìdè meisshwéimyâgà khódánè couttòu khanà θwâ lédé*

máun bà: *khímbyâ shâimhmá ?ayíŋgàde? bámyâ ?athûdû ?ashânzân šìðalê*

shâinšín: *hòu díhmá cì*
pôu lóunjí ?ashâmmyâ manèigàbê yau? ládé
sân cìbá

máun bà: *dí ?ashínhá shânlê shândé, pôulê sitté makâumbûlâ*

máun hlà: *kâundò kâumbáyè kâumbéimè, cou? macaipphû*

shâinšín: *macágín ?ashín ?amyôuzóun yau? lábálèimmé*

SECTION E—CONVERSATION

1. Covering the Burmese of Basic Sentences

With the Burmese covered, practice until you can speak the Burmese for each English sentence without hesitation.

2. Vocabulary Check-Up

Give the Burmese for all English sentences in the *Basic Sentences* as the Leader calls for it.

3. Conversation

Suggested Topics.

1. You are going away on a ship. A friend has come to see you off. He tells you to have a good time and asks you not to forget to write. You assure him that you won't. You say goodbye.

2. You and some new acquaintances get into a card game. Discuss your winnings or losses.

3. You eat with your friends and they ask you how you like the food. You apologize for saying so, but tell them that you find Burmese food a little hot for your taste.

4. You discuss with your friends the time of arrival in Mandalay, the sights of the city, and the appropriate clothes to wear there.

Continue conversation. Additional check-up on the material of the *Basic Sentences* by the Leader if it seems necessary.

Review: Complete check-up on the material of the *Word Study* and *Basic Sentences*.

Finder List

ʔâ nádé	is deterred by fear of offending
ʔacôu ʔacâun	the good and the bad
ʔakóun	the whole, all
ʔathûdû shânzân	strange, unusual things
ʔayîn	capital, stock in trade
bâumbídóu	shorts (short pants)
câun néibeʔ θaŋéjîn	school friend
couttòudeʔ	more than we
dòu	we
dòu bamá	we Burmans
ʔédí	this (that has just been talked about)
ʔêiʔêi	cool
ʔéin	hands at cards
ʔímmatán	very (much)
kán kâundé	is lucky, has good luck
kâumbéimè	although it is good
kazâdé	plays
kazâ néijàdá	the playing
kazâyàʔáun	let's play
kwé	old fellow, my friend
lêdé	changes, exchanges
macágín	before long
májádé	is well, healthy
májâun chájâun	well being, state of health
mámá chájá	state of being well, health
matwèiyàdá	not having the opportunity of meeting
mèidé	forgets
méindé	relishes, enjoys
myándé	is fast
myámmyán	speed
náindé	wins
pádé	accompanies, is with
phê	playing card
phêwâin	card game
phyoutté	loosens, unties
pyautté	disappears, is lost
pyódé	enjoys oneself, is glad
pyóbyó	happiness

pyóbyó šwínšwín happiness, enjoyment
pyôðá pyôbá just say (it)
pyózayá kâundé is fun ('is good for being happy')

sá a writing, something written
sâlòu because one eats
sândé tries, feels
satté is hot tasting, pungent
sâyàʔáun let's eat
seiʔ chàdé feels comfortable and easy in mind
seiʔ shôudé is angry

šaʔ shirt
šallettóu short-sleeved shirt
šôundé loses
šwíndé rejoices, is joyful

taʔéinzí a hand each
thûzândé is strange, unusual
thwettòmé is about to leave
tóudé is short
twèiyàdá the opportunity of meeting

wûn θádé rejoices

yauthlùbí we're almost there
yêidé writes
yêilaippàmé will write (definitely)

zagâ takhûn one word

UNIT 15

SIGHTSEEING

SECTION A—BASIC SENTENCES

ENGLISH EQUIVALENTS	AIDS TO LISTENING
	máun kalaˀ
horse	*myîn*
carriage	*myîn-yathâ*
Rent a carriage for the trip.	*θwâbòu myîn-yathâ hŋâbá*
	kóu sán yà
You don't need to hire one.	*hŋâbòu malóubábû*
We'll just go in my car.	*couˀ mótókânèbê θwâmé*
	máun kalaˀ
How very hot your city of Mandalay is!	*bènélê, khímbyâdòu mândalêi myòu θeiˀ púdé*
	kóu sán yà
season (of the year)	*ˀùdù*
the hot season	*nwéi ˀùdù (=nwéi ˀakhá)*
That's right—it's always very hot like this in the hot season.	*houtté, nwéi ˀùdùhmá dílóu ˀamyê θeiˀ púdé*

the rainy season	*môu ʔùdù (=môu ʔakhá)*
the cold season	*shâun ʔùdù (=shâun ʔakhá)*
heat	*ʔapú (púdé)*
is moderate, comfortable; recovers	*θeθθádé*
In the rainy season and the cold season the heat is moderate.	*môu ʔùdùnè shâun ʔùdùhmá ʔapú θeθθádé*
	máun kalaʔ
remains for a while, lodges	*têdé*
Isn't there a good hotel to stay at in this city?	*dí myòuhmá têbòu kâundè hóté mašìbûlâ*
	kóu sán yà
There is.	*šìbádé*
money	*paisshán*
Why do you want to go stay in a hotel and spend (use up) more money?	*bá phyillòu paisshán póu kóunʔáun, hótéhmá θwâ têjínðalê*
If you want to stay in my house you can.	*couʔ ʔéimhmá têjín-yín, têhnáimbádé*
	máun hlà (to Clark)
That would be very nice.	*dílóu shóuyínlê, θeiʔ kâumbádé*
is different, diverse	*thûdé*
It won't make any difference for a day or two.	*tayeʔ hnayellaunnè mathûbábû*
is long	*šéidé*
Don't make a fuss (about it). (Don't be long winded).	*šéi manéibánè*
Stay right in Mr. San Ya's house.	*kóu sán yà ʔéimhmábê têbá*
[Interval]	

kóu sán yà

Here we are.	*yauppí*
This is my house. There's no reason to stand on ceremony	*dá couʔ ʔéin, bámà ʔâ názayá mašìbábû*
Make yourselves at home. ("You can stay as you like").	*khímbyâdòu θabô šìðalóu néihnáimbádé*
hook	*jeiʔ*
hooks, catches on a hook	*cheitté*
Mr. Clark, take off your coat and hang it on that hook.	*máun kalaʔ, khímbyâ ʔêinjí chuʔ pî, hóu jeiphmá cheiʔ thâlaippá*

máun kalaʔ

I'm very hot.	*couʔ θeiʔʔaitté*
Wouldn't it be (a) good (idea) to take a bath?	*yéi chôuyín, makâumbûlâ*

máun hlà

immediately, right away	*youʔ tayeʔ*
rashly	*ʔayân*
Don't be rash and bathe immediately.	*youʔ tayeʔ yéigóu ʔayân machôunè*
has a fever, is feverish	*phyâdé*
will have a fever, will be feverish	*phyâhmá*
You have to be careful or you'll get sick.	*phyâhmá sôuyéin-yàdé*
cool of the day	*néiʔêi*
It'll be all right to bathe when it gets cool.	*néiʔêihmá chôuyín, kâunlèimmé*

[Interval]

(to kóu sán yà)

maymyo	*méi myòu*
We want to go visit Maymyo.	*couttòu méi myòugóu θwâ léjíndé*
Could you come along with us?	*khímbyâ couttòunè ʔatúdú laithnáimmalâ*

kóu sán yà

I can't say yet for sure.	*couʔ ʔahmán mapyôhnáinðêibû*
I'm busy now.	*ʔakhù ʔalouʔ myâdé*
day after tomorrow	*θabekkhá*
I think I might be able to go along perhaps the day after tomorrow.	*θabekkhálauʔ shóuyín, laithnáinlèimmé, thíndé*

máun kalaʔ

slowly, unhurriedly	*ʔêiʔêi shêizêi*
We'll go the day after tomorrow and take it easy.	*θabekkháhmábê ʔêiʔêi shêizêi θwâmé*
What's your opinion Mg. Hla?	*bélóu θabô yàðalê, máun hlà*

máun hlà

as you say	*pyôðalóu*
I agree with what you say.	*coullê khímbyâ pyôðalóubê θabô yàbádé*

máun kala?

palace	*nândó*
sound of speech	*pyôðán*
hears	*câdé*
I've heard there was a big palace in Mandalay—where is it?	*mândalêi myòuhmá nândójî šìdélòu pyôðán câbûdé, béhmálê*

kóu sán yà

Yes, there is.	*šìbádé*
It's not very far. Do you want to go see it?	*θei? mawêibábû, θwâ cìjínðalâ*

máun hlà

The sun is too hot now.	*?akhù néi θei? púdé*
We'll go see it this afternoon when it gets cool.	*nyà néi?êihmábê θwâ cìmé*

máun kala?

does thoroughly, completely	*hnàndé*
I want to go around and see Mandalay thoroughly in a couple of days.	*mândalêi myòugóu hnayellaunnè hnàn?áun, šau? lé cìjíndé*
You can	*cìhnáimbádé*
day (from sunrise to sunset)	*nèi*
a whole day	*tanéilôun*
If we go see the palace today, there's time to go around the city all day tomorrow.	*dí nèi nândógóu θwâ cìyín, nepphyíŋgá tanèilôun myòudêgóu šau? lébòu ?achéin šìdé*

máun kala?

noon, midday	*nèilé*
What'll we do during the day?	*nèilé bá loummalê*

máun hlà

It's very hot during the day.	*nèilé θei? púdé*
is bored, lazy	*pyîndé*
boredom, laziness	*?apyîn*
gets rid of, loosens, appeases	*pyéidé*
story	*wutthù*
book	*sá?ou?*
reads	*phatté*
I'll just stay home and read books to keep from being bored. (to pass the time)	*?éimhmábê ?apyîn pyéi?áun, wutthù sá?ou? pha? néimé*

kóu sán yà

thinks, intends, plans	*cán sídé*
How do you intend to go to Maymyo?	*méi myòugóu bánè θwâmélòu, cán sí thâðalê*
By train or car?	*mîyathânèlâ, mótókânèlâ*

máun hlà

We thought we'd go by car.	*mótókânè θwâmélòu, sei? kûdé*

máun kala?

arranges, orders	*símándé*
In that case you'll have to arrange for a car.	*dílóu shóuyín, mótókâ hŋâbòu símán-yàlèimmé*

kóu sán yà

It isn't necessary to rent one.	*hŋâbòu malóubábû*
We can go in my car.	*cúndò mótókânè θwâhnáimbádé*

máun hlà

It's cooled off now—let's go see the place.	*ʔakhù néi ʔêi θwâbí, nândógóu θwâ cìjàzòu*
Time interval	

máun kalaʔ

looks attentively, looks after	*cì šùdé*
Is there anything special to see in the palace?	*nândó ʔathêhmá cì šùzayá ʔathû ʔashân šìðalâ*

kóu sán yà

very much	*θeittò*
There isn't very much left that's worth seeing.	*θeittò ʔathû mašìdòbû*
building	*ʔasháun*
is ruined, destroyed	*pyessîdé*
some	*tachòu*
Some of the buildings are in ruins.	*tachòu ʔasháunlê pyessî kóumbí*
exhibition building	*pyádaiʔ*
only one	*takhùðá*
remains, is left	*cándé*
The museum is the only interesting thing left.	*pyàdaiʔ takhùðá ʔathû cándòdé*

máun kalaʔ

When we have seen the museum and the remaining buildings, let's leave.	*cándè ʔasháunnè pyàdaikkóu cì pî, thweʔ pyánjàzòu*

SECTION B—WORD STUDY AND REVIEW OF BASIC SENTENCES

1. Word Study

A. The Seasons

nwéi ʔùdù	the hot season
shâun ʔùdù	the cold season
môu ʔùdù	the rainy season

ʔùdù is a noun meaning 'season, time of year'. There is also another word for it in Burmese: *yáðí* 'season, time of year'. In Unit 5 you learned still another expression, more general, which is used in the same way: *ʔakhá* 'time'. Thus there are three ways in which to mention the seasons:

nwéi ʔakhá, nwéi ʔùdù, nwéi yáðí
shâun ʔakhá, shâun ʔùdù, shâun yáðí
môu ʔakhá, môu ʔùdù, môu yáðí

These expressions are used interchangeably. The first is the commonest, and the last the least common. The times of the year covered by these terms and the names of the months were described in Unit 5.

B. ta . . . lôun 'all, whole'

tanèilôun	all day, the whole day
tamanellôun	all morning, the whole morning
taʔéinlôun	the whole house
bamá pyéi tabyéilôun	the whole of Burma

lôundé as a verb means 'is round', or 'is complete'. It is used as modifier of a noun to which the syllable *ta-* has been prefixed in the sense of 'the whole, all'.

C. More General Particles (See Unit 9)

1. -tò 'as for, concerning'

couttò ŋâjallauʔ náin néibí	As for me, I've won about 5 Rupees.
ʔasàdò nênê náindé	(As for) at first, I won a little.
ʔakhùdò ʔanáin šôun pí, ʔayîmbê	(As for) now I've lost my winnings and am back where I started.

-tò is a general particle. It is added to noun expressions and marks the noun expression as the topic of

the sentence. It may be translated usually as 'as for, concerning' but often need not be represented in the English translation.

2. - *θá* 'only'

pyàdai? takhùðá cándòdé	Only a museum is left.
myòujîhmáðá yàhnáindé	You can get it only in big cities.
pyôðá pyôbá	Just speak up.
kazâðá kazâbá	Just play.

θá is a general particle. It is added to either noun expressions or verb expressions in the meaning 'only, just'.

3. *-lóu* 'fashion, manner'

dílóu ?amyê θei? púdé	It's always hot this way.
θabô šìðalóu néihnáimbádé	You can stay as you like.
coullê khímbyâ pyôðalóubê θabô yàbádè	I too agree with what you say.

-lóu is a general particle which was discussed in Unit 9. It is added to noun expressions, including noun expressions which are derived from verbs by a particle *-té* as in the expressions quoted above. The particle *-té* will be treated in a later unit. It is sufficient now to know that *pyôðalóu* is translated as 'what one says', or 'the way one says'. Similarly *θabô šìðalóu* 'as one is disposed, as one likes'.

D. Subordinating Particles

Verb expressions are marked as *subordinate clauses* by substitution of *subordinating particles* for final particles (see Unit 13). Subordinate clauses precede the main verb expression.

1. *-?áun* 'in order to, so that'

nâ lé?áun, cou? pyô pyàmé	I'll explain so that you will understand.
myòugóu hnàn?áun, šau? lé cìjíndé	I want to go around the city so as to see it thoroughly.
?apyîn pyéi?áun, sá?ou? pha? néimé	I'm going to read a book to keep from being bored.

-?áun is a subordinating particle. It is attached to verb expressions in the meaning 'in order to, so that, so as to'.

2. *-lòu* 'because'

sâlòu kâumbáyè	The meal was good.
thamîn sâlòu méin-yèlâ	Did you enjoy the meal?
ʔímmatán sâlòu méimbádé	I liked it very much.
kóu sán yà náinlòu, wûn θá néidé	I am happy that Mr. San Ya won.

-lòu is a subordinating particle. It is attached to verb expressions and denotes cause. This seldom comes out clearly in the English translation. In the first example *sâlòu kâumbáyè* the literal English rendering might be 'because one eats it is good'. Similarly in the last example *kóu sán yà náinlòu, wûn θá néidé* the literal English rendering might be 'because Mr. San Ya won I am happy'.

You should be careful not to confuse this subordinating particle with the general particle *-lòu* described in Unit 10. Notice that the subordinating particle attaches directly to the verb: *náinlòu* 'because he won'. The general particle *-lòu* attaches to verb expressions with their particles: *náindélòu pyôdé* 'he said that he won'.

3. *-péimè* 'although'

kâumbéimè, hîn nênê satté	Although it was good, the curry was a little hot.
kâumbéimè, couʔ macaipphû	I didn't like it even though it was good.

-péimè is a subordinating particle. It is attached to verbs in the meaning 'although, even if.' There is another use of this form which you will meet later: *dábéimè* 'however, even so' where the particle is attached to a noun.

4. *-yín* 'if, when'

sîyín, . . .	if one rides
yéi ŋayyín, . . .	if one is thirsty
dílóu shóuyín, . . .	if that's the case (*lit.* 'if you say it this way')
šèi tèdè šauʔ θwâyín, nyábekkà šìdé taipphyújîbê	If you walk straight ahead, it's the big white house on the right.
pyôzayá šìyín, pyôðá pyôbá	When (if) you have something to say go ahead and say it.
ʔayîn ŋwéi tashélaunnè kazâyín, ʔahmán náinlèimmé, thíndé	If you play with a capital of about ten rupees you'll surely win I think.

-yín is a subordinating particle. It attaches to verbs in the meaning 'if, when.'

5. *-yínlê* 'if'

dílóu shóuyínlê, θei? kâumbádé	If that's the case it's very nice
šìyínlê, šìlèimmé	Maybe there is. ('If there is there probably is')

-yínlê is a subordinating particle. It attaches to verbs in the meaning 'if'.

6. *pîdé* 'finishes'

sei? tóu pî, sei? shôu manéibánè	Don't be easily offended and get angry.
dí pyissìdéi yú pî, couttòu naukkóu laikkhèbá	Follow us and bring these things.
?akhùdò ?anáin šôun pî, ?ayîmbê	I've lost my winnings and am back where I started.

pîdé 'finishes' is used without a particle at the end of subordinate clauses in constructions where the action or state described in the subordinate clause goes on simultaneously with that of the main clause.

E. *-yà?áun*

sâyà?áun	Let's eat.
θwâyà?áun	Let's go.
θwâ sâyà?áun	Let's go eat.
θwâ cìyà?áun	Let's go and see.

-yà?áun at the end of a sentence marks first-person-plural commands. It has the same force as the particle *-cazòu* (see Unit 13).

2. Covering English and Burmese of Word Study

Give the English equivalents of all Burmese expressions in the *Word Study* and the Burmese for all the English. This is individual study.

3. Review of Basic Sentences

Further oral practice with the first part of the *Basic Sentences*.

SECTION C—REVIEW OF BASIC SENTENCES (*Cont.*)

1. Review of Basic Sentences (*Cont.*)

Further oral practice with the second part of the *Basic Sentences.*

2. Covering the English of Basic Sentences

Check your knowledge of the meaning of all words and phrases in the *Basic Sentences.* This is individual study.

3. What Would You Say?

Give full answers for the following questions.

1. *θwâbòu myîn-yathâ hŋâyàmalâ*
2. *mótókâ hŋâbòu lóuðalâ*
3. *khímbyâ mótókânè θwâmalâ*
4. *mândalêi myòuhmá θeiˀ púðalâ*
5. *nwéi ˀùdùhmá chânðalâ*
6. *shâun ˀùdùhmá môu θeiˀ ywáðalâ*
7. *môu ˀùdùnè shâun ˀùdùhmá ˀapú θeθθáðalâ*
8. *yáŋgóun myòuhmá têbòu kâundè hóté šìðalâ*
9. *bá phyillòu paisshán póu kóunˀáun, hótéhmá θwâ têjínðalê*
10. *cúndò ˀéimhmá têjínðalâ*
11. *khímbyà ˀéimhmá têhnáimmalâ*
12. *hótéhmá têyín, makâumbûlâ*
13. *hóuhmá bélauˀ cájá têmalê*
14. *dí sáˀounnè hóu sáˀouˀ bá thûðalê*
15. *dí sáˀouˀ hóu sáˀoutheˀ cíðalâ*
16. *dá khímbyà ˀéinlâ*
17. *hóu ˀéin badù ˀéinlê*
18. *θabô šìðalóu néihnáinðalâ*
19. *khímbyâ θeiˀ ˀaiθθalâ*
20. *yéi chôuyín, makâumbûlâ*
21. *youˀ tayeˀ yéi chôuyín, kâummalâ*
22. *yéigóu ˀayân chôuyín, phyâhmá sôuyéin-yàðalâ*
23. *méi myòugóu θwâ léjínðalâ*
24. *khímbyâ cúndódòunè ˀatúdú laithnáimmalâ*
25. *ˀakhù ˀalouˀ myâðalâ*
26. *θabekkhálauˀ shóuyín, laithnáinlèimmé, thínðalâ*
27. *ˀêiˀêi θwâyín, bènélê, laithnáimmalâ*
28. *θúdòu bélóu θabô yàðalê*
29. *khímbyâ cúndó pyôðalóu θabô yàðalâ*
30. *mândalêi myòuhmá nândójî šìdélòu, khímbyâ câbûðalâ*

31. *θeiˀ wêiðalâ*

32. *ˀakhù θeiˀ púdalâ*

33. *nyà néiˀêihmá θwâ cìjínðalâ*

34. *myòugóu hnànˀáun, šauˀ lé cìjínðalâ*

35. *šauˀ lébòu ˀachéin šìðalâ*

36. *wutthù sáˀouˀ phacchínðalâ*

37. *bánè θwâmélòu, cán sí thâðalê*

38. *mótókânè θwâmélòu, seiˀ kûðalâ*

39. *mótókâ hŋâbòu símán-yàmalâ*

40. *khímbyâ badúlê*

Make commands of the following statements.

1. *θwâbòu myîn-yathâ hŋâdé*
2. *mótókânè θwâmé*
3. *hótéhmá θwâ têdé*
4. *cúndò ˀéimhmá lá têdé*
5. *ˀêinjí chuˀ pî, hóu jeiphmá cheiˀ thâlaitté*
6. *pyóbyó néidé*
7. *θwâ cìdé*
8. *myámmyán ládé*
9. *thweˀ θwâdé*
10. *ˀakhândêgóu wín ládé*

SECTION D—LISTENING IN

1. What Did You Say?

With the other members of the group give orally your responses to the previous exercise as the Leader calls for them.

2. Word Study Check-Up

Give the Burmese for all English equivalents in the *Word Study* as the Leader calls for them.

3. Listening In

1. When shall we go sightseeing?

máun kalaˀ: *myîn-yathâ tazî hŋâbòu símán-yàlèimmé*

kóu sán yà: *bégóu θwâjínlòulê*

máun kalaˀ: *tanèilôun myòugóu hnànˀáun, šauˀ lémélòu, cán sí thâdé kóu sán yà:* *ˀakhù môu ˀùdù ˀakhá môu ywáhmá sôuyéin-yàdé khímbyâ bágóu θwâ cìjínlòulê*

máun kalaˀ: *cúndó phayâjî θwâ cìjíndé môu maywágín θwâ cìhnáimmalâ*

máun bà: *môu youˀ tayeˀ maywábábû maywágín phayâgóu yauppálèimmé*

máun hlà: *ˀakhù nèilé, θeiˀ néi pyîndé nyànéi ˀêihmá ˀêiˀêi shêizêi θwâjàzòu*

máun kalaˀ: *nyànéi θwâmé shóuyín, cúndò ˀêinjígóu hóu jeiphmá cheiˀ thâlaippá*

2. Have we time to buy books?

máun bà: *hô, hóuhmá sáˀouˀ sháin, wínjàzòu*

máun hlà: *bá sáˀoukkóu wémalòulê*

máun bà: *ˀapyîn pyéiˀáun, phapphòu bé wutthù sáˀoummashóu wéjíndé*

máun hlà: *sáˀouˀ wébòu ˀachéin mašìbû kóu sán yà dòugóu phayâbóhmá θwâ twèiyàmé*

máun bà: *houtté pyàdaitthêhmá twèimélóu, pyô θwâdé dílóu shóuyín, θabekkhábê sáˀoukkóu wédòmé*

3. How's Mr. Williams?

máun kalaˀ: *khímbyâ ˀakhù béhmá tê néiðalê*

máun hlà: *kóu sán yà ˀéimhmá tê néidé*

máun kalaˀ: *têgà paisshán bélauˀ càðalê*

máun hlà: *khímbyâ lúdûbê θaŋéjîn ˀéimhmá néiyín, bé paisshán pêiyàmalê máun wílyán bènélê*

máun kalaˀ: *ˀaphyâ θeθθá lábí*

máun hlà: *θú bá phyillòu sà phyâdálê*

máun kalaˀ: *θú yéi ˀayân θaullòu phyâdé shayáwún θôun-yauˀ cì šùyàdé tachòugà θéimélòu, thínjàdé*

máun hlà: *θú néidè shêiyóun bé nâhmálê*

máun kalaˀ: *nândódêhmá šìdè ˀasháun takhùgóu shêiyóun louˀ thâdé*

máun hlà: *nândó pyessî néibí, mahoupphûlâ bélóu shêiyóun louˀ thâðalê*

máun kalaˀ: *θeittò mapyessîbû cándè ˀasháundéigóu shêiyóun louˀ thâdé*

SECTION E—CONVERSATION

1. Covering the Burmese of Basic Sentences

With the Burmese covered, practice until you can speak the Burmese for each English sentence without hesitation. This is individual study.

2. Vocabulary Check-Up

Give the Burmese for all English sentences in the *Basic Sentences* as the Leader calls for it.

3. Conversation

Suggested Topics:

1. Discuss the weather and the possibility of going sight-seeing with a friend.
2. Discuss the relative merits of staying in a hotel and staying at a friend's house when visiting a strange city.
3. Make plans for seeing the sights tomorrow.
4. Ask your friend about a mutual acquaintance who is in the hospital. What's wrong with him? Where is the hospital?
5. Go to a bookstore and buy some books.

SECTION F—CONVERSATION (*Cont.*)

Continue conversation. Additional check-up on the material of the *Basic Sentences* by the Leader if it seems necessary.

Review: Complete check-up on the material of the *Word Study* and the *Basic Sentences*.

Finder List

ʔapú	heat
ʔapyîn (*pyîndé*)	boredom, laziness
ʔasháun (*sháundé*)	building
ʔathû ʔashân	something special, strange
ʔayân	rashly
cándé	remains, is left
cán sídé	thinks, intends
cheitté	hooks, catches on a hook
cì šùdé	looks attentively, looks after
ʔêi êi shêizêi	slowly, unhurriedly

hnàndé	to do thoroughly, mix up
jei?	hook
lúdû	strange fellow
mâundé	drives (a vehicle)
myîn	horse
myîn-yathâ	carriage
nândó	palace
néi?êi	cool of the day
nèilé	noon, midday
paisshán	money
phatté	reads
phyâdé	has a fever, is feverish
pyàdai?	exhibition building
pyéidé	loosens, unties, appeases
pyîndé	is bored, lazy
pyessîdé	is ruined, destroyed
pyôðalóu	as you say
pyôðán	sound of speech
sá?ou?	book
símándé	arranges, orders, does
šéidé	is long
tachòu	some
takhùðá	only one
tanéilôun	a whole day
têdé	remains for a while, lodges
thûdé	is different, diverse
θabekkhá	the day after tomorrow
θeittò	very much
θeθθádé	is moderate, comfortable; recovers
?ùdù	season
wutthù	story
you? taye?	immediately, right away

UNIT 16

FILL 'ER UP

SECTION A—BASIC SENTENCES

ENGLISH EQUIVALENTS	AIDS TO LISTENING
	máun kalaʔ
horn	*hûn*
blows	*hmoutté*
Blow the horn, Mg. Hla.	*máun hlà, mótókâ hûŋgóu hmoullaiꝑꝑá*
Mg. Ba hasn't come down yet.	*máun bà mashîn láðêibû*
	máun hlà
falls behind, is late	*nauʔ càdé*
He's always late this way whenever we have to go anywhere.	*dílóubê θwâzayá lázayá šìyín, θú ʔamyê nauʔ càdé*
	kóu sán yà
while one talks	*ꝑyôyîn shóuyîn*
Ah, there comes Mg. Ba just as we're talking (about him).	*hô, ꝑyôyîn shóuyîn, máun bà shîn lábí*

	máun bà
slowness	*ʔahnêi (hnêidé)*
happens	*phyitté*
more haste less speed	*ʔayín lóu ʔahnêi phyiʔ*
as the saying goes	*shóuðalóu*
one shoe	*phanaʔ tapheʔ*
'More haste less speed' as the saying goes; I was a long time looking for one shoe.	*ʔayínlóu ʔahnêi phyiʔ shóuðalóu phanaʔ tapheʔ šánéidánè cá θwâdé*
	máun hlà
as for me	*cúndógàdò*
doesn't come (inevitable)	*malaittòbû*
I thought you weren't coming.	*cúndógàdò khímbyâ malaittòbûlòu, thíndé*
	máun kalaʔ
Come on, let's get going.	*kê, sà thweccàzòu*
It's necessary to get to Maymyo before ten o'clock.	*méi myòugóu shénáyí mathôugín yaupphòu lóudé*
	máun bà
Wait. (Just a moment.)	*néibáʔôun*
is ruined, destroyed	*pyetté*
If the car breaks down do you have tools along to fix it?	*mótókâ pyeyyín, pyímbòu pyissîmyâ páyèlâ*
	kóu sán yà
We can get what's needed.	*lóudá yàhnáimbádé*
box	*θittá*
screw	*weʔʔú*

screwdriver	*weʔʔúhlè*
crab	*ganân*
thumb	*lemmà*
monkey wrench	*ganânlemmà*
pliers, tongs	*hnyaʔ*
pump	*léi thôudán*
hammer	*tú*
raises up, elevates	*hmyautté*
auto jack	*mótókâ hmyauʔ jeʔ*
rubber tube	*yóbá cuʔ*
auto tools	*mótókâ pyissî*
There's a set of tools in that box: screwdriver, wrench, pliers, pump, hammer, jack, tube.	*hóu θittádêhmá weʔʔúhlè, ganânlemmà, hnyaʔ, léi thôudán, tú, mótókâ hmyauʔ jeʔ, yóbá cuʔ, mótókâ pyissî ʔasáun šìbádé*

máun bà

accident	*mató tashà*
wheel	*bêin*
pierces, is pierced	*pautté*
What do we do if we accidentally have a puncture on the road?	*lâmhmá mató tashà mótókâ bêin pauʔ θwâyín, bèné loummalê*

kóu sán yà

There's nothing to worry about.	*sôuyéinzayá mahouppábû*
excess, spare, extra	*ʔapóu (póudé)*
There's always a spare in back.	*mótókâ nauphmá bêin ʔapóu takhù ʔamyê pádé*

máun bà

motor, engine	*se?*
oil	*shí*
motor oil	*sesshí*
gasoline	*dasshí*
is sufficient	*lóunlautté*
How about gas and oil? Will there be enough?	*mótókâ sesshínè dasshímyâgô, lóunlauppàmalâ*

kóu sán yà

There'll be enough.	*lóunlauppádé*
iron, metal	*θán*
container	*pôun*
(tin) can	*θámbôun*
gallon	*gálán*
There are five gallons of extra gas in that can.	*hóu θámbôundêhmá dasshi ʔapóu ŋâgálán šìdé*
drives (a vehicle)	*mâundé*
All right, now we'll drive directly to the Maymyo road.	*kâumbí, ʔakhù méi myòu lâŋgóu tèdè mâummé*

[Interval]

máun bà

sound of a horn	*hûn hmouθθán*
I hear a motor horn behind (us).	*naukkà mótókâ hûn hmouθθán câdé*

máun kala?

goes up, ascends, advances, overtakes	*tetté*
I think he's blowing his horn because he wants to pass.	*šèigóu te? θwâjínlòu, hûn hmoutté, thíndé*

avoids, shuns	*šáundé*
Get out of his way and give him room to pass.	*te? θwâbòu lân šáun pêilaippá*

kóu ṣán yà

I can't get out of his way.	*mašáunhnáimbû*
business, affair	*?ayêi*
is very busy is urgent, is in a hurry	*?ayêi cîdé*
We're in a hurry [to go] too.	*couttòulê θwâbòu ?ayêi cîdé*
If his car is fast he'll probably drive past.	*θù mótókâ myán-yín, šèigóu mâun te? θwâlèimmé*

máun kala?

Don't drive too fast.	*θeillê myámmyán mamâumbánè*
is slow, gradual, easy, pleasant, moderate	*phyêidé*
slowly, easily	*phyêibyêi*
slowly and accurately, steadily	*phyêibyêi hmámhmán*
Drive slowly and carefully	*phyêibyêi hmámhmán mâumbá*
guides, 'shows the road'	*lân pyàdé*
sign post	*hmattáin*
something which has been written	*sá yêi thâdá*
I see something written on that signboard up ahead.	*hóu šèigà lân pyà hmattáimhmá sá yêi thâdá myíndé*
read (it)!	*phallai?*
read, will you please	*phallaissâmbá*
Mg. Ba, read it will you please.	*máun bà, phallaissâmbá*

máun bà

Drive up carefully.	*mótókâgóu θadì thâ mâun teppá*
Danger.	*sôuyéinzayá šìdé*

kóu sán yà

mountain, hill	*táun*
foot of a mountain	*táun chéiyîn*
Now we're at the foot of the mountain.	*ʔakhù táun chéiyîn yauppí*
top of a mountain	*táumbó*
from here on	*dígà néi sà pî*
From here on we'll have to drive up to the top [of the mountain].	*dígà néi sà pî, táumbógóu mâun teʔ θwâyàmé*

máun kalaʔ

foot (12 inches)	*péi*
is high, tall	*myìndé*
How high is this mountain?	*dí táun péibâun bélauʔ myìnðalê*

kóu sán yà

is suitable, sufficient	*tódé*
fairly, pretty, enough	*tódó*
It's pretty high; 3200 ft.	*tódó myìndé, péibâun θôundàun hnayá*

máun bà

If it's that high you'll have to drive up very carefully.	*dílauʔ myìn-yín, khímbyâ ʔímmatán θadì thâ mâun teʔ θwâyàléimmé*

kóu sán yà

a road one travels often	*θwâ néijà lá néijà lân*
I'm always travelling these roads; I'm used to them.	*dí lânnè dí khayîgóu, couʔ amyê θwâ néijà lá néijà lân*
Sit quietly back there and come along; I'll do the driving.	*ʔêiʔêi naukkà tháin laikkhè, couʔ mâun teʔ θwâmé*

máun hlà

bends around, is curved	*kwèidé*
is crooked, not straight	*kautté*
curve, corner, bend	*ʔakwèi*
crook, bend	*ʔakauʔ*
The road up the mountain is very crooked—what kind of a road is this?	*táun teʔ lân ʔímmatán ʔakwèi ʔakauʔ myâdé, bèné lânlê*

máun kalaʔ

is straight	*phyàundé*
Talking about roads, who can say that any road is straight? Where did you ever hear that?	*lân shóuyín, bé lâmmashóu phyàundélòu badú pyôhnáinðalê, béhmá câbûðalê*
this fashion, of course	*dílóu pò*
Of course they're like that, my friend.	*dílóu pò. meisshwéi*

máun hlà

What you say is proving to be true.	*khímbyâ pyôdálê hmán ládé*
river	*myiʔ*
I have never read even in books that rivers and roads are straight.	*myimmyânè lâmmyâ phyàundélòu, sáʔoutthêhmálê couʔ maphapphûbû*

máun bà

interjection denoting surprise	*ʔamélêi*
is relieved mentally	*seiʔʔêidé*
right now	*ʔakhùhmàbê*
Well, I'm sure relieved to get to the top of the mountain.	*ʔamélêi, táumbó yaullòu ʔakhùhmábê seiʔ ʔêi θwâdé*

kóu sán yà

time of arrival	*yaukkhá* (=*yauttè ʔakhá*)
We're almost at Maymyo now.	*ʔakhù méi myòu yaukkhá nîbí*
resting place, stage on a journey	*sakhân*
rest station	*tê sakhân*
stiffness, tiredness	*ʔanyâun* (*nyâundé*)
stops to rest, rests	*nâdé*
will stay for a while (pl.)	*nâjàʔôummé*
Shall we stop to rest for a while in that rest house up ahead to get rid of our stiffness?	*šèigà tê sakhâmhmá ʔanyâun pyéi khanà nâjàʔôummalâ*

máun kalaʔ

as for that	*dádò*
That's up to you.	*dádò, khímbyâ θabôbábê*
disputes, argues	*nyîndé*
If you say we'll stay, we won't argue (about it).	*nâmé shóuyínlê, couttòu manyîmbû*

máun bà

There's no need to stay.	*nâbòu malóubábû*
without stopping to rest	*manâbê*
Let's drive to Maymyo without stopping.	*manâbênè méi myòugóu mâun θwâjàzòu*

SECTION B—WORD STUDY AND REVIEW OF BASIC SENTENCES

1. Word Study

A. More Secondary Verb Particles (See Unit 7)

-khè different place or time; change of place.

dígóu lágè	Come here.
dígóu lágèbá	Come here (polite).
couttòu naukkóu laikkhèbá	Follow us.
ʔèiʔèi naukkà tháin laikkhè	Sit quietly back there and come along.
bâumbídóu wukkhèbá	Put on (your) shorts.
manèigà dasshí bé hnagálán wégèðalê	How many gallons of gas did you buy yesterday?
myòudêgóu couʔ kânauphmá tháin laikkhèhnáindé	You can come along to the city in the back of my car.
cúndódòu mótókâgóu šáun thâgèyàmé	We'll have to park our car out of the way.
couʔ búdáyóuŋgóu šinnáyí hnashè ŋâmaniʔ ʔayauʔ lágèmé	I'll get to the station by 8:25.

-khè is a secondary verb particle denoting *different place* or *time* or *change of place*. It is used in both narrative and imperative sentences.

-laiʔ definitive action; action in another situation.

mótókâ hûŋgóu hmoullaippá	Blow the horn.
teʔ θwâbòu lân šáun pêilaippá	Get out of his way and give him room to pass.
phallaiʔ	Read it!
lephmaʔ θôunzáun θwâ wélaippá	Go and buy three tickets.
ŋâmûlauʔ pêilaippá	Give (him) about 8 annas.
ʔacôu ʔacâun ʔakóun yêilaippàmé	I'll write you all about it.
khanaʔ nâlaiʔʔôummé	I'm going to rest for a moment.
ʔakhù θwâlaippáʔôummé	I'll be going now.
sâlaiʔʔôummé	I'm going to eat (and get it over with).

-laiʔ is a secondary verb particle denoting *definitive action*. It is used in both narrative and imperative sentences.

-ôun continuance, repetition, further action (in the future), postponement.

néibáʔôun	Wait a moment.
khanà nâbáʔôun	Stop and rest a while.

khanà yappáʔôun	Stop for a while.
khanà sàumbáʔôun	Wait a while.
khanà sàun néibáʔôun	Wait a while.
phyouʔ pêibáʔôun	Loosen it for me (before we go).
khanà nâjàʔôummalâ	Shall we stop and rest a while?
hóu tê sakhâmhmá nâʔôummalâ	Shall we stop and rest a while in that rest house?
bêin lêyàʔôummé	We'll have to change the wheel (before we do anything else.
ʔawuʔ θwâ lêʔôummé	I'm going to change my clothes (before I go anywhere else).

-ʔôun is a secondary verb particle denoting *continuance, repetition, further action* (*in the future*), *postponement* (*of another action*). It is used in both narrative and imperative sentences. In narrative sentences it is followed by the final particle *-mé*. In imperative sentences it is last: *maθwânèʔôun* 'don't go yet.' It is most often not translated in English.

-tò imminence, inevitability, permission

θwâdòmé	Goodbye (from person leaving).
θwâdò	Goodbye (to person leaving).
θîmbô thwettòmé	The steamer is about to leave.
seʔ maθwâdòbû	The motor won't run.
méi myòugóu θwâdòmalâ	Are you going to Maymyo (right away)?
méi myòugóu myámmyán yaucchímbéimè, cá θwâdòmé	Even though we wanted to get to Maymyo quickly, we'll be late (inevitably).
máin hnashélauʔ cándòdé	There's only about 20 miles left.
malaittòbû	He isn't coming along.
khímbyânèdò bédòmà malaittòbû	I'll never go with you again.
dí ganèi sà pî, mamèidòbû	From now on I won't forget.
kâûndò kâumbáyè, kâumbéimè, couʔ macaipphû	It's all right, but even so I don't like it.

-tò is a secondary verb particle denoting *inevitability, imminence, permission*. It is used in both narrative and

imperative sentences. It is often not translated in the English equivalents.

-cà regularity, the usual thing.

θwâ néijà lá néijà lân	A road one travels regularly.
dí ˀasá khímbyâ sâ néijà ˀasá	This is the food you usually eat.
wuˀ néijà ˀawuˀ	The clothes one always wears.

-cà is a secondary verb particle which is limited to the position shown above. It is used at the end of a verb expression which modifies a noun. It denotes *regularity, constancy, 'the usual thing.'*

-sân polite urgency.

cìzân	Look!
pyôzân	Say (it)!
phallaissâmbá	Read (it)!
khímbyâ pyínlaissâmbá	You fix (it)!
pyô pyàlaissâmbá	Please explain!

-sân is a secondary verb particle denoting *polite urgency*. It is limited to imperative sentences. There is also a verb *sândé* 'feels, tries' *sân cìbá* 'try it and see.'

-hlù imminence, 'about to, on the point of'.

yauthlùbí	It is about to arrive.
θaŋéjîn tayauˀ yauthlùbí	A friend is about to arrive.

-hlù is a secondary verb particle denoting *imminence, 'about to, on the point of.'* It is very infrequent.

B. More General Particles (See Unit 9)

1. -pò 'of course'

dílòu kauyyàdá pò	Of course one has to pick it up this way.
šìdá pò	Of course, there is.
dílòu pò	Of course it's this way.

-pò is a general particle. It follows noun expressions and comes at the end of the sentence. It is usually to be translated 'of course.'

2. -nó expecting acquiescence

θwâdòménó	Goodbye (from person leaving)
θwâdònó	Goodbye (to person leaving).
kâungâun néinó	Be good.

maθwânènó Don't go.

manepphán lábánó Come tomorrow, won't you.

-nó is a general particle. It is used in both narrative and imperative sentences and comes at the end of the sentence. It has a coaxing effect something like the English 'won't you.'

C. Another Subordinating Particle (See Unit 15)

-yîn simultaneous occurrence.

pyôyîn shóuyîn, máun bà shîn lábí Mg. Ba has come down just as we're talking (about him).

pyôyîn shóuyîn hûn hmouθθán câdé While we were talking I heard the sound of an auto horn.

thamîn sâ néiyîn, θaŋéjîn tayau? yau? ládé While he was eating a friend came.

-yîn is a subordinating particle. It denotes *simultaneous occurrence:* while one thing is going on another happens.

D. ma . . . phê 'without'

manâbê without stopping to rest

manâbênè méi myòugóu mâun θwâjàzòu Let's drive to Maymyo without stopping to rest.

SECTION C—REVIEW OF BASIC SENTENCES (*Cont.*)

1. Review of Basic Sentences (*Cont.*)

Further oral practice with the second part of the *Basic Sentences*.

2. Covering the English of Basic Sentences

Check your knowledge of the meaning of all words and phrases in the *Basic Sentences*. This is individual study.

3. What Would You Say?

Give full answers for the following questions.

1. *mótókâ hûn hmouθθán câyàðalâ*
2. *máun bà ?éimbógà mashîn láðèibûlâ*
3. *khímbyâ bá phyillòu ?amyê nau? càðalê*
4. *khímbyâ malaittòbûlâ*
5. *mândalêi myòugóu shè hnanáyí mathôugín, yaupphòu lóuðalâ*

6. *lóudá yàhnáimmalâ*
7. *θwâzayá šìðêiðalâ*
8. *mótókâ pyeyyín, bènè loummalê*
9. *khímbyâhmá sôuyéinzayá mašìbûlâ*
10. *mótókâ nauphmá bêin ˀapóu páðalâ*
11. *khímbyâzíhmá paisshán ˀapóu páðalâ*
12. *mótókâ seˀ pyímbûðalâ*
13. *sáˀouˀ phattá pyîmbòu kâunðalâ*
14. *dasshí béhmá wélòu yàmalê*
15. *sesshígô mawéjímbûlâ*
16. *hóu θámbôundêhmá dasshí bé hnagálán šìðêiðalê*
17. *khímbyâ ˀakhù mâunjínðalâ*
18. *máun bà, mótókâ mâunjínðalâ*
19. *méi myòugóu θwâdòmalâ*
20. *lân šáun pêihnáimmalâ*
21. *khímbyâ θwâbòu ˀayêi cîðalâ*
22. *thamîn myámmyán sâhnáimmalâ*
23. *lâm pyà hmattáimhmá bá sá yêi thâðalê*
24. *dígà néi sà pî, bégóu θwâmalòulê*
25. *dí lân khímbyâ θwâ néijà lá néijà lânlâ*
26. *dí ˀasá khímbyâ sâ néijà ˀasálâ*
27. *dí myiˀ kwèi kauθθalâ*
28. *hóu lâmhmá ˀakwèi ˀakauˀ myâðalâ*
29. *hóu lân phyàunðalâ*
30. *khímbyâ pyôdá hmán-yèlâ*
31. *méi myòu yaukkhá nîbalâ*
32. *hóu tê sakhâmhmá nâˀôummalâ*
33. *nâbòu lóuðalâ*
34. *khímbyâdòu bá phyillòu nyîn néijàðalê*
35. *manâbênè mâun θwâyàmalâ*
36. *phyàundè lâmbóhmá mâumbûðalâ*
37. *méi myòugóu yaupphûðalâ*
38. *kôunáyí mathôugín láhnáimmalâ*
39. *shénáyí makhwêgín maláhnáimbûlâ*
40. *mîyathâ šinnáyí mattîn thwemmalâ*

SECTION D—LISTENING IN

1. What Did You Say?

With other members of your group give orally your responses to the previous exercise as the Leader calls for them.

2. Word Study Check-Up

Give the Burmese for all English equivalents in the *Word Study* as the Leader calls for it.

3. Listening In

1. A flat tire.

máun kalaʔ: *dí lân θeiʔ kwèi kautté, bèné lânlê*

máun hlà: *táun teʔ lân shóuyín, dílóu kwèi kauyyàdá pò*
phyàundè lân cúndó matwèibûbû

máun bà: *ʔamélêi, bêin pautté*
méimyòu myámmyám yaucchímbéimè, cá θwâdòmé

máun hlà: *seiʔ ʔêiʔêi thâbá*
nauʔ càyínlê, ʔayêi macîbábû
táun chéiyîŋgà sàdá maniʔ lêizé šì θwâbí
máin hnashélaupphê cándòdé

kóu sán yà: *shînjà*
bêin lêyàʔôummé

máun kalaʔ: *mótókâ pyissîmyâ béhmálê, hóu θittádêhmálâ*

kóu sán yà: *houtté, mótókâ hmyauʔ jennè hnyaʔ pêibá*

máun kalaʔ: *tú, ganânlemmànè weʔʔúhlè lóujínðalâ*

kóu sán yà: *seʔ bêin ʔapóu mótókânaukkà θwâ yúbá*
ʔayín lóu, ʔahnêi phyiʔ néibí
myámmyán θwâbá
phyêibyêi hnêi manéibánè

máun kalaʔ: *yóbá cuphmá léi mašìbû*
léi thôudán šìðalâ

kóu sán yà: *šìdá pò*
cúndó θeiʔ nyâundé
khímbyâ pyínlaissâmbá
khanà nâlaiʔʔôummé

máun bà: *hô, ʔašèihmá tê sakhân takhù ʔakhùhmàbê myíndé*
couttòu péi bélauʔmyìnðalê shóudá mapyôdapphû

máun hlà: *tódó myìndé*

máun kalaʔ: *khímbyâdòu bá nyîn néijàdálê*

máun bà: *manyîmbábû*

kóu sán yà: *khímbyâgàdò bámà maloupphû bêin pyín pîbí θwâjàzòu*

máun bà: *khanà néibá?ôun cúndò phana? taphe? côu pyou? néibí*

2. They run out of gas.

kóu sán yà: *dasshí kóumbí se? maθwâdòbû ?apóu dasshíbôunlê mapábû sesshí θámbôun tabôumbê pádé*

máun kala?: *manèigà dasshí bé hnagálán wégèðalê*

kóu sán yà: *ŋâgálán wébéimè, khayî ?amyâjî θwâ néilòu kóun θwâbí*

máun kala?: *khímbyâ dasshí ?apóu mótókâbóhmá bá phyillòu mathâðalê*

kóu sán yà: *mèi θwâlòubá dí ganèigà sà pî, mamèidòbû*

máun kala?: *hóu lân pyà hmattáimhmá couttòu bé hnamáin wêiðalêlòu, sá yêi thâðalâ*

kóu sán yà: *?êdádò pú manéibánè dí lânhá θwâ néijà lá néijà lân phyillòu, macágín mótókâ tazî lálèimmé*

máu kala?: *khímbyânè θwâyín, dílóubê khímbyânèdò bédòmà malaittòbû*

kóu sán yà: *hô, pyôyîn shóuyîn, hûn hmouθθán câdé mótókâ tazî ládé*

máun kalannè kóu sán yà: *khanà yappá?ôun, khanà yappá?ôun*

mótókâ máunðamâ: *mótókâ mató tashà taillòu se? pye? néiðalâ*

kóu sán yà: *mahouppábû dasshí kóun θwâlòubá khímbyâhmá dasshí ?apóu páðalâ*

mâunðamâ: *?apóudò mapábû mapábéimè, myòudêgóu cou? kânauphmá tháin laikkhèhnáindé*

máun kala?: *cêizû tímbádé cúndódòu mótókâgóu lân šáun thâgèyàmé khanà sàumbá?ôun*

SECTION E—CONVERSATION

1. Covering the Burmese of Basic Sentences

With the Burmese covered, practice until you can speak the Burmese for each English sentence without hesitation. This is individual study.

2. Vocabulary Check-Up

Give the Burmese for all the English sentences in the *Basic Sentences* as the Leader calls for it.

3. Conversation

Suggested Topics:

1. Take a trip by automobile and discuss the possibilities of trouble along the way.
2. Describe a trip you have taken. Where did you start from and where were you going? How long did it take you? When did you get there? Who was along? Was everybody on time?
3. Describe a trip into the mountains. What was the road like? How high did you go? Where did you stay along the road?
4. You had a blow-out. What did you do? Who changed the tire? What tools did you use and why?
5. You ran out of gas. You stopped a passing motorist for help. What did you say, and what did he say?

Continue conversation. Additional check-up on the material of the *Basic Sentences* by the Leader if it seems necessary.

Review: Complete check-up on the material of the *Word Study* and *Basic Sentences.*

Finder List

ʔahnêi (*hnêidé*)	slowness, slowly
ʔakauʔ (*kautté*)	crook, bend
ʔakhùhmàbê	right now, just this minute
ʔakwèi (*kwèidé*)	curve, corner, bend
ʔamélêi	interjection denoting surprise
ʔanyâun (*nyâundé*)	ache, feeling of stiffness
ʔapóu (*póudé*)	excess, spare
ʔayêi (*yêidé*)	business, affair
ʔayêi cîdé	is busy, is urgent, is in a hurry
bêin	wheel
dádò	as for that
dasshí	gasoline
gálán	gallon
ganân	crab; also, numeral
ganânlemmà	monkey wrench
hmattáin	signboard
hnyaʔ	pliers
hûn	horn
hûn hmouθθán	sound of a horn
kautté	is crooked, not straight
kwèidé	bends around, is curved
léi thôudán	air pump
lemmà	thumb
lóunlautté	is sufficient
manâbê	without stopping to rest
mató tashà	accident, accidentally
mâundé	drives (a vehicle)
mâunðamâ	driver
mótókâ hmyauʔ jeʔ	auto jack
mótókâ pyissî	auto tools
myiʔ	river
myìndé	is high, tall
nâdé	stops to rest, rests
nauʔ càdé	is late, falls behind
nyîndé	disputes, disapproves
pautté	pierces, is pierced
péi	foot (twelve inches)
phyàundé	is straight

phyêidé	is slow, gradual, easy, pleasant, moderate	*taphe?*	one side (classifier)
phyêibyêi	slowly, easily	*táumbó*	upper part of a mountain
phyêibyêi hmámhmán	slowly and accurately	*táun*	mountain
phyitté	happens	*táun chéiyîn*	foot of a mountain
pò	of course	*tê sakhân*	rest house, rest station
pôun	container	*tetté*	climbs, ascends, advances, gains on
pyetté	is ruined, destroyed	*tódé*	is suitable, sufficient
pyôyîn, shóuyîn	while one talks	*tódó*	fairly, pretty much
sakhân	station	*tú*	hammer
sá yêi thâdá	something which has been written	*θámbôun*	tin can, metal container
se?	motor, engine, machine	*θán*	iron, metal
sei? ?êidé	is relieved mentally, is not excited	*θeillê*	too, very much
sesshí	motor oil	*θittá*	box
shé-	ten (combining form)	*θwâ néijà lá néijà lân*	a road one travels often
shí	oil	*we??ú*	screw
shóuðalóu	as the saying goes	*we??úhlè*	screwdriver
šáundé	avoids, shuns	*yaukkhá*	time of arrival
		yóbá cu?	rubber tube, inner tube

UNIT 17

A DAY IN THE COUNTRY

SECTION A—BASIC SENTENCES

ENGLISH EQUIVALENTS	AIDS TO LISTENING
máun kalaʔ	
picnic	*pyóbwêzâ*
Are there any good places to go for picnics in Maymyo?	*méi myòuhmá pyóbwêzâ θwâbòu néiyágâummyâ šìðalâ*
kóu sán yà	
There are a great many places to go.	*θwâbòu néiyá ʔamyâjî šìbádé*
waterfall, cascade, cataract	*yéi tagún*
We can go to a place where there is a waterfall.	*yéi tagún càdè néiyágóu θwâhnáindé*
flower, blossom	*pân*
fence, enclosure	*chán*
flower garden, park	*pânján*
We can also go into the park.	*pânjándêgóulê θwâhnáindé*
side	*nabêi*
side of a mountain	*táunnabêi*
If you want to go to the side of the mountain, it isn't very far.	*táunnabêigóu θwâjín-yínlê, θeiʔ mawêibû*

máun hlà

swims	*yéi kûdé*
As for me I want very much to go to a place where there is a waterfall because I want to swim.	*cúndógàdò yéi kûjíndè ˀatweˀ, yéi tagún càdè néiyágóu θeiˀ θwâjíndé.*
is of one mind, agrees	*θabô túdé*
Do you all agree?	*khímbyâdòu θabô tújàyèlâ*

ˀâlôuŋgà [from all]

We agree.	*θabô tújàbádé*

máun bà

If it's today we're going, we'll have to go now and buy food.	*dí ganèi θwâjàmé shóuyín, ˀakhù sâzayá θaussayá θwâ wéyàlèimmé*

máun kalaˀ

today	*ganèi* (=*dí ganèi*)
tomorrow	*nepphán* (=*nepphyíŋgá*)
If we're going today, don't be arguing about today or tomorrow.	*θwâmé shóuyínlê, ganèi nepphán louˀ manéijàbánè*
Let's go right today.	*dí ganèibê θwâjàzòu*

kóu sán yà

list, account, register	*sayîn*
Write out a list of what you want.	*khímbyâdòu lóujíndágóu sayîn yêibá*
right away, immediately	*checchîn*
I'll go right away and buy it now.	*ˀakhù checchîn couˀ θwâ wémé*

máun kala?

Don't go alone.	*khímbyâ tayautthê maθwâbánè*
We want to go along too.	*cúndódòulê laicchínðêidé*

[Time Interval]

kóu sán yà

tree	*?apín*
Stop the car under that tree.	*mótókâgóu hóu ?apín?auphmá ya? thâbá*
That place isn't far from the place to swim.	*?êdí néiyáhá yéi kûbòu néiyánèlê mawêibû*
tree	*θippín*
shade	*?ayei?*
The shade is good, too.	*θippin ?ayeillê kâundé*

máun hlà

As for me, I want to go take a swim right away.	*cúndógàdò, checchîn yéi θwâ kûjíndé*

máun kala?

is in a hurry, is urgent	*?ayín lóudé*
Don't be in a hurry to swim.	*yéikûbòu ?ayín malóubánè*
puts down, throws down	*chàdé*
helps	*kúdé*
First come and help take the things out of the car.	*pyissîdéigóu mótókâbógà chàbòu ?ayín lá kúbá?ôun*

[Time Interval]

máun hlà

is deep — *netté*
It's fairly deep. — *tódó netté*

And the water is very cold. — *yéilê θei? ?èidé*

máun kala?

is wide, loud — *cédé*
loudness, loudly — *céjé*
fairly loud — *khaccéjé*
Speak up. — *khaccéjé pyôbá*

sound, noise — *?aθán*
I can't hear what you say because of the noise of the falling water. — *yéi càdè ?aθánnè khímbyâ pyôdá macàyàbû*

máun hlà

The water is fairly cold. — *yéi tódó ?èidé*

kóu sán yà

time of swimming — *kûgá (kûdè ?akhá)*
when you start it will be cold — *sàdò ?èihmá*
Of course it's cold when you start. — *kûgá sàdò ?èihmá pò*

the fact that it is cold — *?êihmân*
If you get started and swim a little you won't know that it's cold. — *yéi nênê sà kûlaiyyín, ?êihmân bé θìdòmalê*

	máun bà
is shallow	*téindé*
shallow water	*yéidéin*
I want to swim only in shallow water, I don't know how to swim well.	*yéidéimhmádá kûjíndé cou? kâungâun makûdapphû*
(Show me) how to swim.	*bélóu lou? kûyàmalê*
	kóu sán yà
takes out	*thoutté*
blows up (with air)	*léi thôudé*
neck	*lébîn*
puts on, around, through	*sutté*
Take the tube out of the spare tire, blow it up, put it around your neck and swim.	*?apóu pádè mótókâbêin ?athêgà cukkóu thou?, léi thôu pî, lébîmhmá su? kû*
	máun bà
Well, this way I'll probably be able to swim.	*?èdílóu shóuyín, kûhnáinlèimmé thíndé*
	máun hlà
I'm hungry.	*couttò shábí*
Haven't you had enough swimming yet?	*khímbyâdòu yéi kûlóu matóðèibûlâ*
	máun kala?
It's enough, I think.	*tólauppí, thíndé*
Come on, we'll go and fix lunch.	*lá, sâbòu θwâ pyímmé*

rug, carpet	*kózô*
spreads	*khîndé*
First spread the rug.	*pathamà kózô khîmbá?ôun*

máun bà

opens	*phwìndé*
What do we have along to open the can of fish?	*ŋâ θittá phwìmbòu bá páðalê*

máun kala?

makes a hole in or through	*phautté*
opener	*phaussayá*
We have no opener.	*phaussayádò mapábû*
pocket knife	*mâunjadâ*
Open it with a knife.	*mâunjadânèbê phau?*
touches	*thìdé*
Open it carefully so that you don't cut your hand.	*lekkóu mathì?áun, θadî thâ phau?*

máun bà

while cutting	*phauyyîn*
is cut	*pyatté*
While opening it, my finger got cut.	*phauyyîn, cou? lekkóu dâ pya? θwâdé*
wound, scar	*dán-yá*
wraps around	*patté*
piece of cloth, rag	*?awussou?*
Don't you have a piece of cloth to tie up the cut?	*dán-yá papphòu ?awussou? mašìbûlâ*

máun kalaˀ

The knife cut isn't very big. *dâ dán-yá θeiˀ macîbábû*

handkerchief *lekkáin pawá*
tears *shoutté*
I'll tear up my handkerchief for you. *couˀ lekkáin pawágóu shouˀ pêimé*

máun bà

is clean *síndé*
You wrap it up for me, please, after we wash it clean. *yéi sínˀáun shêi pî, khímbyâ kóudáimbê paˀ pêibá*

kóu sán yà

It's time to return home. *ˀéin pyámbòu ˀachéin tóbí*

Let's go back. *pyánjàzòu*

SECTION B—WORD STUDY AND REVIEW OF BASIC SENTENCES

1. Word Study

A. Auxiliary Verbs

Auxiliary verbs function both as full verbs and as modifiers immediately following full verbs. They precede the particles, secondary and final, in verb complexes. In negative sentences the negative particle *ma-* is never attached to an auxiliary verb.

1. ˀâdé 'is free, disengaged, at liberty'

ˀakhân θôuŋgân ˀâ néibádé There are three rooms vacant.
khímbyâ ˀâyín, θwâ cìjímbádé I'd like to go see [them], if you are free.
cúndó ˀakhù maˀâbû I am not at liberty now.
khímbyâ θwâˀâðalâ Are you free to go?
maθwâˀâbû I am not free to go.

The first three sentences show *ʔâdé* in its use as a full verb. Sentences 4 and 5 show it as an auxiliary verb.

2. *lautté* 'is enough, sufficient'

lóunlautté	It is enough, there's enough.
malóunlaupphû	There isn't enough.
làgà sâlauθθalâ	Is your salary sufficient to live on?
masâlauppábû	It isn't enough to live on.

lautté is infrequent as a full verb.

3. *séidé* 'sends, causes to do'

dí ʔatweʔ khímbyâgóu ʔalouʔ mamyâzéijímbû	I don't want to make a lot of work for you about this.
pyôzéijíndé	I want to have him speak.
mapyôzéijímbû	I don't want to have him speak.
lousséidé	I had [him] do [it].
malousséibû	I didn't have him do it.

séidé is infrequent as a full verb.

4. *tatté* 'knows how to; is customary, is the usual course'

myîn sîdaθθalâ	Can you ride horseback?
myîn masîdapphû	I can't ride horseback.
shêileiʔ θauttatté	I can (or usually do) smoke cigars.
shêileiʔ maθauttapphû	I don't smoke.
bamâ zagâ pyôdəθθalâ	Can you speak Burmese?
bamâ zagâ taθθalâ	Can you speak Burmese?
mapyôdapphû	I cannot
matapphû	I cannot.

5. *yàdé* 'gets, obtains;' as auxiliary verb 'has the opportunity of'

pyôðán câyàdé	I heard (had the opportunity of hearing) a voice
macâyàbû	I didn't hear (hadn't the opportunity of hearing) it.

There is also a secondary particle *-yà-* meaning 'necessity' (Unit 7).

šáun thâgèyàdé	I had to move it out of the way.

The position of the particle *-yà-* is different from that of the auxiliary *-yàdé*. Notice that in the example quoted the particle *-yà-* is preceded by another particle *-khè*. In many expressions the position is ambiguous. That is, if there is only a verb followed by a syllable *-yà*, only the context determines whether the *-yà* is the auxiliary verb or the secondary verb particle.

Other auxiliary verbs will be called to your attention in later units.

B. *-séi* commands: first-person-singular and third person

néibázéi	Don't bother ('let it remain')
θwâbázéi	Let him (them) go.
θwâjàbázéi	Let them go.
θwâbayàzéi	Let me go.
maθwâbázéinè	Let him (them) not go.
maθwâbayàzéinè	Let me not go.

-séi is a secondary verb particle (Unit 7) marking first-person-singular and third-person commands.

C. *Commands*

The commands in Burmese are as follows:

Concerning yourself:

θwâbayàzéi	Let me go.

Concerning yourself and others:

θwâjàzòu	Let's go.
θwâyàʔáun	Let's go.

Concerning the person to whom you are talking:

θwâ	Go.
θwâbá	Go. (polite)

Concerning more than one person to whom you are talking:

θwâjà	Go.
θwâjàbá	Go. (polite)

Concerning a third person:

θwâbázéi	Let him go.

Concerning more than one third person:

θwâjàbázéi	Let them go.

2. Covering English and Burmese Word Study

Give the English equivalents of all Burmese expressions in the *Word Study* and the Burmese for all the English. This is individual study.

3. Review of Basic Sentences

Further oral practice with the first part of the *Basic Sentences*.

1. Review of Basic Sentences (*Cont.*)

Further oral practice with the second part of the *Basic Sentences.*

2. Covering the English of Basic Sentences

Check your knowledge of the meaning of all words and phrases in the *Basic Sentences.* This is individual study.

3. What Would You Say?

Give full answers to each of the following questions.

1. *dí myòuhmá pyóbwêzâ θwâbòu néiyámyâ šìðalâ*
2. *θwâbòu néiyá ˀamyâjî šìyèlâ*
3. *yéi tagúnnâhmá pânján šìðalâ*
4. *taúnnabêihmá θippímmyâ šìyèlâ*
5. *khímbyâ yéi kûdaθθalâ*
6. *yéi kûbòu ˀakhù θwâjinðalâ*
7. *dí néiyáhmá yéi kûhnáinðalâ*
8. *khímbyâdòu θabô tújàyèlâ*
9. *khímbyâ díganèi yéi kû θwâmalâ*
10. *khímbyâ ˀakhù yéi chôujínðalâ*
11. *khímbyâ yéi ŋaθθalâ*
12. *khímbyâgô yéi θaucchíndalâ*
13. *θauyyéi béhmá yàhnáinðalê*
14. *leˀ shêijínðalâ*
15. *sâzayá θaussayá béhmá yàmalê*
16. *θú tayautthê θwâmalâ*
17. *khímbyâdòulê laicchínðalâ*
18. *hóu ˀapín ˀauphmá nâjínðalâ*
19. *dí néiyáhá yéi kûbòu néiyánè θeiˀ wêiðalâ*
20. *dí θippín ˀayeiˀ kâunðalâ*
21. *pyissîdéigóu kâbógà chàbòu lá kúmalâ*
22. *yéi téinðalâ, neθθalâ*
23. *máun bà céjé pyôdaθθalâ*
24. *khímbyâ dílóu ˀamyê céjé pyôdaθθalâ*
25. *yéi téindéimhmáðá kûjínðalâ*
26. *lébîmhmá cuˀ sullòu, yéi kûmalòulâ*
27. *dílóu shóuyín, yéi kûhnáimmalâ*
28. *yéi kûlòu matóðêibûlâ*
29. *sâzayámyâ θwâ pyímmalâ*
30. *pathamà kózô khín-yàmalâ*
31. *ŋâ θittá bé hnakhù phwìn-yàmalê*
32. *phaussayá mašibûlâ*
33. *khímbyâzíhmá mâunjadâ páyèlâ*

34. *bá phyiθθalê, dâ pya? θwâðalâ*
35. *dâ dán-yá cîðalâ*
36. *béhmá dâ pya? θwâðalê*
37. *yéi sín?áun shêi pîbalâ*
38. *lekkáin pawánè pa? pêiyàmalâ*
39. *?éin pyámbòu ?achéin tóbalâ*
40. *?akhù bé hnanáyí thôubalê*

SECTION D—LISTENING IN

1. What Did You Say?

With other members of the group give orally your responses to the previous exercise as the Leader calls for them.

2. Word Study Check-Up

Give the Burmese for all English equivalents in the *Word Study* as the Leader calls for it.

3. Listening In

1. "How about a picnic?"

máun kala?: *pyóbwêzâ θwâyà?áun*

máun bà: *bé néiyágóu θwâyín, kâummalê*

kóu sán yà: *θwâjín-yín, táunnabêigà pânjánhá pyóbwêzá θwâbòu kâundé*

máun kala?: *yéi kûbòu néiyá šìyèlâ*

kóu sán yà: *šìdé, yéi tagún càdè néiyáhmá yéi kûhnáindé*

máun kala?: *?êdí néiyáhmá yéi téinðalâ, neθθalâ*

kóu sán yà: *lébîn ?athî netté*
yéi kûbòu ?atóbê

máun bà: *cúndódò yéi kâuŋgâun makûdapphû*

kóu sán yà: *keissà mašìbû*
yóbá cukkóu léi thôu pî, lébîmhmá su? kûhnáindé

máun kala?: *?êdí pânjándêhmá θippín ?ayeimmyâ šìyèlâ*

kóu sán yà: *θippín khaccîjîmyâ šìdé*
dájàun θippín ?ayei? θei? kâundé

máun bà: *bé nèi θwâjínlòulê*

máun kala?: *khímbyâdòu laimmé shóuyín, ganèi nepphán lou? manéibánè couttò dí nèi θwâmé* kóu sán yà: kâumbí, máun bà θabô tûyín, dí nèi θwâyà?áun

2.

máun hlà: mótókâ bé nâhmálê

máun bà cí: ?éinnabêihmá ya? thâgèdé khímbyâ bégóu θwâmalòulê

máun hlà: cúndò kózô sou? néilòu, kózô shâimhmá θwâ pêimalòu ?éimbógà chàbòu khanà lá kúbá?ôun

máun bà cí: khímbyà ?akhân cébéimè, kózôjîgóu khîn thâlòu cìlòu kâundé

máun hlà: wégá sàdò dáde? póu cìlòu kâundé

máun bà cí: ?ô, khímbyâgóu pyôbòu mèi θwâdé díganèi ?âlôun sháindéi maphwìmbû

3.

máun hlà: khímbyâ bá yêi néiðalê

máun bà: zêi sayîn yêi néidé

máun hlà: khímbyâ ?akhù checchîn zêigóu θwâyín cúndò ?atwellê ŋâ θittá wégèbá

máun bà: cúndò hmá šìdé khímbyâ lóujín-yín hóu θittádêgà thou? yúbá

máun hlà: phaupphòu bá šìðalê

máun bà: phaussayádò mašìbû dí mâunjadânè phau?

máun hlà: cúndò le? pya? θwâbí bá louyyàmalê

máun bà: dán-yágóu sín?áun shêi, lekkáinpawágóu shou?pî, ?awussou? lou?, pa?thâbá

SECTION E—CONVERSATION

1. Covering the Burmese of Basic Sentences

With the Burmese covered, practice until you can speak the Burmese for each English sentence without hesitation.

2. Vocabulary Check-Up

Give the Burmese for all the English sentences in the *Basic Sentences* as the Leader calls for it.

3. Conversation

Suggested Topics:

1. You want to go on a picnic. You discuss the various places you might go. You want to go to a park. You want to swim. You want to go to the mountains, and so on.
2. You discuss the problem of when to go—today, tomorrow, right now, three o'clock.
3. You discuss the problem of how to go—automobile, streetcar, train, boat.
4. You discuss the swimming place. How deep is the water? How cold is it? You ask how to swim. Your friend tells you to inflate an inner tube and put it around you.
5. Your friend asks you where he can get an opener for a can of fish. You tell him to use your knife. He cuts himself and you tell him to wrap it up in his hankerchief.

SECTION F—CONVERSATION (*Cont.*)

Continue conversation. Additional check-up on the material of the *Basic Sentences* by the Leader if it seems necessary.

Review: Complete check-up on the material of the *Word Study* and *Basic Sentences*.

Finder List

ʔapín	tree
ʔaθán	sound, noise
ʔawussouʔ	piece of cloth, rag
ʔayeiʔ	shade, shadow
ʔayín lóudé	is in a hurry, is urgent

cédé	is wide, loud (of a voice)
céjé	wideness, loudness, loudly
chàdé	puts down, throws down
chán	fence, enclosure
checchîn	right away, immediately
dán-yá	wound, scar
ˀêihmá	it will be cold
ˀêihmân	the fact that it is cold
ganèi (= *dí ganèi*)	today
khaccéjé	fairly loudly
khîndé	spreads
kózô	rug, carpet
kúdé	helps
kûgá (= *kûdè ˀakhá*)	time of swimming
lekkáin pawá	handkerchief
lébîn	neck
léi thôudé	blows up with air
mâunjadâ	pocket knife
nabêi	side
nepphán (= *nepphyíŋgá*)	tomorrow
netté	is deep
pân	flower
pânján	flower garden, park
patté	wraps around
phaussayá	opener
phautté	makes a hole in or through
phauyyîn	while cutting
phwìndé	opens
pyatté	is cut
pyóbwêzá	picnic
sàdò	when starting
sayîn	list, account, register
shoutté	tears
síndé	is clean
sutté	puts on, into, through
táunnabêi	side of a mountain
téindé	is shallow
thìdé	touches
thoutté	takes out
θabô túdé	are of one mind, agree
θippín	tree
yéidéin	shallow water
yéi kûdé	swims
yéi tagûn	waterfall

UNIT 18

REVIEW

SECTION A—SENTENCE REVIEW

To the Leader: Begin this review of the work so far by having a session in which you call out at random English sentences from Parts I and II (the first twelve units) and ask members of the class to give the Burmese. The members of the class should not prepare in any special way for this. You can take the sentences you ask for from Sections B and C of Units 6 and 12, but take them in random order.

SECTION B—SENTENCE REVIEW

Practice saying out loud the Burmese for the following sentences. Keep at them until you know them all thoroughly. Do not write anything down. This is individual study.

I

1. Where is the railroad station?
2. Where are the tickets sold?
3. They're sold at this window.
4. What time does the Prome train leave?
5. Which platform does the Prome train leave from?
6. There's nothing to worry about.
7. (I) can't say for sure.
8. (I) won't stay long.
9. Come on, let's go.
10. Take these things away.

II

1. Hurry up, old man.
2. Don't worry.
3. How goes it, Mr. Clark?
4. How about you?
5. Come on, let's go eat.
6. I haven't seen you for a long time.
7. Is everybody all right?
8. Very pleased to meet you.

9. Did you enjoy the meal?
10. Don't take offense, please.

III

1. I'll explain so that you understand.
2. You can stay as you like.
3. I agree with what you say.
4. Just speak up.
5. I didn't like it even though it was good.
6. Maybe there is.
7. If that's the case, it's very nice.
8. Follow us and bring these things.
9. Let's go and see.
10. If you have something to say, go ahead and say it.

IV

1. Come on, let's get going.
2. Wait a moment.
3. There'll be enough.
4. Don't drive too fast.
5. Get out of his way and give him room to pass.
6. Drive slowly and carefully.
7. Danger!
8. That's up to you.
9. There's no need to stay.
10. I'll be going now.

V

1. Do you all agree?
2. We agree.
3. Let's go right today.
4. Don't go alone.
5. We want to go along too.
6. It's time to return home.
7. Come on, we'll go and fix lunch.
8. The water is fairly cold.
9. The water is very cold.
10. It's fairly deep.

SECTION C—HOW DO YOU SAY IT?

Quiz by the Group Leader on the sentences in Section B, asking various members of the group to give the Burmese equivalents of the English sentences.

SECTION D—HOW WOULD YOU SAY IT?

Practice the Burmese equivalents of the following sentences until you know them thoroughly. This is individual study.

I

1. The first-class charge is very expensive.
2. It's very crowded in the third class.
3. The steamer is about to leave.
4. Let's get off.
5. Let's get on.
6. Will you go by train?
7. I'm going by steamer.
8. What time is it?
9. It's 8:20.
10. Ah, we've arrived.

II

1. Don't stay long.
2. What did you ask?
3. I don't have a rupee on me.
4. Did you forget to come?
5. I haven't been to the market for a long time.
6. Where have you been?
7. I'm going for a walk.
8. Do you intend to go by rickshaw?
9. To whom are you writing?
10. To a friend.

III

1. The curry was a little hot (tasting).
2. It won't rain right away.
3. It's the middle of the day; the sun is very hot.
4. Let's go in the afternoon when it's cool and take our time.
5. Where are you staying now?
6. You're a strange fellow.
7. How's Mr. Williams?
8. His fever is better.
9. There's no time to buy books.
10. If that's the case I'll buy the books day after tomorrow.

IV

1. I'll get to the station by 8:25.
2. Give (him) about 8 annas.
3. Shall we stop and rest for a while?
4. The motor won't run.
5. It's all right, but even so I don't like it.
6. You fix it!
7. Come tomorrow, won't you.
8. Let's drive to Maymyo without stopping.
9. I'll have to change the tire.
10. I'm very stiff.

V

1. Are you free to go?
2. There isn't enough.
3. I want to have him speak.
4. Can you speak Burmese?
5. I can (speak Burmese).
6. Don't bother.
7. I don't know how to swim well.
8. What day do you want to go?
9. I forgot to tell you.
10. I cut my hand.

SECTION E—HOW DID YOU SAY IT?

Quiz by the Group Leader on the sentences in Section D, asking various members of the group to give the Burmese equivalents of the English sentences.

SECTION F—CONVERSATION REVIEW

Hold a series of conversations on any of the topics covered so far. All members of the group should have a chance to take part. Here are some suggested topics.

1. Discuss with a friend the best way of going to Mandalay from Rangoon. Discuss the classes of travel, the prices and the advantages and disadvantages of each.
2. Have dinner with a friend in a restaurant and discuss the Burmese food. Have a third member act as waiter. Order a meal, pay for it, discuss its quality.
3. Tell a friend about a card game you were in last night. How much did you win or lose? What did you start with and what did you take away?
4. You have just arrived in Rangoon and you meet a Burman. Discuss the weather with him. Ask him where you can stay. You ask about a hotel. He suggests that you stay with him at his home. You are coy but give in.
5. Tell someone about plans you had with a friend to go sightseeing. It's too hot today. Let's wait till tomorrow. Can't wait till tomorrow—tomorrow you're going to Prome. It gets cool and you hire a

car to take you around the city. You see the ruined palace, pagodas, and so on.

6. Tell about a trip to Maymyo. People were late. You were worried about the car breaking down. You had a flat tire and ran out of gas. Tell what you did about it.

7. You are riding with a reckless driver. Give him instructions as to how to drive. You hear a horn from behind: tell him so and tell him to get out of the way. Your friend says he can't—that you're in a hurry too. Tell him not to drive so fast. Tell him to take the other road. Point out the dangers of the road. He tells you that he knows the road and that you can just sit back in silence and come along for the ride.

8. Discuss plans for a picnic. Where to go? What to do? What to take? Why?

9. Your friend cuts himself. He asks you to help him bandage it. Do so discussing the operations necessary.

10. You meet a Burman and discuss your families. How many children? How are they? Where are your wives? What are you doing in Burma? What are your plans?

PART FOUR

UNIT 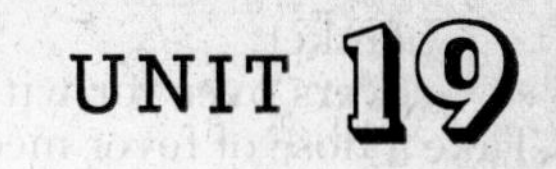

THE HOSPITAL

SECTION A—BASIC SENTENCES

ENGLISH EQUIVALENTS	AIDS TO LISTENING
	máun kalaʔ
what really happens	*phyiphmân*
I don't know what's happening now.	*couʔ ʔakhù bá phyiphmân maθìbû*
I don't feel well	*néilòu makâumbû*
	máun hlà
Mr. San Ya, feel his hand and see.	*kóu sányà, θù lekkóu sân cìlaissâmbá*
	kóu sán yà
body	*kóu*
His body is hot; I think he has a fever.	*kóu púdé, phyâ néidé thíndé*
	máun bà
medicine, tobacco, drug	*shêi*
fever medicine	*ʔaphyâzêi (ʔaphyâ phyasshêi)*

blanket	*sáun*
covers over (or with a blanket)	*chóundé*
Take a dose of fever medicine and then cover up with a blanket and sleep.	*ʔaphyâzêi takhwellauʔ θauʔ pî, sáun chóun ʔeiʔ néibá*
aches (also bites)	*kaitté*
My hand aches a little too.	*couʔ lellê nênê kaitté*

máun hlà

unties, unrolls, unfolds, answers (a question)	*phyéidé*
If it aches why don't you loosen the bandage that's wrapped around it?	*kaiyyín, paʔ thâdè ʔawukkóu phyéi thâbálâ*

máun bà

an ache; a bite	*ʔakaiʔ (kaitté)*
It doesn't ache so much now. (Only now the ache is relieved.)	*ʔakhùhmàbê ʔakaiʔ θeθθádé*

kóu sán yà

conveys, conducts (to a person or a place)	*pòudé*
We'll take Mr. Clark to the hospital tomorrow.	*nepphyíŋgáhmà máun kalakkóu shêiyóun pòumé*

[Interval]

máun hlà

last night	*nyàgà*
sleeps well	*ʔeillòu pyódé (ʔeiʔ pyódé)*
Did you sleep well last night, Mr. Clark?	*kóu kalaʔ, nyàgà ʔeillòu pyóyèlâ*

	máun kalaʔ
No, I didn't.	*ʔeillòu mapyóbû*
My fever was high all night.	*tanyàlôun ʔaphyâ tetté*
	máun bà
My hand's aching more than before.	*cúndò lellê ʔayíŋgàdeʔ póu kaitté*
I want to go to the hospital.	*shêiyóuŋgóu θwâjíndé*
	máun hlà
ready	*ʔashínðìn*
If you want to go get everything ready.	*θwâjín-yin, ʔashínðìn pyín thâ*
I'll go get the car out.	*cúndó mótókâ θwâ thóummé*
	máun kalaʔ
I'll need pyjamas ('pants and coat') to wear when I sleep (at night)	*cúndó nyà ʔeittè ʔakhá wuʔ ʔeipphòu ʔêinjínè bâumbí lóumé*
puts or places in	*thèdé*
Please put everything in the box and bring it [along].	*θittádêhmá ʔasóun thè yúgèbá*
[*shêiyóuŋgóu θwâjàbí*]	[*shêiyóuŋgà sayêimêi*]
	sayêi
disease	*yôgá*
What's the matter? What's your complaint?	*bá phyiθθalê, bélôu yôgálê*

kóu sán yà

He's sick. *θú phyâ néidé*

sayêi

takes medicine *shêi sâdé*

Do you want to stay at the hospital for treatment? *shêiyóumhmá te? shêi sâ néijínðalâ*

máun kala?

That's right. *houppádé*

before it disappears, is lost *mapyaukkhín*

I want to stay at the hospital till [the fever] goes away. *mapyaukkhíndò shêiyóumhmá néijímbádé*

sayêi

leaf *ywe?*

sheet of paper, form *sáywe?*

district, address *néiya?*

Write your name and address and the rest of it on this form. *dí saywe ppóhmá khímbyâ náménè néiya? ?acôu ?acâun yêibá*

máun kala?

Look here. *díhmá cìbá*

Is this written right? *dílóu yêidá houyyèlâ*

sayêi

Yes. That's right. *houppádé*

Follow that nurse. *khímbyâ hóu shayámà naukkóu lai? θwâbá*

shayámà

cot, couch, bedstead — *kadín*
lies at full length; throws down from an erect posture — *hlêdé*
Lie down on that cot for a while, sir. — *šín, hóu kadímbóhmá khanà hlê néibá*

The doctor will come right away. — *shayáwún ʔakhùbê lábálèimmé*

shayáwún

as soon as (one) gets sick — *(ʔa) phyâ phyâjîn*
Did you take (drink) any medicine as soon as you got the fever? — *(ʔa) phyâ phyâjîn, ʔaphyâzêimyâ θauθθêiðalâ*

máun kalaʔ

quinine — *kwínáin*
fever medicine (quinine) — *ʔaphyâ phyasshêi*
I took a dose of fever medicine called quinine. — *kwínáin khó ʔaphyâ phyasshêi takhwettò θauppádé*

Even so, it didn't make any difference in the fever. — *θauppéimè, ʔaphyâ ʔatweʔ bámà mathûbábû*

shayáwún

blood — *θwêi*
feels the pulse — *θwêi sândé*
I'll take your pulse and see. — *khímbyâ lekkóu θwêi sân címé*

mouth — *bazaʔ*
opens — *hàdé*
compares, measures, estimates — *tâindé*
Open your mouth; I'll take your temperature. — *bazaʔ hà, ʔapú tâin cìmé*

thermometer	*ʔapúdâin*
enclose, cover up, shut in (or in the mouth)	*ŋóundé*
Hold this thermometer in your mouth—don't bite it.	*dí ʔapúdâiŋgóu bazatthêhmá ŋóun thâ, makainnè*
temperature	*ʔapú chéin*
decimal	*dàθamà*
Your temperature is 103.4	*ʔapú chéin tayà θôunnè lêidàθamà šìdé*
	kóu sán yà
What kind of fever do you think it is, doctor?	*shayáwún, bélóu ʔaphyâlòu khímbyâ thínðalê*
	shayáwún
bird	*hŋeʔ*
malaria, jungle-fever	*hŋepphyâ*
He has a high fever; I think it's malaria.	*ʔaphyâ cîdé. hŋepphyâ thíndé*
bleeds, lets blood by opening a vein	*θwêi phautté*
We'll probably have to take a sample of blood and see.	*θwêi phauʔ cìyàlèimmé*
How about you? What's wrong?	*khímbyâdòugô, bá phyiθθalê*
	kóu sán yà
nose	*hná [hnakhâun]*
has a cold in the nose	*hná sîdé*
coughs, has a cough	*châun shôudé*
I have a cold in the head and a cough.	*cúndó hná sîdé, châun shôudé*
As for him, he has a knife cut on his hand.	*θúgàdò lephmá dâ pyattè dán-yá šìdé*

shayáwún

prescription	*shêizá* [*shêi sá*]
asks for, demands	*tâundé*
Very well, the one with the cold go with this prescription to that room and ask for medicine.	*kâumbábí, hná sîdè lú dí shêizánè hóu ʔakhâmhmá shêi θwâ tâun yúbá*
The one with the knife cut on his hand follow me.	*lephmá dán-yá šìdè lú couʔ naukkóu laikkhè*
is ill, is in pain	*nádé*
pain, disease, sore	*ʔaná*
I'll put some medicine on the sore place for you	*ʔanágóu shêi thè pêimé*

máun bà

cries out, screams	*ʔódé*
the sound of shouting, a shout, a scream	*ʔóðán*
I hear screams from that room, doctor. What's wrong?	*shayáwún, hóu ʔakhândêgà ʔóðán câdé. bá phyiθθalê*

shayáwún

just now	*khùdíŋgàbê*
hits, strikes against	*taitté*
hits (by accident, implying inadvertence)	*taimmìdé*
breaks (crosswise)	*côudé*
Just now there was an automobile accident and a man broke his leg.	*khùdíŋgàbê lú tayauʔ mótókâ taimmìlòu chéi côu θwâdé*
patient, sick person	*lúná*
treats (medically) gives medicine	*kùdé*
amputates	*phyaʔ kùdé*
We're going to have to amputate.	*ʔêdí lúnágóu phyaʔ kù néiyàdé*

knee	*dû*
abrades, bruises, scrapes	*pûndé*
Nurse, wash that patient's bruised knee and put some medicine on it.	*shayámà, hóu lúná tayauʔ dû pûndágóu yéi shêi pî, shêi thèlaippá*
[Interval]	
	tachâ lúná tayauʔ [another patient]
What sort of complaint did you come to the hospital for?	*khímbyâ bélóu yôgánè shêiyóun teθθalê*
	máun kalaʔ
Malaria.	*hŋepphyâ yôgábê*
How about you, what's your complaint?	*khímbyâgô bélóu yôgálê*
	tachâ lúná
belly	*wûn*
has dysentery	*wûn kaitté*
two weeks	*hnapaʔ*
I've been in the hospital two weeks with dysentery.	*wûn kaiʔ yôgánè shêiyóun teʔ néidá hnapaʔ šìbí*
ear	*nâ*
ear aches	*nâ kaitté*
I came to the hospital once before with an earache.	*ʔayíngàlê nâ kaillòu, shêiyóun takhá tepphûdé*
	máun kalaʔ
when I was little	*ŋéŋédôuŋgà*
time and again	*khanà khanà*
head	*gâun*
head aches	*gâun kaitté*

tooth	*θwâ*
tooth aches	*θwâ kaitté*
When I was little, in America, from time to time I had headaches and toothaches.	*cúndólê ŋéŋédôuŋgà ʔaméiyìkán pyéihmá khanà khanà gâun kaitté, θwâ kaitté*
later (on)	*nauʔ*
one (of respected persons)	*taʔû*
Later on I met a good doctor and before long I was cured.	*nauʔ, shayágâun taʔûnè θwâ twèilòu macágín pyauʔ θwâdé*

lúná

cuts in half	*khwêdé*
splits, cuts lengthwise	*seitté*
does surgery	*khwê seiʔ phyaʔ kùdé*
I have heard that your American surgeons are quite good.	*khímbyâdòu ʔaméiyìkán pyéigà shayáwúmmyâ khwê seiʔ phya kùdè néiyáhmá tódó kâundélòu, pyôðán câbûdé*

máun kalaʔ

That's right.	*hmámbádé*
praises	*chîmûndé*
You can praise (admire) them if you want to.	*chîmûmmé shóuyínlê, chîmûnhnáimbádé*

SECTION B—WORD STUDY AND REVIEW OF BASIC SENTENCES

1. Word Study

A. More Secondary Verb Particles

-mì- 'inadvertence'

loummìdé	I did it inadvertently.
pyômìdé	I misspoke; 'it slipped out.'
mêimìdé	I raised the question unintentionally.
néiyá hmâpî, tháimmìdé	I sat in the wrong place.
khímbyâ ʔêinjí hmâpî, wummìdé	I put on your shirt by mistake.
cúndò sáʔoukkóu myímmìðalâ	Did you happen to see my book?
khìmbyâ ságóu phammìdé	I read your letter (I'm sorry—I didn't mean to).
dí sá cúndò há thínlòu phammìdé	I read this letter thinking it was mine.
khímbyâgóu mató tashà taimmìdé	I bumped you accidentally.

-mì- is a secondary verb particle denoting *inadvertence.* Whatever was done wasn't done intentionally, and often the speaker implies that he is sorry. This particle occurs in narrative sentences.

-pálâ 'urgent imperative'

dígóu lágèbálâ	Why don't you come here?
laiʔ θwâbálâ	Why don't you go along?

laikkhèbálâ	Come along!
laiʔ lábálâ	Why don't you come along.
yéi θwâ chôulaippálâ	Go ahead and take a bath.
ʔeicchín-yín, θwâ ʔeillaippálâ	If you're sleepy, go ahead and sleep.
θìjín-yín, θwâ mêibálâ	If you want to know, go and ask.
sá maphacchín-yín, youššímbwêgóu θwâ cìbálâ	If you don't want to study, go see a movie.
sâjín-yín, khímbyâ kóudáin khwê sâbálâ	If you want to eat it, cut it yourself and eat it.

-pálâ denotes an urgent imperative.

B. Another General Particle

-hmà 'only, just'

nepphyíŋgàhmà máun kalakkóu shêiyóun pòumé	We'll take Mr. Clark to the hospital tomorrow.
ʔakhùhmàbê seiʔ êi θwâdé	Only now have I relaxed.
hóu ʔakhândêhmá mêimmà tayauphmà mašìbû, wínðá wín θwâbá	There isn't a single woman in that room. Go ahead in.
cúndòzíhmá paisshán tabyâhmà mašìbû	I don't have a single pice.
bámà maloucchímbû	I don't want to do anything.
bámà mahmámbû	It's all wrong. Nothing is correct.
bá phyillòu bámà mašíðalê	Why is it that you don't have anything?
mîyathâ takháhmà masîbûbû	I have never once ridden on a train.
bédòhmà maládòbû	I'll never come again to your house.

-hmà (sometimes *-mà*) is a general particle. It is attached to noun expressions. It is usually translated as 'only.'

C. More Subordinating Particles

1. *-hmà* 'only'

ʔalouʔ pîhmà, pyóbwêzâgóu laithnáimmé	I can come along only when the work is done.
máun bà cí pyán yauphmà thamîn sâjàzòu	Let's have dinner after Mg Ba Kyi gets back (not before).
bamá zagâgóu bamá tayauʔ θín pêihmà kâuŋgâun pyôdammé	You will be able to speak Burmese well only if a Burman teaches (you).
paisshán šìhmà, pyóbyó šwínšwín néihnáindé	You can be happy only if you have money.
myámmyán θwâhmà, mîyathâgóu hmímé	You'll catch the train only if you hurry.
ʔapúdâinnè tâin cìhmà θìhmá pò	We'll know, of course, only when we've taken your temperature.
shêi θauphmà, ʔaphyâ phyauphmá pò	Of course you'll get rid of your fever only if you take medicine.

-hmà is a subordinating particle. It is usually translated as 'only when, only if.'

2. *-chîn* 'as soon as, immediately after'

phyâ phyâjîn, ʔaphyâzêimyâ θauθθêiðalâ	Did you take any medicine as soon as you got the fever?
manèi nyàgà thweʔ thweʔ θwâjîn, môu ywádé	It rained just as I went out yesterday.
ʔéiŋgóu yauʔ yaucchîn thamîn θwâ sâdé	Immediately upon arrival.

-chîn is a subordinating particle. It is usually translated 'as soon as, immediately after.'

D. *ʔahmân* 'the facts about'

couʔ ʔakhù bá phyiphmâm maθìbû, néilòu makâumbû	I don't know what's happening (but) I don't feel well.
cúndó béhmá néihmâŋgóu θìyàʔáun, ʔéin námbaʔ yêi pêilaimmè	I'll write my address for you so that you'll know where I live.
shêizágóu bé shayawún yêi pêihmân maphyéihnáinlòu, sháinšíŋgà shêi mayâunlaipphû	Because I couldn't say which doctor wrote the prescription the druggist wouldn't sell me the medicine.
hmâhmân θìdé	I knew it was wrong.
hmámhmân θìdé	I knew it was right.
yéi téinhmân maθìbûlâ	Didn't you know the water was shallow?
θú thweʔ θwâhmân maθìlaipphû	I didn't know that he had gone out.
kâumhmân θìdé	I knew it was good.
bá louyyàhmân maθìbû	I don't know what I should do.

ʔahmân is a noun meaning 'the facts about.' It is modified by a preceding verb expression, the whole then followed usually by the verb *θìdé* 'knows.'

2. Covering English and Burmese of Word Study

Give the English equivalents of all Burmese expressions in the *Word Study* and the Burmese for all the English. This is individual study.

3. Review of Basic Sentences

Further oral practice with the first part of the *Basic Sentences*.

1. Review of Basic Sentences (*Cont.*)

Further oral practice with the second part of *Basic Sentences*.

2. Covering the English of Basic Sentences

Check your knowledge of the meaning of all words and phrases in the *Basic Sentences*. This is individual study.

3. What Would You Say?

Give full answers for each of the following questions.

1. *ʔakhù bá phyiʔ néiðalê*
2. *khímbyâ néilòu kâun-yèlâ*
3. *θú lekkóu sân cìðalâ*
4. *khímbyâ kóu púðalâ*
5. *θú phyâ néiðalâ*
6. *ʔaphyâzêi θauʔ pîbalâ*
7. *sáun chóun ʔeiʔ néiyàmalâ*
8. *khímbyâ leʔ kaiθθalâ*
9. *leʔ kaiyyín, ʔawuʔ paʔ thâjínðalâ*
10. *ʔakhù ʔakaiʔ θeθθáðalâ*
11. *nepphyíŋgá máun kalakkóu shêiyóun pòumalâ*
12. *khímbyâ leʔ ʔayíŋgàdeʔ póu kaiθθalâ*
13. *pyissîdéi ʔashíndìn pyín thâyàmalâ*
14. *cúndó móotókâ θwâ thouyyámalâ*
15. *θittádêhmá ʔasóun thè pîbalâ*
16. *khímbyâ yôgá, bé yôgálê*
17. *ʔaphyâ mapyaukkhíndò shêiyóumhmá néijínðalâ*
18. *dí sáyweppóhmá bá yêiyàmalê*
19. *shayáwún bédò lámalê*
20. *manèigà pyóbwêzâ θwâðalâ*
21. *kwínáin khó ʔaphyâ phyasshêi khímbyâ θaupphûðalâ*
22. *shêi θauʔ pî, ʔaphyâ θeθθáðalâ*
23. *bazaʔ mahàyín, ʔapú bélóu tâimmalê*
24. *bazatthêhmá bá ŋóun thâðalê*
25. *ʔapú chéin bélaullê*
26. *ʔapú dílauʔ šìyín, sôuyéinzayá šìðalâ*
27. *dí ʔaphyâ, hŋepphyâ thínðalâ*
28. *θwêi phauʔ cìyàmalâ*
29. *khímbyâ hná sî, châun shôuðalâ*
30. *shêigóu badù shígà tâun-yàmalê*
31. *hóu ʔakhâmhmá shêi θwâ tâun-yàmalâ*
32. *ʔanágóu shêi thè pêiyàmalâ*

33. *hóu lú bá phyillòu ʔó néiðalê*
34. *khímbyâ bédôuŋgà chéi côuðalê*
35. *phyaʔ kùyàmalâ*
36. *dû bélóu pûn θwâðalê*
37. *shêi thè pêimalâ*
38. *khímbyâ wûn kaiθθalâ*
39. *nâ kaiθθalâ*
40. *gâun kaiθθalâ*
41. *θwâ kaiθθalâ*
42. *leʔ náðalâ*
43. *chéidauʔ náðalâ*

SECTION D—LISTENING IN

1. What Did You Say?

With other members of your group give orally your responses to the previous exercise as the Leader calls for them.

2. Word Study Check-Up

Give the Burmese for all English equivalents in the *Word Study* as the Leader calls for it.

3. Listening In

1. How's your family's health?

máun bà: *khímbyâ ʔakhù béhmá néiðalê*

máun séin: *lâmmadó néiyaphmá néidé cúndó béhmá néihmângóu θìyáʔáun khímbyâzíhmá sáyweʔ páyín, ʔéin námbaʔ yêi pêilaimmé*

máun bà: *cúndòhmá ʔashínðìn sekkú pádé yêi pêiyín, cêizûbábê*

máun séin: *manèinyàgà ʔéiŋgà thweʔ thweʔ θwâjîn, môu ywádé ywábéimè, pyînlòu tareisshán-yóuŋgóu θwâdé*

máun bà: *dájàun khímbyâ hná sîdágóu: nyàgà ʔeillòu pyóyèlâ*

máun séin: *ʔciʔ pyóbádé*

máun bà: *khímbyà khalêi bélóulê néi kâun-yélâ*

máun séin: *díganèi manekkàbê paisshán tabyâgóu ŋóun thâlòu, bazakkóu hà thouyyàdé*

máun bà: *khímbyà khalêigóu ʔímmatán cì šùyàdénó hóu tabakkàbê châun shôu nâ kaitté, mahoupphûlâ*

máun séin: *houtté, dílóu dû pûnlaiʔ, ʔaná paullaiʔ phyippéimè, hŋepphyâlóu ʔaphyâ yôgá ʔacî ʔacédò takkháhmà mapyàðêibû*

máun bà: *khímbyâlê ŋéŋédôuŋgà dìlóubê mahoupphûlâ*

máun séin: *houppádé*

2. I think I have a fever.

máun θín: *khímbyâ bá phyiθθalê cìyàdá néi makâumbû, thíndé*

máun có: *cúndò kóu sân cìbá*

máun θín: *lennè sânlòu bé phyimmalê ʔapúdâinnè tâin cìhmà θìhmá pò*

máun có: *ʔapú ʔachéin bélaullê*

máun θín: *θeiʔ mašìbábû kôuzè kôu daθθamà lêi šìdé dábéimè, kadímbóhmá hlê pî, sáun chóun néi*

máun có: *cúndò θwêi sân cìbáʔôun*

máun θín: *θwêi sân cìbòu malóubábû, bá ʔó néidálê*

máun có: *shayawún taʔû khó pî, shêi kùyín, makâumbûlâ*

máun θín: *khóbòu malóubábû kóu sán yàzígà ʔaphyâ phyasshêi takhwellauʔ tâun θauyyín, kâun θwâlèimmé*

[Interval]

máun có: *khímbyâ bá phyillòu dílauʔ cáyàdálê*

máun θín: *kóu sán yàhmá shêi kóun θwâlòu shêizáiŋgóu θwâyàdé*

máun có: *shêi yàgèðalâ*

máun θín: *shêizágóu bé shayawún yêi pêihmân maphyéihnáinlòu sháinšíŋgà shêi mayâunjímbù ʔakhùdò máun bàgóu shayawún náménè shêi wébòu pòulaippí*

máun có: *nauʔ takhá shóuyín, takhádê shayáwún námé pá yú θwâbòu mamèinè*

3. Go get it yourself!

máun hlà: *cúndó wûn shádé bé θiθθîmashóu khwê pêibá*

máun bà tín: *khùdíŋgàbê thamîn sâ pîðêidé ʔakhù checchîn shá néibí dílauʔ khanà khanà sâ néiyín, wûn kaillèimmé*

máun hlà: *wûn makaippábû*
khwê pêibá

máun bà tín: *lúnálóu lou?, manéibánè sâjín-yín, khímbyâ kóudáin khwê sâbálâ khwê sâ pîyín, dâgóu šá yàdè néiyáhmá pyán thè thâbòu, mamèinè*

4. Did you hear about the accident?

máun hlà: *manèigà ?éin šèihmá mótókâ hnasî taittá myínlaiθθalâ*

máun bà tín: *mamyínlaipphû*
mótókâdêhmá pádè lúdéi dán-yá ?acî ?acé yàðalâ

máun hlà: *mótókâ mâunðamâ tayauphmá gâun kwê θwâdé*
tachâ mâunðamâhmádò θwâ θôunjâumbê côu θwâdé

máun bà tín: *dîlóu dán-yá nênê yàdá chîmûnzayábê*

máun hlà: *dán-yá ?acî yàyínlê, keissà mašìbábû*

máun bà tín: *bá phyilloulê*

máun hlà: *dí myòuhmá khwê sei? phya? kùbòu shayáwúŋgâundéi šìlòubá*

SECTION E—CONVERSATION

1. Covering the Burmese of Basic Sentences

With the Burmese covered, practice until you can speak the Burmese for each English sentence without hesitation. This is individual study.

2. Vocabulary Check-Up

Give the Burmese for all the English sentences in the *Basic Sentences* as the Leader calls for it.

3. Conversation

Suggested Topics:

1. Tell your friend that you don't know what's wrong but that you don't feel well. Ask him to take your temperature and feel your pulse. Tell him that you didn't sleep well all night and that you had a fever. He tells you you'll have to take some medicine for the fever.
2. You go to a hospital. The clerk asks you to fill out a form. A nurse takes you to a doctor. The doctor

examines you and tells you to lie down. You tell him your symptoms. You tell him that you took quinine. You tell him that you want to stay in the hospital until you are better.

3. You hear a patient groaning in another room. You ask why. Another patient tells you that a man had his leg broken in an accident and that they are going to amputate. You ask about surgeons in Burma. He tells you that they are very good.

SECTION F—CONVERSATION (*Cont.*)

Continue conversation. Additional check-up if necessary.

Finder List

ʔakaiʔ (*kaitté*)	ache; bite
ʔaná (*nádé*)	pain, disease; sore
(*ʔa*)*phyâ phyâjîn*	as soon as one gets sick
ʔaphyâ phyasshêi (=*ʔaphyâzêi*)	fever medicine
ʔaphyâzêi (=*ʔaphyâ phyasshêi*)	fever medicine
ʔapú ʔachéin	temperature
ʔapúdâin	thermometer
ʔashínðin	ready
bazaʔ	mouth
châun shôudé	coughs, has a cough
chîmûndé	praises
chóundé	covers (as with a blanket)
côudé	breaks (crosswise)
dàθamà	decimal, tenth
dû	knee
ʔeillòu pyódé	sleeps well
ʔeiʔ pyódé	sleeps well
gâun	head
hàdé	opens
hlêdé	lies at full length, throws down from an erect position
hná (=*hnakhâun*)	nose
hnapaʔ	two weeks
hná sîdé	has a cold in the head
hŋeʔ	bird
hŋepphyâ	malaria, jungle fever
kadín	cot, couch, bedstead
kaitté	aches, bites

khanà khanà	time and again
khùdíŋgàbê	just now
khwêdé	cuts in half
khwê sei? phya? kùdé	does surgery
kóu	body
kùdé	treats (medically)
kwínáin	quinine
lúná	patient, sick person
mapyaukkhín	before it disappears, is lost
nâ	ear
nádé	is in pain
nâ kaitté	ear aches
nau?	later on
néiya?	district, address
nyàgà	last night
ŋéŋédôungà	when (I) was little
ŋóundé	enclose, cover up, shut in (as in the mouth)
?ódé	cries out, screams
?óðán	the sound of shouting, a shout, a scream
phya? kùdé	amputates
phyéidé	loosens, unrolls, unfolds; answers (a question)
phyéi thâbálâ	loosen (it)!
phyiphmân	what really happens
pòudé	conveys, conducts (to a person or place)
pûndé	abrades, bruises, scrapes
sáun	blanket
sáywe?	sheet of paper, form
seitté	splits, cuts lengthwise
shêi	medicine, tobacco, drug
shêi sâdé	takes medicine
shêizá	prescription
taimmìdé	hits (by accident, implying inadvertence)
tâindé	compares, measures, estimates
taitté	hits, strikes against
ta?û	one (of respected persons)
tâundé	asks for, demands
thèdé	puts, places in
θwâ	tooth
θwâ kaitté	tooth aches
θwêi	blood
θwêi sândé	feels the pulse
wûn	belly
wûn kaitté	has dysentery
wûn shádé	is hungry
yôgá	disease
ywe?	leaf

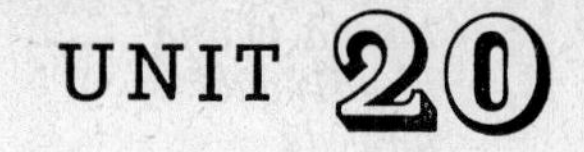

AGRICULTURE

SECTION A—BASIC SENTENCES

ENGLISH EQUIVALENTS	AIDS TO LISTENING
	máun kala?
farmer	*táunθú*
farmer	*léθamâ*
in most cases, generally	*?amyâ ?â phyìn*
holds, takes hold of	*káindé*
works, performs work	*lou? káindé*
sets, plants, erects	*saitté*
plants	*pyôudé*
sets out, plants	*sai? pyôudé*
What do the farmers in Burma usually raise?	*bamá pyéihmá táunθú léθamâ ?amyâ ?â phyìn, bámyâgóu lou? káin sai? pyôujàθalê*
	kóu sán yà
irrigated rice field	*lé*
paddy	*sabâ*
In general the people living in Lower Burma work rice fields and plant paddy in the rainy season.	*?au? bamá pyéihmá néidè lúmyâ ?amyâ ?â phyìn, môu ?akháhmá lé lou?, sabâmyâgóu sai? pyôujàdé*

máun kala?

I'd like to see how they do it. *bélóu lou? káindé shóudá, cúndó cìjíndé*

kóu sán yà

bank of a river, lake, sea — *kân*

that side — *hóu bekkân*

I have a great many farmer friends in Dala on the other side of the river from Rangoon. — *yáŋgóun myòu hóu bekkân šìdè dalàhmá cúndò meisshwéi léðamâ ?amyâjî šìbádé*

If you want to go there and see how it is done you can probably see it yourself. — *hóuhmá bélóu louttê shóudá θwâ cìjín-yín, khímbyâ kóudáin twèiyàbálèimmé*

[Interval]

?û phôu chóu

Well, if it isn't Mg. San Ya. Where are you going; what brings you here? — *máun sán yàbálâ, bé θwâjàmalòulê bá keissà ?atwe? lájàðalê*

kóu sán yà

No special business. — *?athû keissà mašìbábû*

to you (to an older man) — *?û shígóu (?ûzígóu)*

I brought my friend to you because he wanted to see how rice fields were worked. — *cúndò θaŋéjîn, lé bélóu louttê shóudá cìjíndé shóudánè ?û shígóu khó ládé*

?û phôu chóu

is it so — *houllâ = houθθalâ*

Oh, is that so? What's your name? — *?ô houllâ, khímbyâ námé bélóu khóðalê*

máun kala?

My name is Mg. Clark—I'm an American.	*cúndò námé máun kala?, cúndó ?améiyìkán pyéiðâbê*

?û phôu chóu

We are very happy to have the opportunity of meeting Americans in Burma.	*couttòu bamá pyéihmá ?améiyìkán pyéiðâmyânètayaunnè tayau? twèiyàdè ?atwe?, ?amyâjî wûn θábádé*

máun kala?

I am very grateful for what you have said.	*?û dílóu pyôdá cúndó ?amyâjî cêizû tímbádé*

kóu sán yà

is interested	*sei? pádé*
When it's a matter of farming, he's quite interested in the work.	*θú táunðú léðamâ ?alou? shóuyín, tódó loupphòu sei? pádé*
a little bit, please	*tashei?*
If you are free please take us along and show us how paddy is planted.	*sabâ bélóu sai? pyôudé shóudágóu ?û ?âyín, cúndódòugóu tashei? lai? pyàbá*

?û phôu chóu

I am on the point of going into the fields—come along with me.	*cou? akhù lédêgóu θwâmalòubê, counnè laikkhèbá*
I myself will go along and show you everything ('so that it will be complete').	*cou? kóudáin sóun?áun, lai? pyàmé*

	máun kala?
earth, ground, soil	*myéi*
How do you prepare the soil for planting the paddy?	*myéigóu bélóu lou? pî, sabâgóu saiyyàðalê*
	?û phôu chóu
buffalo	*cwê*
bull, ox, cow	*nwâ*
scatters, throws about, sows	*cêdé*
ploughs, harrows	*thúndé*
First after there has been three or four months of heavy rainfall, the ground is ploughed by means of buffaloes and bulls for the planting of rice.	*pathamà môu kâuŋgâun θôun lêilà ywádè ?akhá, cwê nwâmyânè myéigóu sabâ saithnáin cêhnáin?áun, thún thâyàdé*
	máun kala?
Can't they plant paddy when there isn't any water?	*yéi mašìyín, sabâ masaithnáimbûlâ*
	?û phôu chóu
If there isn't any water at planting time, you can't plant.	*sabâ saittè ?akhá, yéi mašìyín, masaithnáimbú*
only having planted	*sai? pîhmà*
reaps	*yeitté*
Only when it has been planted about four mon s with lots of water, do you have the opportunity of harvesting paddy.	*yéi myâmyânè lêilàlau? sai? pîhmà, sabâgóu yei? yúyàdé*
	máun kala?
is tired, fatigued; is tiresome	*pímbândé*
Having to work rice fields would be fairly tiresome, I think.	*lé ?alou? louyyàdá tódó pímbânlèimmé, thíndé*

ʔû phôu chóu

work and eat, make a living	*lou? káin sâ θautté*
Even though it is tiring, because there isn't other work to do we always have to make our living at this rice field labor.	*pímbâmbéimè, dì pyín loussayá ʔalou? mašìdè ʔatwe?, dí lé ʔaloukkóubê ʔamyê lou? káin sâ θau? néiyàdé*

kóu sán yà

What time is it, Mr. Clark?	*ʔachéin bélau? šìbalê, máun kala?*

máun kala?

is or goes beyond, exceeds	*lúndé*
It's now 15 minutes past nine.	*ʔakhù kôunáyí thôu pîlòu, shè ŋâmani? lún θwâbí*

ʔû phôu chóu

song	*tachîn*
sings a song	*tachîn shóudé*
picks up	*kautté*
transplants (rice)	*kau? saitté*
Hurry, I still want to show the women singing and transplanting rice over there.	*lá, lá, hóuhmá mêimmàmyâ tachîn shóu, kau? sai? néidágóu pyàjínðèidé*

máun kala?

As far as I can see, they're having a lot of fun.	*cìyàdá θei? pyózayá kâundé*
has come to be, has happened	*phyi? θwâdé*
Seeing them transplanting, I feel like doing it myself.	*θúdòu· kau? sai? néidá myín-yàdò, cou? kóudáin kau? saicchínðalóu phyi? θwâdé*

There aren't many men where they transplant rice.	*kau? saittè néiyáhmá yauccâ mamyâbû*
Why are there more women?	*bá phyillòu mêimmà póu myâðalê*

?û phôu chóu

Men aren't as good as women at this work.	*dí ?alouphmá yauccâmyâgà mêimmàmyâlau? makâumbû*
woman transplanter stick plants	*kau? saimmà* *dou?* *sai? káindé*
That's the reason why more women are hired, some to do the transplanting by means of sticks and some by hand.	*dájàun kau? saimmàmyâgóu póu hŋâ pî, tachòulê dounnè tachòu lennè myámmyán sai? káin-yàdé*

máun kala?

Do they have to harvest paddy in the rainy season?	*môu ?ùdùhmá sabâ yei? yúyàðalâ*

?û phôu chóu

No—they start harvesting near the end of the cold season.	*mahoupphû, shâun ?ùdù kóuŋgánîhmá sà yei? yúyàdé*
At harvesting time you have to be very careful so as not to run across snakes.	*sabâ yeittè ?akhá mwéinè matwèi?áun, ?ímmatán θadì thâyàdé*
You have to worry about snakes whenever you come or go—rainy season, cold season, hot season, any season, any time at all.	*môu ?ùdù shâun ?ùdù nwéi ?ùdù bé ?ùdù bé ?akhámashóu, θwâdè ládè ?akhá mwéi ?atwe? ?ímmatán sôuyéin-yàdé*

máun kala?

a cultivated piece of ground (not irrigated)	*yá*
Are there lots of people who do dry-farming in lower Burma?	*?au? bamá þyéihmá yá louttè lú myâðalâ*

?û phôu chóu

farmer	*yáðamâ*
There aren't many dry farmers in lower Burma.	*?au? bamá þyéihmá yáðamâ θei? mamyâbû*
There are lots of rice farmers.	*léðamâ θei? myâdé*

máun kala?

Mr. Phou Cho, now that you have explained I know how some farmers work.	*?û phôu chóu þyô pyàdè ?atwe?, tachòu léðamâ ?acâuŋgóu nâ lébábí*
Now please tell me about dry farming.	*yáðamâ ?acâuŋgóu tashei? pyôbá?ôun*

?û phôu chóu

It doesn't rain much in upper Burma even in the rainy season.	*?athe? bamá þyéihmá môu ?akháhmálê môu θei? maywábû*
Lots of people work the dry fields because you can't get a great deal of water in the hot season either.	*nwéi ?akhálê yéi myâmyâ mayàhnáindè ?atwe?, yá louttè lú myâdé*

máun kala?

What do they plant in the dry fields?	*yáhmá bámyâ saiθθalê*

ʔû phôu chóu

sesamum	*hnân*
cotton	*wágûn*
corn	*pyâumbû*
tobacco	*shêi*
peppers, chilies	*ŋayouʔ*
onions	*ceθθún*
peanuts	*myéibê*
When they have finished plowing the field they sow semamum, cotton, corn, and then they plant tobacco, peppers, onions and peanuts.	*yágóu thún pîdè ʔakhá, hnân wágûn pyâumbûmyâ cê pî, shêi ŋayouʔ ceθθún myéibê saiccàdé*

máun kalaʔ

How about paddy?	*sabâmyâgô bènélê*

ʔû phôu chóu

In a place near water people who plant paddy, plant and harvest twice a year because they can get lots of water.	*yéinè nîdè néiyáhmá sabâ saittè lúmyâ yéigóu myâmyâ yàhnáindè ʔatweʔ, tahniphmá hnakhá sabâ saiʔ yeiʔ yúyàdé*

máun kalaʔ

We are very grateful for your explanation about farming.	*ʔû táunðú léðamâ ʔacâungóu pyô pyàdè ʔatweʔ cúndódòugà, amyâjî cêizû tímbádé*
We'll have to be going, good-bye.	*θwâzayálê šìðêidé, θwâdòmé*

ʔû phôu chóu

Goodbye.	*θwâdònó*

SECTION B—WORD STUDY AND REVIEW OF BASIC SENTENCES

1. Word Study

A. The position of *-pá-* (Secondary Verb Particle, see Unit 7)

1. *θwâdé, θwâbádé* — he goes, went
   θwâmé, θwâbámé — he will go
   θwâbí, θwâbábí — he has gone
   maθwâbû, maθwâbábû — he doesn't go, didn't go, won't go
   θwâ, θwâbá — go, hasn't gone
   maθwânè, maθwâbánè — Don't go

As you learned in Unit **7** the secondary verb particle *-pá-* is used in narrative and imperative sentences and denotes *politeness*. The effect of this particle is to reduce the abruptness of a bare statement. We shall now look at some verb expressions containing more than one secondary verb particle.

2. *-cà-* 'plurality' (Unit 14)

θwâjàdé, θwâjàbádé — They went.
θwâjà, θwâjàbá — Go (to more than one person)

cájá manéijàbánè — Don't be long.

3. *-khè-*

lágèdé, lágèbádé — (He) came.
lágè, lágèbá — Come!

4. *-lai?*

pêilaitté, pêilaippádé — (He) gave.
pêilai?, pêilaippá — Give!

5. *?ôun*

?awu? θwâ lê?ôummé, ?awu? θwâ lêbá?ôummé — I'm going to change clothes.
néi?ôun, néibá?ôun — Wait!
maθwânè?ôun, maθwâbánè?ôun — Don't go yet.

6. *-tò*

θwâdòmé, θwâbádòmé — Goodbye (by person leaving)

θwâdò, θwâbádò — Goodbye (to person leaving)

Only Narrative Sentences

7. *-chín*

θwâjíndé, θwâjímbádé — (I) want to go.

8. *-hnáin*

θwâhnáindé, θwâhnáimbádé	(I) can go.

9. *-hlù*

yauthlùbí, yauthlùbábí	has almost arrived, is almost here

10. *-lèin*

θwâlèimmé, θwâbálèimmé	(I')ll probably go.

11. *-mì*

pyômìdé, pyômìbádé	(I) spoke inadvertently.

12. *-phû*

θwâbûdé, θwâbûbádé	(I) have gone (formerly)

13. *-θêi*

wêiðêidé, wêibáðêidé	It is still far.

14. *-yà*

pyán lágèyàdé, pyán lágèyàbádé	(He) had to come back.

Only Imperative Sentences

15. *-sân*

pyôzân, pyôzâmbá	Speak up. Just say it.

16. *-séi*

θwâzéi, θwâbázéi	Let him go.
θwâjàzéi, θwâjàbázéi	Let them go.

In third-person commands the form with *-pá-* is the more frequent.

17. *-sòu*

θwâjàzòu, θwâjàbázòu	Let's go.

B. Verb complexes which consist of more than two or three secondary verb particles are infrequent. Here are a few which you have met.

mapyôhnáinðêibû	(I) can't say as yet.
laithnáinlèimmé *laithnáimbálèimmé*	(I'll) probably be able to come along.
θwâyàlèimmé *θwâyàbálèimmé*	(I'll) probably have to go.
θwâ sâlai??ôummé *θwâ sâlaippá?ôummé*	(I'm) going to eat.
θwâlai??ôummé *θwâlaippá?ôummé*	(I'll) be going.
khanà nâjà?ôummalâ *khanà nâjàbá?ôummalâ*	(We'll) stop and rest awhile.

bêin lêyà?ôummé *bêin lêyàbá?ôummé*	(I'll) have to change the tire.
thâgèyàmé *thâgèyàbámé*	(I'll) have to put (it somewhere).

C. Auxiliary Verbs with *-pá-*

θwâ?âdé, θwâ?âbádé	(I'm) free to go.
lóunlautté, lóunlauppádé	It is sufficient.
pyôzéidé, pyôzéibádé	(I) allowed (him) to speak.
louttatté, louttappádé	I know how to do (it).
câyàdé, câyàbádé	I heard (it).

The particle *-pá-* always follows an auxiliary verb.

2. Covering English and Burmese of Word Study

Give the English equivalents of all Burmese expressions in the *Word Study* and the Burmese for all the English. This is individual study.

3. Review of Basic Sentences

Further oral practice with the first part of the *Basic Sentences*.

SECTION C—REVIEW OF BASIC SENTENCES (*Cont.*)

1. Review of Basic Sentences (*Cont.*)

Further oral practice with the second part of the *Basic Sentences*.

2. Covering the English of Basic Sentences

Check your knowledge of the meaning of all words and phrases in the *Basic Sentences*. This is individual study.

3. What Would You Say?

Give full answers to the following questions.

1. *máun sami?, léðamâ ?acâun θìðalâ*
2. *bamá pyéihmá bámyâ sai? pyôujàðalê*
3. *khímbyâ ?alou? ?akáin bálê*
4. *khímbyâ béhmá ?alou? louθθalê*
5. *khímbyâ kúlí ?alou? lou? káimbûðalâ*
6. *?améiyìkán pyéihmá sabâ sai? pyôujàðalâ*
7. *bélóu lou? káindé shóudá, khímbyâ cìjínðalâ*

8. *dalà myòuhmá meisshwéimyâ šìðalâ*
9. *yáŋgóun myòu hóu bekkân šìdè myòu, dalà myòulâ*
10. *hóuhmá bélóu louttè shóudá θwâ cìjínðalâ*
11. *khímbyâ bá keissànè lábáðalê*
12. *khímbyâ θaŋéjîŋgóu makhógèbûlâ*
13. *khímbyâ námé bélóu khóðalê*
14. *khímbyâ ʔaméiyìkán pyéiðâlâ*
15. *θú bá phyillòu wûn θá néiðalê*
16. *khímbyâdòu hnàyauʔ tayaunnè tayauʔ twèiyàdá wûn θájàyèlâ*
17. *khímbyâ ʔalòuphmá seiʔ páyèlâ*
18. *khímbyâ ʔakhù ʔâðalâ*
19. *cúndò ʔakhâŋgóu laiʔ pyàhnáimmalâ*
20. *sabâ saiʔ mapyôugín myéigóu bélóu louyyàðalê*
21. *khímbyâ kóudáin sabâ saiʔ pyôubûðalâ*
22. *sabâ cêbûðalâ*
23. *lê thúmbûðalâ*
24. *yéi mašìyín, sabâ masaithnáimbûlâ*
25. *sabâgóu yeiʔ yúbûðalâ*
26. *sabâ bédò yeiʔ yúyàmalê*
27. *khímbyâ pímbânðalâ*
28. *khímbyâ pímbândè ʔalouʔ loupphûðalâ*
29. *khímbyâ bá phyillòu pímbânðalê*
30. *lé ʔalouʔ tódó pímbânlèimmé thínðalâ*
31. *bá louʔ káinðalê*
32. *bá louʔ káin sâ θauθθalê*
33. *khímbyâ tachîn shóudaθθalâ*
34. *bá tachîmmyâ shóudaθθalê*
35. *hóuhmá mêimmàmyâ tachîn shóu, kauʔ saiʔ néidágóu myínjínðalâ*
36. *kauʔ saittè néiyáhmá bá phyillòu mêimmà myâðalê*
37. *bamá pyéihmá dounnè kauʔ saiθθalâ, lennè kauʔ saiθθalâ*
38. *mwéi kaiphmá sôuyéinzayá šìðalâ*
39. *khímbyâ mwéi cauttaθθalâ*
40. *mwéi ʔacâuŋgóu pyô pyàhnáinðalâ*
41. *ʔauʔ bamá pyéihmá yáðamâ myâðalâ*
42. *ʔatheʔ bamá pyéihmá léðamâ šìðalâ*
43. *yáhmá bámyâ saiθθalê*
44. *yéinè nìdè néiyáhmá tahniʔ bé hnakhá saithnáinðalê*
45. *táunðú léðamâ ʔacâuŋgóu pyô pyàhnáinðalâ* ....

SECTION D—LISTENING IN

1. What Did You Say?

With the other members of your group give orally your responses to the previous exercise as the Leader calls for them.

2. Word Study Check-Up

Give the Burmese for all English equivalents in the *Word Study* as the Leader calls for it.

3. Listening In

1. U Pho Cho asks Mr. Clark about farming in America.

ʔû phôu chóu: *ʔaméiyìkán pyéihmá táunðú léðamâ θeiʔ myâðalâ*

máun kalaʔ: *θeiʔ myâdé*

ʔû phôu chóu: *khímbyâ bá louʔ káin sâ θauθθalê*

máun kalaʔ: *cúndó ʔaméiyìkán pyéihmá néidôuŋgà yá saiʔ pyôudé*

ʔû phôu chóu: *ʔaméiyìkán pyéihmá sabâ ʔacî ʔacé lé saiʔ pyôu louʔ káinjàðalâ*

máun kalaʔ: *cúndódòu pyéihmá bamá pyéilauʔ sabâ masaiʔ pyòujàbû*
cúndò yáhmádò hînðî hîn-yweʔ ceθθûn pyâumbûnè wâgûn saiʔ pyôudé
dì pyín néiyámyâhmá shêi myéibê ŋayouʔ saiccàdé

ʔû phôu chóu: *hnân masaipphûlâ*

máun kalaʔ: *hnân saiθθalâ, masaiθθalâgóu cúndó hmámhmám mapyôhnáimbû*

ʔû phôu chóu: *khímbyâ shíhmá sennè myéi thúndélòu câdé bènélê, hmán-yèlâ*

máun kalaʔ: *hmámbádé*
sennè lé thúnlòu cwê nwâmyâ mapímbâmbû

2. They hear women singing and investigate.

máun kalaʔ: *tachîn shóuðán câdé*
bégà láðalê

ʔû phôu chóu: *hóuhmá kauʔ saimmàdwéi kauʔ saiʔ néidôun tachîn shóu néidé*

máun kalaʔ: *houllâ*
dílóu shóuyín, θúdòu pyólòu tachîn shóu néidágóu cúndó wûn θábádé

dábéimè, θúdòu ʔalouphmá bèné seiʔ pámalê

ʔû phôu chóu: *kauʔ saittáhmá seiʔ pábòu malóubû*

máun kalaʔ: *θúdòu sabâ cêdôun yeittôunlê tachîn shóujàðalâ*

ʔû phôu chóu: *ʔamyâ ʔâ phyìn, mêimmàdwéi sabâ mayeiccàbû*

θadì thâ, hóuhmá mwéi tagáunlóu myínlaitté
douʔ tachâun kauʔ thâ

máun kalaʔ: *cúndó cauʔ θwâbí*
cúndògóu hóubekkân tasheiʔ pòubá hóu mótókâdêhmá badú páðalêlòu, myínlaiθθalâ

ʔû phôu chóu: *lún θwâlòu mamyínhnáimbû*

SECTION E—CONVERSATION

1. Covering the Burmese of Basic Sentences

With the Burmese covered, practice until you can speak the Burmese for each English sentence without hesitation. This is individual study.

2. Vocabulary Check-Up

Give the Burmese for all English sentences in the *Basic Sentences* as the Leader calls for it.

3. Conversation

Suggested Topics:

1. Quiz a friend on farming in Lower Burma. Ask what the Burmese farmer raises, when he plants, when he harvests. Ask about the transplanting of paddy: who does it and how.
2. Quiz a friend on farming in Upper Burma. Ask what they plant and how. Find out the reasons for the difference between Upper Burma and Lower Burma.
3. Explain to a friend about farming in America. How does it differ from Burma. What do they plant, when, and how?

Continue conversation. Additional check-up if necessary.

Finder List

ʔamyâ ʔâ phyìn	in most cases, generally
cautté	fears, is afraid
cêdé	scatters, throws about, sows
ceθθûn	onions
cwê	buffalo
douʔ	stick
hnân	sesamum
hóubekkân	that side
houllâ (= *houθθalâ*)	is it so?
káindé	holds, takes hold of
kân	bank of a river, lake, sea
kauʔ saimmà	woman transplanter (of paddy)
kauʔ saitté	transplants (paddy)
kautté	picks up
lé	irrigated rice field
léðamâ	farmer
louʔ káindé	works, performs work
louʔ káin sâ θautté	works and eats, makes a living
lúndé	is or goes beyond, exceeds
myéi	earth, ground, soil
myéibê	peanuts
nwâ	bull, ox, cow
ŋayouʔ	peppers, chilies
phyiʔ θwâdé	has come to be, has happened
pímbândé	is tired, fatigued; is tiresome
pyâumbû	corn, maize
pyôudé	plants
sabâ	paddy
saiʔ káindé	plants
saiʔ pîhmà	only having planted
saiʔ pyôudé	sets out, plants
saitté	sets, plants, erects
seiʔ pádé	is interested
shêi	tobacco (see 19)
tachîn	song
tachîn shóudé	sings a song
tasheiʔ	a little bit, please
táunðú	farmer
thúndé	ploughs, harrows
wágûn	cotton
yá	cultivated piece of ground (not irrigated)
yáðamâ	farmer
yeitté	reaps (see 8)

UNIT 21

A VISIT

SECTION A—BASIC SENTENCES

ENGLISH EQUIVALENTS	AIDS TO LISTENING
	ʔû phôu chóu
breakfast ('morning-meal')	*manessá*
Have you had your morning meal?	*manessá sâ pîjàbalâ*
If you haven't eaten yet, I'll cook (something).	*masâyàðêiyín, chellaimmé*
	máun kalaʔ
Don't cook.	*macheppánè*
We had breakfast in the city this morning.	*ʔakhù maneʔ couttòu myòugà manessá sâgèdé*
	ʔû phôu chóu
dinner ('night meal')	*nyàzá*
How about dinner—will you eat here?	*nyàzá ʔatwekkô, díhmá sâjàmalâ*
	kóu sán yà
takes, receives, accepts, experiences	*khándé*
goes to a lot of trouble	*pímbân khándé*

boils	*pyoutté*
cooks	*che? pyoutté* (=*chetté*)
gives a meal, feeds	*cwêidé*
Don't bother—don't go to a lot of trouble to cook specially for us.	*néibazéi, ?û phôu chóu, couttòu ?atwe? pímbân khán pî, ?athû che? pyou? cwêi manéibánè*

?û phôu chóu

resolves, determines; considers	*θabô thâdé*
I don't consider it troublesome.	*pímbândélòu, θabô mathâbábû*
If I cook, it won't take long.	*cheyyín, macábábû*

kóu sán yà

O.K. . . Go ahead and cook—we'll come and eat dinner here.	*kâumbábí, che? thâbá, cúndódòu nyàzá díhmá lá sâmé*
[Interval]	

máun kala?

invites	*pheitté*
What time did Mr. Po Cho invite us to dinner?	*?û phôu chóugà bé ?achéin thamîn sâ phei? thâðalê*

kóu sán yà

arrival	*?ayau?* (*yautté*)
He said to come at six.	*chaunnáyị ?ayau? lábálòu phei? thâdé*

máun kala?

How long will it take to get to his house from here?	*dígà ?û phôu chóu ?éiŋgóu θwâyín, bélau? cámalê*

	kóu sán yà
one half	*tawe*ʔ
half an hour	*náyíwe*ʔ
It'll take about half an hour.	*náyíwellau*ʔ *θwâyàlèimmé*
What time is it now?	ʔ*akhù bé hnanáyí šìbalê*
	*máun kala*ʔ
splits, divides into two, parts, halves	*khwêdé*
It's about 5:30.	*ŋânáyí khwêdòmé*
It's time to go.	*θwâbòu* ʔ*achéin tóbí*
looks forward to, expects, anticipates	*hmyódé*
Mr. Po Cho will be looking for us. Let's go.	ʔ*û phôu chóu hmyó néi lèimmé, θwâjàzòu*
[Interval]	
	*máun kala*ʔ
Why are you taking off your shoes, Mr. San Ya?	*kóu sán yà, khímbyâ bá phyillòu phana*ʔ *chu*ʔ *néidálê*
	kóu sán yà
custom, manner, way, precedent	*thôunzán*
We Burmans don't have the custom of wearing shoes in the house.	*cúndódòu bamá lúmyôu* ʔ*éindêhmá phana*ʔ *sîdè thôunzán mašìbû*
	*máun kala*ʔ
head dress	*gâumbâun*
Aren't you going to take off your gaungbaung?	*khímbyâ gâumbâun machupphûlâ*

kóu sán yà

hat, cap	*ʔoutthouʔ*
You Americans, when you go in a house, don't take off your shoes, but do take off your hats.	*khímbyâdòu ʔaméiyìkán lúmyôu ʔéindêgóu θwâdè ʔakhá phanaʔ chuʔ maθwâbû, ʔoutthouʔ chuʔ θwâdé*
head	*gâun*
collects into one, puts on (a turban)	*pâundé*
When Burmans, on the other hand, go into a house they take off their shoes. Wherever they are they always wear a turban on their head.	*bamá lúmyôulê ʔéindêgóu θwâdè ʔakhá phanaʔ chuʔ θwâdé, gâumbâuŋgóu bé néiyá mashóu θwâdè ládè ʔakhá ʔamyê gâumhmá pâun thâdé*

ʔû phôu chóu

You have arrived just as Ma Pu and I were talking about you.	*ʔakhùbê couʔ khímbyâdòu ʔacâuŋgóu mà pùnè pyô néiyîn, yauʔ lájàdé*
living room ('guest room')	*ʔêgân*
Come into the living room.	*ʔêgândêgóu lábá*

kóu sán yà

Come and sit in this chair, Mr. Clark.	*máun kalaʔ, dí kalatháimhmá lá tháimbá*

máun kalaʔ

How about you—where are you going to sit?	*khímbyâdòugô, béhmá tháimmalê*

kóu sán yà

mat	*phyá*
We'll sit on mats.	*phyáhmá tháimmé*
We Burmans always sit on mats.	*couttòu bamá lúmyôu ʔamyê phyáhmá tháinjàdé*

máun kala?

In that case I'll sit on a mat too. *dílóu shóuyín, cúndólê phyáhmábê tháimmé*

?û phôu chóu

It's embarrassing that you have to sit on a mat this way. *khímbyâ dílóu phyábóhmá tháin-yàdá, ?â nábòu kâundé*

máun kala?

Don't give it a thought, sir. *dí ?atwe? keissà mašìbábû, khímbyá*

We soldiers can sit any way at all. *cúndódòu siθθâ shóudá bélóu mashóu tháinhnáimbádé*

kóu sán yà

You'll probably eat sitting this way at dinner too. *thamîn sâdè ?akhálê dílóubê tháin sâyàlèimmé*

?û phôu chóu

uses *θôundé*
partakes of food (very polite) *θôunzáundé*
Please have some tea and a cigar before we have dinner. *thamîn masâgín lapheyyéinè shêileimmyâ θôunzáumbá?ôun*

[Interval]

kóu sán yà

Mr. Clark, are you going to eat with a knife and fork? *máun kala?, zûn khayînnè sâmalâ*

máun kala?

How about you, how are you going to eat? *khímbyâdòugô, bélóu sâmalê*

kóu sán yà

We'll eat with our fingers. *couttòu lennè sâmé*

Here are a knife and fork for you. *khímbyâ ʔatweʔ zûn khayîn díhmá*

máun kalaʔ

I too would like to eat with my fingers the way you do. *cúndólê khímbyâdòulóu lennè sâjíndé*

ʔû phôu chóu

Since when have you known how to eat with your fingers? *khímbyâ bédôuŋgà lennè sâbòu taθθalê*

máun kalaʔ

I can't yet. *mataθθêibû*

learns, studies; teaches *θíndé*

I thought I'd learn now. *ʔakhù θímmelòu*

dó pù

is sweet *chóudé*

is sour *chínde*

relish, savory *chóu chín*

Here's tea, relish, fruit, please have some. *díhmá lapheyyéi, chóu chín θiθθîmyâ θôunzáumbá*

ʔû phôu chóu

mango *θayeθθî*

slices *hlîdé*

Bring a knife to cut the mangoes, please. *θayeθθî hlîbòu dâ yú lábáʔôun dó pù*

Did you enjoy your meal, Mr. Clark? — *máun kalaʔ, thamîn méin-yèlâ*

máun kalaʔ

I enjoyed it very much. — *ʔímmatán méimbádé*

salad — *leθθouʔ*
shrimp salad — *bazún leθθouʔ*
What with the shrimp salad there's no question about it. — *bazûn leθθouʔ shóudò, bé pyôzayá šìdòmalê*

kóu sán yà

We're very grateful [to you] Mr. Pou Cho for giving us this dinner. — *ʔû phôu chóu, thamîn cwêidè ʔatweʔ cêizû tímbádé*

If you will excuse us we have some place else to go. — *cúndódòu θwâzayá šìðèidé*

instructs, gives instruction — *hmádé*
orders, gives orders or instructions — *hmá thâdé*
And the carriage we ordered has come too. — *hmá thâdè yathâlê díhmá yauʔ lábí*

ʔû phôu chóu

rejoices, is elated — *wûn myautté*
I am delighted to have had the opportunity of having you to dinner. — *cúndógàlê khímbyâdòugóu thamîn cwêilaiyyàdá ʔímmatán wûn myauppádé*

SECTION B—WORD STUDY AND REVIEW OF BASIC SENTENCES

1. Word Study

A. *Coordinate Verb Expressions*

che? pyoutté	cooks ('cooks and boils')
sâ θautté	lives (on) ('eats and drinks')
lou? káindé	words ('does and holds')
lou? káin sâ θautté	does for a living
sabâ saithnáin cêhnáindé	can plant and sow paddy

A phrase consisting of more than one verb expression which are coordinated we call a *Coordinate Verb Expression.* Often they are sets of expressions which complement each other.

B. *Subordinate Verb Expressions*

díhmá lá sâmé	(We'll) come and eat here.
tháin sâyàlèimmé	(You'll) have to eat sitting down.
dâ yú lábà?ôun	Come bringing a knife
pyán ládé	(He) came back.
pyán lá néidé	(He) is coming back.
khó ládé	(He) invites (comes having called).
lún θwâdé	(It) has gone past.
póu myâdé	(It) is more.
póu myìndé	(It) is taller.
póu cîdé	(It) is bigger.
póu myándé	(It) is faster.
sâ pîbí	(He) has finished eating.

Subordinate verb expressions precede the main verb.

díhmá lá masâbû	(He) didn't come here to eat.
tháin masâyàbû	(You) don't have to eat sitting down.
pyán malábû	(He) didn't come back.
pyán lá manéibû	(He) wasn't (isn't) coming back.
khó malábû	(I) didn't bring (him) along.
póu mamyâbû	(It) isn't more.
póu macîbû	(It) isn't bigger.

The main verb is negated in subordinate verb expressions.

θú mashîn láðêibû	He hasn't come down yet.

Infrequently a verb other than the main verb is negated.

C. Subordinate Noun Expressions

1. No Particle

thamîn sâdé	(He) eats (a meal).
thamîn shádé	(He) is hungry.
thamîn méindé	(He) enjoyed the meal.
manessá sâgèdé	(He) ate breakfast.
phanaʔ chutté	(He) takes off his shoes.
ŋânáyí khwêdòmé	It's almost half past five.
shêileiʔ θauppá	Have a cigar.
cêizû ʔamyâjî tímbádé	Thanks a lot.
keissà mašìbû	Never mind.
kâuŋgâun loutté	(He) works well.
tèdè θwâbá	Go straight ahead.
ʔathû cheʔ pyouʔ cwêi manéibánè	Don't do any special cooking.

A subordinate noun expression precedes the main verb expression.

In Unit 5 you learned the use and force of the noun particles *-hmá*, *-kóu*, *-kà*, and *-nè*. You will have noticed that in many cases where the situation is unambiguous two sentences may be heard which are exactly the same except for the presence or absence of one of the noun particles.

bé néiyáhmá néihmân maθìbû *bé néiyá néihmân maθìbû*	I don't really know where he lives.
ʔéiŋgóu pyán ládé *ʔéin pyán ládé*	(He) came back home.
cúndógàlê dílóu pyôdé *cúndólê dílóu pyôdé*	I said so too.
bá hînnè sâmalê *bá hîn sâmalê*	What curry will (you) eat?

2. Covering English and Burmese of Word Study

Give the English equivalents of all Burmese expressions in the *Word Study* and the Burmese for all the English. This is individual study.

3. Review of Basic Sentences

Further oral practice with the first part of the *Basic Sentences*.

SECTION C—REVIEW OF BASIC SENTENCES

1. Review of Basic Sentences (*Cont.*)

Further oral practice with the second part of the *Basic Sentences*.

2. Covering the English of Basic Sentences

Check your knowledge of the meaning of all words and phrases in the *Basic Sentences*. This is individual study.

3. What Would You Say?

Give full answers to the following questions.

1. *thamîn sâ pîbalâ*
2. *thamîn chettaθθalâ*
3. *manessá ˀéinhmá sâgèðalâ, thamînzáimhmá sâgèðalâ*
4. *nyàzá thamîn béhmá sâmalòulê*
5. *dí nèinyà badú thamîn cwêimalê*
6. *khímbyâ ˀakhù pímbânðalâ*
7. *khímbyâ θaŋéjîn θabô kâun-yèlâ*
8. *cúndògóu khímbyâ θaŋéjînlòu θabô thâðalâ*
9. *nyàzá díhmá lá sâmalâ*
10. *khímbyâgóu badú thamîn sâ pheiˀ thâdalê*
11. *khúnnanáyí ˀayauˀ lágèbálòu pheiˀ thâðalâ*
12. *dígà θù ˀéiŋgóu θwâbòu bélauˀ cámalê*
13. *náyíwellauˀ θwâyàlèimmé, thínðalâ*
14. *dígà néi pî, θùzígóu yauˀˀáun, bélauˀ cájá θwâyàmalê*
15. *ˀakhù hnanáyí khwêdòmalâ*
16. *ˀakhù θôunnáyí thôudòmalâ*
17. *ˀakhù lêináyí thôugá nîbalâ*
18. *badùgóu hmyó néiðalê*
19. *bamá ˀéindêhmá phanaˀ chuˀ θwâjàðalâ*
20. *ˀaméiyìkán ˀéindêhmá ˀoutthouˀ chuˀ thâjàðalâ*
21. *ˀaméiyìkán lúmyôu gâumbâun pâunjàðalâ*
22. *khimbyâzíhmá ˀoutthouˀ bé hnalôun šìðalê*
23. *dí ˀakhândêhmá kalatháin bé hnalôun šìðalê*
24. *khímbyâ phyábóhmá tháimbûðalâ*
25. *khímbyâ khanà khanà phyâðalâ*
26. *khímbyâ kalatháimbóhmá tháinjínðalâ, phyábóhmá tháinjínðalâ*
27. *khímbyâ ˀêgândêhmá phyá mašìdè ˀatweˀ ˀâ ná néiðalâ*
28. *siθθâ shóuyín bélóu mashóu tháinhnáinðclâ*
29. *siθθâ shóuyín bé néiyá mashóu ˀeithnáinðalâ*
30. *ˀakhù khimbyâzíhmá zûnnè khayîn páðalâ*

31. *khímbyâ lennè sâdaθθalâ*
32. *ˀakhù khímbyâ bá θín néiðalê*
33. *khímbyâ chóu chín sâbûðalâ*
34. *khímbyâ yathâ hmá thâðalâ*
35. *bá phyillòu khímbyâ dílauˀ wûn θá wûn myauθθalê*
36. *khímbyâ θùgóu cwêijínðalâ*
37. *khímbyâ lâmhmá badúnè zagâ pyô néiðalê*
38. *khímbyâ bá phyillòu nauˀ càðalê*
39. *khímbyâgòu θín pêi néidá mêimmàlâ, yauccâlà*
40. *khímbyâhmá θâ θamî bé hnayauˀ šìðalê*

SECTION D—LISTENING IN

1. What Did You Say?

With the other members of your group give orally your responses to the previous exercise as the Leader calls for them.

2. Word Study Check-Up

Give the Burmese for all English equivalents in the *Word Study* as the Leader calls for them.

3. Listening In

1. Will you have breakfast with me?

máun bà: *khímbyâgóu thamîn cwêijíndé bé neì ˀâmalê*

máun kalaˀ: *θabekkhálauˀ ˀâlèimmé manessálâ, nyàzálâ*

máun bà: *manessá ˀatweˀ pheicchíndé bamá thôunzándò ˀéimhmábê cwêidé dabéimè, cúndò mêimmà pyéi myòugóu ˀalé θwâlòu, khímbyâgóu thamînzáimhmábê cwêiyàlèimmé*

máun kalaˀ: *thamînzáimhmá cwêibòu ˀâ manábánè bé thamînzáimhmá cwêijínðalê*

máun bà: *máun pù thamînzáimhmá khímbyâgóu shé náyígwêlauˀ hmyó néimé nauˀ macàzèinè*

2. In Mg. Pu's restaurant.

máun bà: *khímbyâ ˀatweˀ sàun néidá náyíweˀ šì θwâbí bá phyillòu nauˀ càdálê*

máun kalaˀ: *máun hlànè lâmhmá zagâ pyô néiyîn, ˀachéin kóumhmân maθìlòu cá θwâdé máun bà:* *cúndó thamîn sâbòu bazúnhîn ceθθâhînnè θayeθθî leθθou? hmá thâdé khímbyâ ?acai? bá hmájín ðêiðalê*

máun kala?: *ŋajó hmájíndé*

máun bà: *hînjóugô, bélóu hînjóu θaucchínðalê*

máun kala?: *chóu chín hînjóu hmáðá hmálaippá*

máun bà: *sháinšín, ŋayouθθî hlîbòu dâ tachâunnè leθθouppawá yúgèbá thamîn sâ méin-yèlâ*

máun kala?: *méimbádé dílóu chetta??áun, θínjíndé*

máun bà: *cúndò mêimmà θabô kâumbádé θínjín-yín, θú pyán ládè ?akhá θín pêilèimmé*

máun kala?: *khímbyà mêimmà θín pêimé shóudá ?ímmatán wûn myauppádé*

3. A visit to a Burman.

máun bà: *máun kalappálâ ?êgándêgóu wín lábá khímbyâ ?outthoukkóu hóu jeippóhmá chei? thâlaippá*

máun kala?: *khímbyâ gâumbáun cìlòu kâundé cúndólê pâun cìjíndé*

máun bà: *?îngalei? ?awunnè shóuyín, bé cì kâummalê gâumbâun pâunjín-yín, lóunjí ?êinjíbá wuyyàlèimmé*

máun kala?: *lóunjí ?éinjíbá wuttá pò dílóu wuyyín, ?apú ?apóu khánhnáimmé*

máun bà: *shêilei? θôunzáumbá*

SECTION E—CONVERSATION

1. Covering the Burmese of Basic Sentences

With the Burmese covered, practice until you can speak the Burmese for each English sentence without hesitation. This is individual study.

2. Vocabulary Check-Up

Give the Burmese for all English sentences in the *Basic Sentences* as the Leader calls for it.

3. Conversation

Suggested Topics:

1. Invite a friend to have dinner with you. He tells you not to go to a lot of trouble. Tell him you don't consider it a lot of trouble. He asks you what time to come. You tell him. He asks you how long it will take to get to your house. You tell him. You say that you will be looking forward to seeing him. He thanks you.
2. Tell a friend about the customs of the Burmese. Explain that Burmans take off their shoes before they go into the house. Tell him that the Burmans do not take off their headdress in the house; they sit on mats; they do not eat with knives and forks.
3. Tell a Burman about the customs of the Americans. Americans do not take off their shoes when they go into a house; they do not wear their hats; they sit on chairs; they do not eat with their fingers.
4. Take the part of a Burman. Ask a friend to come in, to sit down, to have a cigar and a cup of tea, and so on.
5. Go to a restaurant and order a meal.

Continue conversation. Additional check-up if necessary.

Finder List

ˀayauˀ (yautté)	arrival
bazún leθθouˀ	shrimp salad
cheˀ pyoutté	cooks
chíndé	is sour
chóu chín	relish, savory
chóudé	is sweet
cwêidé	gives a meal, feeds
ˀêgân	living room ('guest room')
gâumbâun	headdress, turban
gâun	head
hlîdé	slices
hmádé	instructs, gives instructions
hmá thâdé	orders, gives orders or instructions
hmyódé	looks forward to, expects, anticipates
khándé	takes, receives, accepts; experiences
khwêdé (see 19)	halves, divides into two parts
leθθouˀ	salad
manessá	morning meal, breakfast
náyíweˀ	half an hour
nyàzá	night meal, dinner
ˀoutthouˀ	hat, cap
pâundé	collects into one, puts on (headdress)
pheitté	invites
phyá	mat
pímbân khándé	goes to a lot of trouble
pyoutté	boils
taweˀ	one half
thôunzán	custom, manner, way, precedent
θabô thâdé	resolves, determines; considers
θayeθθî	mango
θíndé	learns, studies; teaches
θôunzáundé	partakes of food (very polite)
wûn myautté	rejoices, is elated

UNIT 

AROUND THE HOUSE

SECTION A—BASIC SENTENCES

ENGLISH EQUIVALENTS	AIDS TO LISTENING
	máun bà cí
bed, sleeping place	*ʔeiyyá*
Is there a bed to sleep on in that bedroom Maung Thin?	*máun θín, hóu ʔeikkhândêhmá ʔeipphòu kadín šìyèlâ*
	máun θín
mattress	*mwèiyá*
pillow	*gâunʔôun*
There is also a mattress and a pillow on the bed.	*kadímbóhmá mwèiyánè gâunʔôunlê šìbádé*
	máun bà cí
mosquito netting	*chíndáun*
Is there a blanket, mosquito net, and the rest?	*sáun chíndáun ʔasóun šìyèlâ*
	máun θín
There's a blanket and mosquito net.	*sáunnè chíndáun šìdé*

pillow slip	*gâun?ôunzu?*
bed sheet, spread	*?eiyyágîn*
As for the pillow slips and sheets, I sent them to the laundry.	*gâun?ôunzunnè ?eiyyágîndò dóubígóu pêilaitté*
cupboard	*bídóu*
There are towels in that cupboard.	*myethnaθouppawá hóu bídóudêhmá šìdé*

máun kala?

sets up, in an upright position	*tháundé*
Why do you have to set up mosquito netting to sleep?	*bá phyillòu chíndáuŋgóu tháun, ?eiyyàðalê*

máun θín

mosquito	*chín*
When you sleep at night without using (putting down) a mosquito net you run the risk of getting malaria from the mosquito bites.	*nyà ?eittè ?akhá chíndáun chà ma?eiyyín, chín kaillòu hŋepphyâ phyâhmá sôuyéin-yàdé*

máun kala?

If that's the case I sure won't sleep without a mosquito net.	*dílóu shóuyín, chíndáun mašìbê cúndó ma?eipphû*

---

máun bà cí

Who is going to cook today?	*dí nèi badú thamîn chemmalê*

máun θín

fireplace, hearth	*mîbóu*
kitchen	*mîbóugân (mîbóujáun)*
fries	*códé*
pot, jar	*ʔôu*
large iron pot, pan	*déʔôu*
Are there pots and pans in the kitchen to do the cooking?	*mîbóugândêhmá cheppphòu cóbòu ʔôunè déʔôu šiyèlâ*

máun bà cí

There's all kinds.	*ʔasóun šìdé*
Are you going to cook?	*khímbyâ chemmalâ*

máun θín

Yes I will, but . . .	*chettò chemmé*
even so, I won't wash the dishes.	*dábéimè, ʔôu khwemmyâ mashêihnáimbû*

máun bà cí

Never mind.	*keissà mašìbû*
glass	*phán*
drinking glass, tumbler	*phaŋgweʔ*
I'll wash these dishes and glasses.	*dí pagánlôun pagambyánè pháŋgwemmyâgóu couʔ shêibámé*

máun θín

hold in the ground, pit — *twîn*
well — *yéidwîn*
drum, cark, barrel — *sí*
tub — *síbâin*
is full — *pyèidé*
dips up, draws water — *khatté*

Maung Ba Kyi, (with the aid of a can) please fill the tub with water from the well. — *máun bà cí, yéidwîŋgà yéigóu θámbôunnè síbâin pyèi?áun, kha? thèlaippá*

[Interval]

máun θín

button — *céðî*
is unloosened by severing of some part — *pyoutté*
puts in, fixes — *tatté*
thread — *?acchí*

My shirt button has come off, will you please get me a needle and thread to sew it back on? — *cúndò ša? ?êinjí céðî pyou? θwâlòu, pyán tapphòu ?annè ?acchí yú pêibá*

máun kala?

drawer — *?ánzwê*
spool of thread — *?acchílôun*

Maung Ba Kyi, will you please go and get him a spool of thread and a needle from the drawer upstairs? — *máun bà cí, ?éimbógà ?ánzwêdêhmá šìdè ?acchílôunnè ?a? θwâ yú pêilaippá*

máun bà cí

sock, stocking — *chéizu?* (= *chéi?ei?*)
iron, flat iron — *mîbú*

irons, presses — *mîbú taitté*
burns (a hole) — *mî pautté*
mends, patches — *phádé*

I also have to darn a pair of socks which were burnt while ironing (my clothes). — *cúndòhmálê chéizukkóu mîbú taiyyîn, mî pauʔ θwâlòu pháyàʔôummé*

máun θín

eye (human) — *myessì*
is dim (as the eye), is blurred — *hmóundé*
eye of a needle — *ʔappauʔ*

Because my eyes are dim, I can't thread the needle. — *cúndò myessì hmóunlòu ʔappautthêgóu ʔacchí thôulòu mayàbû*

Please thread it for me. — *khímbyâ tasheiʔ ʔacchí thôu pêibá*

máun bà cí

window glass, mirror — *hmán*
eye glasses, spectacles — *myephmán*

If your eyes are bad, you should have an optician test them and buy a pair of glasses. — *khímbyâ myessì hmóun-yín, shayawúnzíhmá khímbyà myessìgóu sân cì pî, myephmán taleʔ wébòu kâundé*

máun kalaʔ

It isn't that your eyes are bad. — *khímbyà myessì hmóunlòu mahouppábû*

is dark — *hmáundé*
probably (because)

It's probably (because) the room is dark. — *ʔakhân hmáunlòu phyippálèimmé*

electric light — *dammî*

Why don't you turn on the light? — *dammîgóu phwìnlaippálâ*

máun bà

electric wire	*daccôu*
You won't be able to turn on the lights because the wire is broken.	*daccôu phyaʔ néidè ʔatweʔ mî phwìnlòu yàhmá mahoupphû*
light	*ʔalîn*
is light	*lîndé*
window	*padîmbauʔ*
door	*tagabauʔ*
If you want light, open the doors and windows.	*ʔalîn-yáun lóujín-yín, hóu padîmbaunnè tagabauttéigóu phwìnlaippá*

máun θìn

flashlight	*lethneiʔ dammî*
connects, joins, unites	*shetté*
Mr. Ba Kyi, look with the flashlight for the place where it's broken and please fix (connect) it up.	*máun bà cí, bé néiyáhmá côu pyatté shóudá lethneiʔ dammînè laiʔ šá pî, pyán shellaippá.*

máun bà cí

post, column	*táin*
adheres to, is attached to (flatwise)	*katté*
wall clock	*táin kaʔ náyí*
Take a look and see what time it is by the wall clock in the house.	*bé ʔachéin šìbalê shóudá, ʔéindêgà táin kaʔ náyígóu cìlaippá*

máun θìn

The wall clock is stopped.	*táin kaʔ náyí yaʔ néidé*

wrist watch	*leppaˀ náyí*
It's 5:30 by my wrist watch.	*couˀ leppaˀ náyí ŋânáyí khwêbí*

máun kalaˀ

Does your watch keep good time?	*khímbyâ náyí ˀachéin hmámhmán θwâyèlâ*
pocket, bag	*ˀeiˀ*
carries, bears	*sháun dé*
pocket watch	*ˀeiˀ sháun náyí*
[As for] my [pocket] watch [it] is ten minutes faster than yours.	*cúndò ˀeiˀ sháun náyígàdò khímbyâ náyídeˀ shémaniˀ myándé*

máun bà cí

photograph	*dappóun*
takes a photograph	*dappóun yaitté*
sunlight	*néiyáun*
Mr. Clark, if you want to take pictures why don't you get them while there is sunlight.	*máun kalaˀ khímbyâ dappóun yaicchín-yín, néiyáun šìdôun yàlaippalâ*

máun kalaˀ

All right—you go over to the side of the house where there is a sunny place.	*kâumbábí, khímbyâdòu hóu ˀéinnabêigà néiyáun šìdè néiyágóu θwâbá*

máun bà cí

mud	*šùn*
mud puddle	*šùmbweˀ*
There's a mud puddle there.	*hóu néiyáhmá šùmbweˀ šìdé*
Will it be all right for taking pictures?	*dappóun yaillòu kâumbàmalâ*

máun θín

What difference does it make if there's a mud puddle. — *šùmbweʔ šìyíngô, bá phyiθθalê*

sand — *θê*
throws into or upon, fills up partially or entirely (as a pit) — *phòudé*

Well, get some sand from the back yard and cover it up. — *ʔéinnauphmá šìdè θê yú phòulaittá pò*

SECTION B—WORD STUDY AND REVIEW OF BASIC SENTENCES

1. Word Study

A. Noun Expressions

1. As we have seen nouns are modified in various ways. A modifying noun precedes the noun modified.

twîn 'hole in the ground'	
yéi 'water'	*yéidwîn* 'well'
	twîn-yéi 'well-water'
daʔ 'electricity'	
shí 'oil'	*dasshí* 'gasoline'
yathâ 'carriage'	*dayyathâ* 'street-car'
côu 'rope'	*daccôu* 'electric wire'
mî 'fire'	*dammî* 'electricity'
póun 'picture'	*dappóun* 'photograph'

mîbú 'iron'	*dammîbú* 'electric iron'
ʔakhân 'room'	
mîbóu 'fire-place, hearth'	*mîbóugân* 'kitchen'
ʔeiyyá 'bed'	*ʔeiyyágân* 'bed-room'
ʔêðé 'guest, visitor'	*ʔêgân* 'living room'
ʔathê 'interior'	*ʔakhândê* 'interior of the room'

Notice that the *ʔa-* of the second member of such compounds disappears.

hîn 'curry'	
ŋâ 'fish'	*ŋâhîn* 'fish curry'
weʔ 'pig' *ʔaθâ* 'flesh'	
weθθâ 'pork'	*weθθâhîn* 'pork curry'
ceʔ 'chicken'	

ceθθâ 'chicken meat'	*ceθθâhîn* 'chicken curry'
ʔaθî 'fruit' *ʔaywe*ʔ 'leaf'	*hînðî hin-ywe*ʔ 'vegetables'

2. In some cases the tone of the modifying noun, if tone I or II, is replaced by tone III.

cúndó 'I'	*cúndò sáʔouʔ* 'my book'
θú 'he'	*θù θaŋéjîn* 'his friend'
badú 'who'	*badù ʔéinlê* 'whose house?'
ʔaméi 'mother' *shí* 'presence'	*ʔamèizígóu* 'to mother'
khímbyâ 'you'	*khímbyà ʔéin* 'your house'
lúmyâ 'people'	*lúmyà θâðamî* 'other people's children'

There is considerable difference in usage in the matter of tone change in various parts of Burma. Imitate what you hear. Note that the change usually indicates a possessive relationship. The same change occurs before the noun particles *-kóu* and *-hmá*.

θùgóu 'him'	*θùhmá* 'at him'
cúndògóu 'me'	*cúndòhmá* 'at me'

3. Noun expressions derived from verb expressions by means of the particles *-mé* and *-té* precede the noun modified and the particles are replaced by *-tè* *-mè*.

lú kâundé 'the man is good'	*kâundè lú* 'a good man'
lú shôudé 'the man is bad'	*shôudè lú* 'a bad man'
θé ʔéinnauphmá šìdé	There is sand in the back yard.
ʔéinnauphmá šìdè θé	The sand which is in the back yard.
θú gâunʔôun wédé	He bought pillow slips.
θú wédè gâunʔôun	The pillow slips which he bought.
sabwê tagabaunnâhmá šìdé	There is a table near the door.
tagabaunnâhmá šìdè sabwê	The table near the door.
nyà ʔeittè ʔakhá	When one sleeps at night.
θwâdè ládè ʔakhá	When one comes and goes.
daccôu pyattè ʔatweʔ	Because the wire is broken.
θwâyàdè ʔatweʔ	Because one has to go.
θwâmè ywágóu	The village to which we are going.

…pressions derived from verb expressions by … of the particle *-phòu* precede the noun …ed.

…ou yéi	Water for drinking.
…ibòu yéi	Water for washing the hands.
…âbòu lân	The road we should go.
…eipphòu kadîn	A bed for sleeping.
chepphòu cóbòu ʔôunè déʔôu	Cooking utensils.
pyán tapphòu ʔannè ʔacchí	A needle and thread to sew it back on.

5. Noun expressions plus *-kà* and *-nè* precede the noun modified.

yéidwîngà yéi	Water from the well.
ʔèdí bandaikkà manéijá	The manager of this bank.
θú cúndónè ʔímmatán khíndè θaŋéjîmbê	He is a very dear friend of mine.

6. Certain verb expressions follow the noun modified.

khêdé 'is hard'	*yéigê* 'ice'
chóudé 'is sweet'	*yéijóu* 'fresh water'
ŋándé 'is salty'	*yéiŋán* 'salt water'
sêindé 'is raw, uncooked'	*yéizêin* 'fresh water i.e. unboiled'
kâundé 'is good'	*lúgâun* 'a good man'
shôudé 'is evil'	*lúzôu* 'a bad man'
pyîndé 'is lazy, bored'	*lúbyîn* 'a lazy person'

mádé 'is well' *mamábû* 'is not well' *lúmamá* 'a sick person, patient'

7. Some verb expressions immediately precede the noun modified. Modifiers of this type are limited in occurrence. They occur only where a parallel phrase may be spoken in which the modified noun is preceded by a noun modifier of the type described in paragraph 4.

θautté 'drinks'	*θauyyéi* 'drinking water' [= *θaupphòu yéi*]
θôundé 'uses'	*θôun-yéi* 'general purpose water'
leʔ shêidé 'washes the hands'	*leʔ shêiyéi* 'water for washing the hands'
yéi chôudé 'bathes'	*chôuyéi* 'bath water'

B. Interrogative Nouns

The interrogative nouns *bá* 'what' and *bé* 'which', and

noun expressions in which they occur, are accompanied in questions by the interrogative particle *-lê*.

bá lóujínðalê	What do you want?
bágóu lóujínðalê	What do you want?
bá phyillòulê	Why?
vájàunlê	For what reason?
bá keissà šìðalê	What's (your) business?
bá phyiθθalê	What happened?
bámyâgóu wéjínðalê	What do you want to buy?
bá ʔadeipbélê	What does it mean?
béhmá néiðalê	Where do you live?
bé θwâmalòulê	Where are you going?
bégóu θwâmalòulê	Where are you going?
bégà láðalê	Where did you come from?
bélóu louθθalê	How is it done?
bélaullê	How much?
bélauʔ wêiðalê	How far is it?
bédò yaummalê	When will he arrive?
bé ʔachéin mîyathâ thwemmalê	What time will the train leave?
bénâhmá šìðalê	Near where is it?
badúlê	Who?
mà hlà cí shóudá badúlê	Who is Ma Hla Kyi?
badùgóu myínðalê	Whom do you see?
bènélê	How?
bè hnayauʔ šìðalê	How many (of people) are there?
shín nè hnakáun myínðalê	How many elephants do you see?

bélauʔ is often spoken *balauʔ*, and *badú* is often spoken *béðú* or *baðú*.

2. The nouns *bá*, *bé*, and expressions in which they occur, are also used in sentences which are not questions. In these sentences they do not occur alone.

bá phyiphyiʔ	whatever happens.
badú phyipphyiʔ	whoever it is.
badú mashóu	anyone at all.
bé néiyá mashóu	anywhere at all.
bégóu θwâ θwâ	wherever one may go.
bélóu pyô pyô	whatever one may say.

3. The nouns *bá*, *bé*, and expressions in which they occur, are used in negative sentences with *-mà*, *-hmà*.

bámà mapyôbû	He didn't say anything.
bégóumà maθwâbû	He didn't go anywhere.
badúmà malábû	Nobody came.

C. Space Relationships

ʔapyín thweʔ θwâdé	He went outside.
ʔathê wín lábá	Please come in.
ʔauʔ shîn lábá	Please come downstairs.
hóu ʔauphmá thâlaiʔ	Put it underneath.
dí nâhmá thâgè	Leave it near here.
ʔawêigóu maθwânè nó	Don't go far, will you.
ʔapóhmá šìdé	It's on top.
ʔapyíŋgà kalatháindéi θwîn yúgè	Bring the chairs in from outside.
šèigà mótókâ námbaʔ bálê	What's the number of the car ahead?
ʔanaukkóu hlè cìzân	Look behind.
ʔanaukkà néi pî, bá ʔó néiðalê	You behind there—what are you shouting about?

The preceding examples display some of the uses of nouns which describe position. The following examples display a commoner use of the nouns—describing relationship in space with regard to something else which is mentioned.

ʔéimbó teʔ lábá	Please come upstairs.
mótókâbógà mashîndòbûlâ	Aren't you going to get out of the car?
sabwêbóhmá tín thâlaiʔ	Put it on the table.
ʔéinʔauphmá bá šìðalê	What's under the house?
kalatháinʔaukkà šá twèidé	He found it under the chair.
ʔéíndê wín lábá	Come into the house.
θittádêhmá thè thâlaiʔ	Put it inside the box.
mótókîdêgà šá twèidé	I found it in the car.
θù ʔakhândêgóu wín maθwânè	Don't go into his room.
ʔéinšèihmá pânján šìdé	There is a garden in front of the house.
ʔéinnaukkà yéidwîmhmá yéi šìyèlâ	Is there water in the well behind the house?
ʔéinnabêihmá mótókâ yaʔ thâdé	He stopped the car beside the house.
θippínjâhmá myíndé	I see it between the trees.

2. Covering English and Burmese of Word Study

Give the English equivalents of all Burmese expressions in the *Word Study* and the Burmese for all the English. This is individual study.

3. Review of Basic Sentences

Check your knowledge of the meaning of all words and phrases in the *Basic Sentences*. This is individual study.

1. Review of Basic Sentences (*Cont.*)

Further oral practice with the second part of the *Basic Sentences*.

2. Covering the English of Basic Sentences

Check your knowledge of the meaning of all words and phrases in the *Basic Sentences*. This is individual study.

3. What Would You Say?

Give full answers to the following questions.

1. *dí ˀakhândêhmá ˀeiphòu kadín šìðalâ*
2. *kadímbóhmá mwèiyánè gâunˀôun šìðalâ*
3. *sáunnè chíndáun díhmá šìðalâ*
4. *myethnaθouppawá béhmá yàhnáimmalâ*
5. *chíndáun tháun ˀeiyyèlâ*
6. *dí pyéihmá chín kaiyyín, hŋepphyâ phyâhmá sôuyéinzayá šìðalâ*
7. *khímbyâ chíndáun mašìbê ˀeiθθalâ*
8. *khímbyâ kóudáin thamîn chettaθθalâ*
9. *hóu ˀakhân mîbóujáunlâ*
10. *pháŋgweˀ bánè louθθalê*
11. *dí nâhmá yéidwîn šìðalâ*
12. *ˀôu khwemmyâgóu shêiyàdá pímbânðalâ*
13. *yéidwîmhmá yéi chôubûðalâ*
14. *ˀêinjíhmá céðî taˀ pêihnáimmalâ*
15. *khímbyâ wuˀ thâdè chéizuˀ bá ˀayáunlê*
16. *dóubí bé nèi lámalê*
17. *bamá pyéihmá dammîbú wélòu yàhnáimmalâ*
18. *khímbyâ bá phyillòu myephmán taθθalê*
19. *padîmbaukkóu bá phyillòu peiˀ thâðalê*
20. *cúndò ˀoutthouˀ béhmálê*
21. *khímbyâ dappóun yaipphûðalâ*
22. *dammî bá phyillòu phwìnlòu mayàbûlê*
23. *ˀéinnabêihmá badú kazâ néiðalê*
24. *ˀakhù dappóun yaicchínðalâ*
25. *dí ˀakhândêhmá béˀachéin nèiyáun thôu wínðalê*
26. *bá šá néiðalê*
27. *khímbyâ leppaˀ náyí ˀachéin hmán-yèlâ*
28. *khímbyâzíhmá paisshán bélauˀ páðalê*
29. *môu ywádè ˀakhá lâmbóhmá šùmbweˀ myâðalâ*
30. *dappóun yaillòu kâumbàmalâ*
31. *dí sháimhmá ˀacchílôun yâunðalâ*
32. *dí bâumbígóu phá pêihnáimmalâ*
33. *ˀéimbóhmá bá louˀ néiðalê*

34. *môu ywáyín, bá loummalê*
35. *shayawún béhmá šá yàhnáimmalê*
36. *ŋânáyí khwêbalâ*
37. *cúndò ʔeitthêhmá bá šìdé shóudá khímbyâ pyôhnáimmalâ*
38. *cúndò myephmán myímmìðalâ*
39. *dí ʔakhân bá phyillòu hmáunðalê*
40. *myephmán matayyín, ʔawêigóu mamyínhnáimbûlâ*

SECTION D—LISTENING IN

1. What Did You Say?

With the other members of the group give orally your responses to the previous exercise as the Leader calls for them.

2. Word Study Check-up

Give the Burmese for all English equivalents in the *Word Study* as the Leader calls for it.

3. Listening In

1. Did you know Mg. Pyu was married?

máun séin: *máun phyú ʔéindáun càbí shóudá khímbyâ θìyèlâ*

máun hlà: *θìbádé*
manéigàbê θùgóu sháimhmá mwèiyánè gâunʔôun wé néidá myíŋgèdé

máun séin: *gâunʔôunzunnè ʔeiyyágîn chíndáundòugô, mawébûlâ*

máun hlà: *gâunʔôunzukkóudò wéjíndé, thíndé dábéimè, sháimhmá šìdè gâunʔôunzuttéihá θú wédè gâunʔôunnè matólòu mawélaipphû*
ʔeiyyágînnè chíndáuŋgóudò θù ʔadózígà lessháun yàlòu wébòu malóubû

máun bà: *θù ʔaméi θùgóu bá lessháun pêiðalê*

máun hlà: *bídóu talôun déʔôunè chepphòu ʔôu ʔamyôuzóun pêidé*

máun bà: *θú badúnè ʔéindáun càðalê*

máun séin: *mà hlà cínè ʔéindáun càdé*

máun bà: *mà hlà cí shóudá badúlê*
θùgóu takhámà mamyímbûbû, thíndé

máun séin: *θúdòu hnayau? ?atúdú yai? thâdè dappóun cúndòzíhmá šìdé*
hô, díhmá, cìbá

máun bà: *?ô, myephmánnèbálâ*

máun séin: *houtté*
θù myessì hmóunlòu myephmán sà tayyàdá hnahnillau? šì θwâbí

2. Let's take a bath.

máun séin: *lá, yéidwîmhmá yéi kha? chôuyà?áun*

máun bà: *kâumbí, dí nèidò khímbyâ yéi khayyàlèimmé*
cúndò le? ná néidé

máun séin: *cúndó ?ató kán kâundé síbâindêhmá yéi ?apyèibálâ*

máun bà: *cúndódòu yéi chôulòu myéijî šùmbwe? phyi? kóumbí*

máun séin: *mapúbánè*
θênè phòulaippàmé

máun bà: *khímbyâ lóunjí pau? néidé pháyàlèimmé*

máun séin: *houtté, manèigà mîbú taiyyîn, pau? θwâdé ?annè chígóu šálòu mayàlòu mapháyàðêibû*

máun bà: *?ánzwêdêhmá šá cìyèlâ*
manèigàbê cúndò ša? ?éinjíhmá céðî pyoullòu, pyán ta? pî, ?êdí néiyáhmá thâgèdé

máun séin: *?anzwêdêhmá mašáyàðêibû chéizu? ?êinjí wu? pîyín, lai? šá čìmé*

3. What's wrong with the lights?

máun sán: *mîbóugâŋgà dammî pye? néidé*
bé néiyáhmá pye? néidé shóudá θìyà?áun, le? hnei? dammî yúgèbá

máun khín: *bé néiyáhmá pye? néidágóu θìyínlê, bá thûmalê*
khímbyâ pyímbòu tayyèlâ

máun sán: *nênê nâ lédé*
táin ka? náyínâhmá šìdè sabwêbóhmá we??úhlè tachâun šìdé
θwâ yúgèbá

máun khín: *?êdí sabwêbóhmá šálòu mayàbû*

máun sán: *tagabaunnâhmá šìdè sabwêbóhmá šá cìyèlâ*

máun khín: *macìgèbû*

máun sán: *θei? ?aitté maθwâgín padîmbaukkóu phwìnlaippá*

máun khín: *padîmbaukkóu phwìn-yín, chíndéi wín pî, cúndódòugóu kaillèimmé*

máun khín: *yò, díhmá we??úhlè*

máun sán: *dí dammî côugóu she? néidôun, cúndò leppa? náyígóu khanà yú thâbá ?â, dammî yàbí hóu pháŋgwekkóu táun thâlaippá*

SECTION E—CONVERSATION

1. Covering the Burmese of Basic Sentences

With the Burmese covered, practice until you can speak the Burmese for each English sentence as without hesitation. This is individual study.

2. Vocabulary Check-Up

Give the Burmese for all English sentences in the *Basic Sentences* as the Leader calls for it.

3. Conversation

Suggested Topics:

1. Ask a friend about the furnishings of his rooms. Make him describe the location of the bed, chairs and so on.
2. Ask your friend questions about fixing the lights if they won't go on.
3. Discuss a mutual friend who has gotten married. To whom? What did they get as presents? From whom?
4. Describe taking a bath in Burma.
5. Discuss taking pictures.

Continue conversation. Additional check-up if neccessary.

Finder List

ˀacchí	thread
ˀacchílôun	spool of thread
ˀalîn (lîndé)	light
ˀánzwê	drawer
ˀappauˀ	eye of a needle
bídóu	cupboard
céðî	button
chéizuˀ	sock, stocking
chín	mosquito
chíndáin	mosquito netting
códé	fries
daccôu	electric wire
dammî	electric light
dappóun	photograph
dappóun yaitté	takes a photograph
déˀôu	large iron pot, pan
ˀeiˀ	pocket, bag
ˀeiˀ sháun náyí	pocket watch
ˀeiyyá	bed, sleeping place
ˀeiyyágîn	bed sheet, spread
gâunˀôun	pillow
gâunˀôunzuˀ	pillow slip
hmán	window glass, mirror
hmáundé	is dark
hmóundé	is dim (as the eye), is blurred
katté	adheres to, is attached to (flatwise)
khatté	dips up, draws water
leppaˀ náyí	wrist watch
lethneiˀ dammî	flashlight
lîndé	is light
mî	fire
mîbóu	fireplace, hearth
mîbóugân	kitchen
mîbóujáun	kitchen
mîbú	iron, flat iron
mîbú taitté	irons, presses
mî pautté	burns a hole
mwèiyá	mattress
myephmán	eye glasses, spectacles
myessì	eye (human)
néiyáun	sunlight
ˀôu	pot, jar

padîmbau?	window
phádé	mends, patches
phán	glass
pháŋgwe?	drinking glass, tumbler
phòudé	throws into or upon; fills up partially or entirely (as a pit)
pyèidé	is full
pyoutté	is unloosed by severing of some part
sháundé	carries, bears
shetté	connects, joins, unites
sí	drum, cork, barrel
síbâin	tub
šùmbwe?	mud puddle
šùn	mud
tagabau?	door
táin	post, column
táin ka? náyí	wall clock
tatté	puts in, fixes
tháundé	sets up, in an upright position
twîn	hole in the ground, pit
θê	sand
yéidwîn	well

UNIT 23

POST OFFICE AND BANK

SECTION A—BASIC SENTENCES

ENGLISH EQUIVALENTS	AIDS TO LISTENING
	máun kalaʔ
pen	*kaláundán*
ink	*hmín*
bottle of ink	*hmín ʔôu*
Mr. Ba Kyi, please give me some paper, a bottle of ink, and a pen; I want to write a letter.	*máun bà cí, cúndó sá yêijínlòu, sá yêi sekkú kaláundánnè hmínʔôu tasheiʔ pêibá*
	máun bà cí
Whom do you intend to write?	*badùzígóu sá yêimalòulê*
	máun kalaʔ
relatives	*shwéimyôu*
I'm going to write to my relatives in America so that they'll know I'm all right.	*ʔaméiyìkán pyéihmá šìdè shwéimyôumyâzígóu cúndó câmmájâuŋgóu θìyàʔáun, sá yêimalòu*

máun bà cí

pencil	*khêdán*
I don't have a pen—I have a pencil.	*cúndòzíhmá kaláundán mašìbû, khêdán šìdé*
Do you want it?	*khímbyâ lóujínðalâ*

máun kala?

Yes, please.	*lóujímbádé*

máun θín

but you said . . .	*shóu*
But you said you were going to write to your girl.	*khímbyâ yîzâzígóu sá yêimé, shóu*

máun kala?

the other day	*tanéigà*
I wrote my girl the other day.	*yîzâzígóu hóu tanèigà yêilaitté*

máun θín

so that's the reason	*dájàummòu*
So that's the reason you're so happy.	*dájàummòu khímbyâ sei? þyó néidágóu . . .*
post-man, letter carrier	*sábòuðamâ*
Mr. Ba Kyi, hasn't the postman brought the mail yet?	*máun bà cí, dí nèi mane? sábòuðamâ sá lá mapêiðêibûlâ*

máun bà cí

He hasn't come yet.	*maláðêibû*

máun θín

envelope	*sá?ei?*
is fit, sufficient	*tándé*
mark made by stamping, a seal	*tazei?*
postage stamp	*tazei? gâun*
How much postage do you have to put on the envelope if you mail it to America?	*khìmbyâ ?améiyìkán pyéigóu sá pêiyín, sá?eippóhmá bélauttán tazei? gâun ka? thèyàmalê*

máun kala?

I can't say for sure how much it'll be.	*bélau? càmalê, shóudá, cúndó ?ahmán mapyôhnáinðêibû*
We'll go to the postoffice and find out.	*sádaikkóu θwâ mêi cì?ôummé*
every time	*khádâin*
If it's as usual it will probably come to 3 rupees, I think.	*khádâinlóu shóuyíndò, θôunja? càlèimmé, thíndé*

máun θín

When are you going to the postoffice?	*sádaikkóu bédò θwâmalê*
sends a telegram	*cêinân yaitté*
telegraph wire, iron cable, chain	*θánjôu*
telegraph station	*θánjôuyôun*
I have to go to the telegraph office too to send a telegram.	*cúndólê cêinân yaipphòu θánjôuyôuŋgóu θwâzayá šìdé*

máun bà cí

You don't have to go to the telegraph station.	*θánjôuyôuŋgóu θwâbòu malóubábû*

You can send telegrams at the post office too.	*sádaiphmálê cêinân yaithnáimbádé*
If you're going now, I want to go along too because I have to send some money.	*khímbyâdòu ʔakhù θwâyín, cúndólê ŋwéi pòuzayá ʃìdè ʔatweʔ laicchíndé*

máun kalaʔ

If you're coming along, hurry up.	*laimmé shóuyín, myámmyán louʔ*
reaches, attains to, overtakes	*hmídé*
tries to catch, arrests	*phândé*
I want to be sure to catch that car.	*hóu dayyathâ hmíʔáun, phânjíndé*

máun bà cí

Be careful.	*θadì thâ*
You're liable to get hit by a car.	*mótókâ taimmìlèimmé nó.*
even this much	*dílauttáun*
is in a hurry	*lôdé*
Don't be in such a terrific hurry to cross the street.	*lâŋgóu phyaʔ kûbòu dílauttáun lô manéibánè*

máun kalaʔ

is closed, closes	*peitté*
The window where (stamps) are usually sold is closed.	*khádâin yâun néidè ʔapaukkóu peiʔ thâdé*
Where can I buy a stamp?	*bé néiyáhmá tazeiʔ gâuŋgóu wélòu yàmalê*

máun bà cí

You can buy stamps at this window.	*khímbyâ dí ʔapauphmá tazeiʔ gâuŋgóu wéhnáimbádé*

máun θín

one anna denomination	*tabêdán*
Mr. Clark, please buy four one anna stamps for me.	*máun kala?, cúndò ?atwellê tabêdán tazei? gâun lêigâun wélaippá*

máun kala?

one's self	*kòuhá kóu*
employs, asks (to do)	*khâindé*
You're certainly a fellow who knows how to ask people to do things for you.	*khímbyâ kòuhá kóu mawébênè lúmyâdéigóu khâimbòu tattè lúbê*

máun bà cí

money order from	*mánní ?ódá pháun*
I have to go fill out a money order blank to send some money.	*cúndó ŋwéi pòubòu mánní ?ódá pháun θwâ yêiyà?ôummé*

máun θín

sends a telegram	*θánjôu yaitté*
I have to go send a telegram too.	*cúndólê θánjôu θwâ yaiyyà?ôummé*

máun kala? (to a clerk)

How much postage do I have to put on this envelope?	*dí sá ?eippóhmá bélauttán tazei? gâun ka? thèyàmalê*

sádai? sayêi

How do you want to send the letter?	*khímbyâ dí ságóu bélóu pòujínðalê*
airplane	*léiyímbyán*
Do you want to send it by boat or by plane?	*θîmbônè pòujínðalâ, léiyímbyánnè pòujínðalâ*

máun kala?

I want to send it by air.	*léiyímbyánnè póujíndé*
weighs	*chéindé*
Please weigh this letter and see how much it will cost.	*bélau? càmé shóudá, dí ságóu chéin cìbá*

sayêi

It will be Rs. 2—12as.	*θôunja? mattîn càlèimmé*

máun kala?

one unit	*takhù*
Here's the money, please give me two one rupee stamps and one twelve anna stamp.	*díhmá paisshán, tajattán gâun hnakhùnè θôummattán gâun takhù pêibá*
is pretty	*hlàdé*
is really pretty	*hlàðâbê*
These stamps are rather pretty.	*dí tazei? gâundéihá ?ató hlàðâbê*

---

máun kala?

Have you finished your business?	*khímbyâdòu ?alou? pîjàbalâ*

máun θín

We're finished.	*couttòu ?alou? pîbábí*
Where else do you want to go?	*khímbyâ bégóu θwâjínðêiðalê*

máun kala?

I still have to go to the bank to draw out some money.	*cùndó ŋwéi thoupphòu bándaikkóu θwâzayá šìðêidé*
Do you want to go along?	*khímbyâ laicchínðalâ*

máun bà cí

Mr. Thin, if you want to go with (him) go ahead.	*máun θín, khímbyâ laicchín-yin, lai? θwâbálâ*
telephone	*télíphôun*
I still have to call a friend on the telephone.	*cúndó télíphôunnè θaŋéjînzígóu zagâ pyôzayá šìðêidé*

máun θín

Which bank do you want to go to Mr. Clark?	*máun kala?, bé bándaikkóu θwâjínðalê*

máun kala?

citizen, fellow countryman	*?amyôuðâ*
I want to go to the National Bank.	*?amyôuðâ bándaikkóu θwâjíndé*

máun θín

manager	*mánéijá*
The manager of that bank is an old school mate of mine.	*?êdí bándaikkà mánéijáhá, cúndónè câun néibe? θaŋéjîn-*
If we go, we can have a talk with him too.	*θwâyín, θúnèlê zagâ pyôhnáimbádé*

máun kala?

If you're going along, come on, we'll go. — *laimmé shóuyín, lá, θwâmé*

taxi — *taissí* [or *taksí*]

Let's take that cab. — *hóu taissígóu hŋâ sîyà?áun*

[At the bank]

máun kala?

check — *ce? lephma?*

Here's a check. — *díhmá ce? lephma?*

I'd like to take out some money. — *cúndó ŋwéi thoucchíndé*

ŋwéi thêin sayêi [teller]

puts in — *θwîndé*

This is where you deposit money. — *dí néiyá ŋwéi θwîndè néíyá*

Go to that window to draw money out. — *ŋwéi thoupphòu hóu ?apaukkóu θwâbá*

máun θín

borrows, lends (money) — *chîdé*

When you get the money can you lend me about five rupees. — *ŋwéi thoullòu yàdè ?akhá cúndògóu ŋâjallau? chîhnáimmalâ*

máun kala?

Yes I can. — *chîhnáimbádé*

SECTION B—WORD STUDY AND REVIEW OF BASIC SENTENCES

1. Word Study

A. shóudé

1. shóudé 'speaks, says, tells'
shóu

khímbyâ yîzâgóu sá yêimé, shóu	I was under the impression you were going to write your sweetheart.
khímbyàhmá khêdán wézayá šìdé, shóu	But you said you had to buy pencils.
malaipphû, shóu	I thought you said you weren't coming.

shóu at the end of a statement denotes surprise at what was said. It may be translated 'but you said . . ., they say . . ., didn't you say?'

2. shóudá

bélau? càmalê shóudá, cúndó ?ahmán mapyôhnáinðeibû	I can't say for sure how much it will be.
bélau? càmé shóudá, dí ságóu chéin cìbá	Please weigh this letter and see how much it will cost.
?û séin dáin shóudá, hóu sháiŋgà mánijá, mahoupphûlâ	Mr. Sein Daing is the manager of that store, isn't he?
?adeiphé bálê shóudá, cúndó maθibû	I don't know what the meaning is.

shóudá follows expressions about which a general remark is to be made. 'The fact that. . .' Seldom translated in an English equivalent.

3. shóuyín, 'if'

khádâinlóu shóuyíndò, θôunja? càlèimmé, thíndé	If it's as usual it will probably come to 3 rupees I think.
laimmé shóuyín, myámmyán lou?	If you're coming along, hurry up.
laimmé shóuyín, lá, θwâmé	If you're going along, come on, we'll go.
sá daikkóu θwâmé shóuyín, cúndò ?atwe? tamûdán gâun chaukkhù tasheillau? wégèbá	If you go to the post office please buy me six 2 anna stamps.
dílóu shóuyín. . .	If that's the case. . .

shóuyín subordinates a preceding expression in the meaning 'if, if you suppose, if we put the case'.

4. *shóuðalóu*

ʔayín lóu ʔahnêi phyiʔ shóuðalóu	'More haste less speed' as the saying goes.

shóuðalóu follows proverbial statements in the meaning 'as the saying is'.

B. More particles.

1. *-θâ* 'approving comment'

houθθâbê	That's very true.
hlàðâbê	It's rather pretty.
ʔató hlàðâbê	It's really rather pretty.
θú pyôdá hmánðâbê	What he says is quite right.

-θâ is a particle which makes nouns from verbs. It is most often used with a following *-phê* (Unit 9)

2. *-dáun* 'even'

dílauttáun	even this much
díhádáun loupphòu matapphû	(He) doesn't even know how to do this
cúndódáun maθìbû	Even I don't know.
shé máindáun mawêibû	It isn't even 10 miles away.
kôu náyídáun thôu θwâbí	It's nine o'clock already.
ŋâ jattáun càdé	It cost as much as 5 rupees.
yángôun myòuhmádáun wélòu mayàbû	You can even buy it in Rangoon.
θùzígàdáun paisshán chîhnáinðêidé	I can borrow money even from him.
dádáun kâunðêidé	Even this is better.

-táun is a *general particle* which is attached to noun expressions. It is best translated as 'even'.

C. -tâin

1. *-tâin* 'every, each'

khádâin dílóujîbê	It's always like this.
lúdâin dílóubê pyô shóujàdé	Everybody talks this way.
nèidâin sá phaθθalâ	Do you read every day?
hnittâin yáŋgóun myòugóu ʔalé θwâdé	I go to Rangoon every year.
ʔéindâimhmá šìdé	It's in every house.
lúdâiŋgóu pyôlaippá	Tell everybody.

The syllable *-tâin* occurs in noun expressions and is translated as 'every, each'.

D. Numerals

The cardinal numbers from 1 to 9 are as follows:

1. *tiʔ* (*ta-*)
2. *hniʔ* (*hna-*)
3. *θôun*
4. *lêi*

5. *ŋâ*
6. *chau?*
7. *khúnni?* (*khúnna-*)
8. *ši?*
9. *kôu*

Immediately preceding a classifier, *ti?*, *hni?*, and *khunni?* are replaced by the forms *ta-*, *hna-* *khúnna-*.

The *tens* from 10 to 90 consists of *shé* immediately preceded by a digit.

10 *tashé*	60 *chaussh*é
20 *hnashé*	70 *khúnnashé*
30 *θôunzé*	80 *šisshé*
40 *lêizé*	90 *kôuzé*
50 *ŋâzé*	

The numerals from 11 to 99, except for the tens, consist of *shè* (note tone) immediately preceded by a digit, and followed by a digit. From 11 to 19 there occur also numerals which consist of *shè* followed by a digit.

11 *tashè ti?* or *shè ti?*	57 *ŋâzè khúnni?* or *ŋâzè khún*
12 *tashè hni?* or *shè hni?*	68 *chausshè ši?*
13 *tashè θôun* or *shè θôun*	79 *khúnnashè kôu*
24 *hnashè lêi*	81 *šisshè ti?*
35 *θôunzè ŋâ*	92 *kôuzè hni?*
46 *lêizè chau?*	

The hundreds consist of *yá* immediately preceded by a digit.

100 *tayá*	600 *chauyyá*
200 *hnayá*	700 *khúnnayá*
300 *θôun-yá*	800 *šiyyá*
400 *lêiyá*	900 *kôuyá*
500 *ŋâyá*	

The numerals from 101 to 999, except for the hundreds, consist of *yà* (note tone) immediately preceded by a digit and followed by a number.

101 *tayà ti?*	678 *chauyyà khúnnashè ši?*
202 *hnayà hni?*	724 *khúnnayà hnashè lêi*
330 *θôun-yà θôunzé*	863 *šiyyà chausshè θôun*
446 *lêiyà lêizè chau?*	999 *kôuyà kôuzè kôu*
555 *ŋâyà ŋâzè ŋâ*	

Variants of the numerals from 11 to 999 consist of *shé* or *yá* immediately preceded by a digit and followed by the noun particle *-nè* and the whole expression followed by a number.

88 *šisshénè ši?*	*šisshè ši?*
101 *tayánè ti?*	*tayà ti?*
330 *θôun-yánè θôunzé*	*θôun-yà θôunzé*
678 *chauyyànè khúnnashè ši?*	*chauyyà khúnnashè ši?*

The numerals from 1,000 to 9,999 consist of *tháun* used as follows.

1,000 *tatháun*
1,001 *tatháun ti?; thàun ti?; tatháunnè ti?*
1,100 *tathàun tayá; thàun tayá; tatháunnè tayá*
1,101 *tathàun tayà ti?;* and as above
5,000 *ŋâdáun*
8,000 *šittháun*
1,946 *tathàun kôuyà lêizè chau?*

From 10,000 on the numerals are formed as in the preceding paragraph, using as a basis the following list:

10,000 *taθâun*
100,000 *taθêin*
1,000,000 *taθân*
10,000,000 *tagadéi*

1,500 *tathàun ŋâyá*
15,000 *taθâun ŋâdáun*
150,000 *taθêin ŋâðâun*
1,500,000 *taθân ŋâðêin*
15,000,000 *tagadéi ŋâðân*
150,000,000 *shè ŋâgadéi*
123,456,789 *shè hnagadéi θôunðân lêiðêin ŋâðâun chautthául khúnnayà šisshè kôu*

Burmans learn this series by memorizing the list: *khù, shé, yá, tháun, θâun, θêin, θân, gadéi*

There is a special list of *ordinal numerals*.

1st *pathamà*
2nd *dùtìyà*
3rd *tatìyà*

Usually the cardinal number is used:

khúnnatân	7th standard (in school)
θôundân	3rd standard (in school)
lêidân	4th standard (in school)
làzân taye?	1st day of the new moon
làzou? hnaye?	2nd day after the full moon

2. Covering English and Burmese of Word Study

Give the English equivalents of all Burmese expressions in the *Word Study* and the Burmese for all the English.

3. Review of Basic Sentences

Further oral practice with the second part of the *Basic Sentences*.

SECTION C—REVIEW OF BASIC SENTENCES (*Cont.*)

1. Review of Basic Sentences (*Cont.*)

Further oral practice with the second part of the *Basic Sentences.*

2. Covering the English of Basic Sentences

Check your knowledge of the meaning of all words and phrases in the *Basic Sentences*. This is *Individual Study.*

3. What Would You Say?

Give complete answers to the following questions.

1. *khímbyâ khêdânnè yêidaθθalâ, hmínnè yêidaθθalâ*
2. *khímbyâ shwéimyôumyâ béhmá néiðalê*
3. *hóu tanéigà sábòuðamâ sá lá pêiðalâ*
4. *manèigà badú sá lá pêiðalê*
5. *dí ganèi khímbyâ sá tazáun yàðalâ*
6. *nepphyíŋgá sá yêimalòulâ*
7. *khímbyâ bamá pyéigóu sá yêiðalâ*
8. *sá ʔeippóhmá bélauttán tazeiʔ gâun thèyàðalê*
9. *cêinân yaicchínðalâ*
10. *θánjôuyôun béhmálêlòu, khímbyâ θìðalâ*
11. *sádaiphmá cêinân yaithnáinðalâ*
12. *bamá pyéigóu ŋwéi pòuzayá šiðalâ*
13. *hóu dayyathâ hmímalâ*
14. *khímbyâ ʔéiŋgóu pyán-yín, lân phyaʔ kûyàðalâ*
15. *dí ʔachéin zêi peiʔ thâðalâ*
16. *kòuhá kóu zêi wédaθθalâ*
17. *dí ságóu bégóu pòujínðalê*
18. *khímbyâ léiyímbyán sîbûðalâ*
19. *khímbyâ tayouʔ pyéigóu léiyimbyánnè θwâbûðalâ*
20. *khímbyâ bamá pyéigóu léiyímbyánnè sî láðalâ*
21. *télíphôun béhmá šibáðalê*
22. *khímbyâ bá ʔamyôuðâlê*
23. *dí néiyá ŋwéi θwîndè néiyálâ*
24. *dí néiyá ŋwéi thouttè néiyálâ*
25. *dí myòuhmá taissí yàhnáinðalâ*
26. *khímbyâ ʔû séin dáiŋgóu twèibûðalâ*
27. *khímbyânè máun kalaʔ θaŋéjînlâ*
28. *máun kalaʔhá khímbyà θaŋéjînlâ*
29. *ʔû séin dáin khímbyà ʔaphéilâ*
30. *léiyímbyánnè sî ládôun máun kalakkóu twèigèðalâ*
31. *khímbyâ kóu sán yàgóu θabô bélóu šìðalê*
32. *khímbyâ léiyímbyán mâundaθθalâ*
33. *máun bà cí mîyathâ mâunðamâlâ*
34. *khímbyâ myîn sîbûðalâ*
35. *θîmbô sîbûðalâ*
36. *ʔachéin ʔamyâjî šìðêiðalâ*
37. *ʔachéin bélauʔ šìðeiðalê*
38. *ŋânáyí khwê pîbalâ*
39. *taissí khólaiyyàmalâ*
40. *ʔakhù θwâdòmalâ*

SECTION D—LISTENING IN

1. What Did You Say?

With the other members of the group give orally your responses to the previous exercise as the Leader calls for them.

2. Word Study Check-Up

Give the Burmese for all English equivalents in the *Word Study* as the Leader calls for it.

3. Listening In

1. Will you buy some stamps for me?

máun bà: *khímbyâ ʔû séin dáiŋgóu twèibûðalâ*

máun bà cí: *ʔû séin dáin shóudá, hóu sháiŋgà máníjá, mahouppûlâ*

máun bà: *houppádé*

máun bà cí: *hóu tanèigàbê mândalêigà yáŋgóuŋgóu léiyímbyánnè sî ládôun twèigèdé*

máun bà: *khímbyâ ʔû séin dáiŋgóu θabô bélóu šìðalê*

máun bà cí: *cúndódò ʔû séin dáinhá ʔamyôuðâ ʔacôugóu ʔamyê θìdattè lúlòu, thíndé*

máun bà: *dájàummòu lúdâin θùgóu chîmûnjàdágóu....*

máun bà cí: *cúndó télíphôun shessayá šìðêidé sádaiʔ mapeikkhín θwâlaiʔʔôummé*

máun bà: *sádaikkóu θwâmé shóuyín, cúndò ʔatweʔ tamûdán gâun chaukkhù sáʔeinnè mánníʔódá pháun tasheillauʔ wégèbá*
dábéimè khímbyâ ʔakhù chechhîn θwâbòu lô manéibánè
hmíbálèimmé
ʔachéin ʔamyâjî šìbáðêidé

máun bà cí: *paisshán yú lábòu mèi θwâdé shéjallauʔ khanaʔ chîbá*

2. I have to go to the bank.

máun θín: *cúndòhmá θôunzayá ŋwéi mašìdòbû cheʔ lephmaʔ yêi pî, bándaiphmá ŋwéi θwâ thouyyàʔôummé*

máun máun thûn: *bándaikkóu θwâyín, cúndò ʔatweʔ ŋwéi ŋâzé θwîŋgèbá*

máun θín: *cúndògóu makhâimbênè kòuhá kóu laiʔ θwîn-yín, kâunlèimmé, thíndé*
khímbyâhmá hmín kaláundán khêdán wézayá šìdé, shóu
cúndónè ʔatúdú laikkhèbálâ

máun máun thûn: houθθàbê
taisshí talôun khólaippá
cúndólê laikkhèmé

3. Did you hear about Mg. Tin Maung?

máun máun thûn: tín máuŋgóu palei? twèi phâmmìbílòu
?akhùbê câgèdé

máun θín: θù shwéimyôumyâzígóu θánjôu
yaiyyín, kâunlèimmé, thíndé

máun máun thûn: houtté
θù mêimmà ?ímmatán wûn nêhmábê
θù θamîgalêigàlê hlàdé
θúdòu hnayaukkóu cì šùbòu lú
mašìdòbû

SECTION E—CONVERSATION

1. Covering the Burmese of Basic Sentences

With the Burmese covered practice until you can speak the Burmese for each English sentence without hesitation. This is individual study.

2. Vocabulary Check-Up

Give the Burmese for all English Sentences in the *Basic Sentences* as the Leader calls for it.

3. Conversation

Suggested Topics:

1. Tell a friend that you want to write a letter. Ask him for a pen and ink. He asks about the letter—whom are you writing? Where do they live, etc.? How much is the postage? How long does it take?
2. Tell a friend that you want to send a telegram. He tells you that in Burma you send telegrams from the post office. He says he wants to go along—he has to go to the bank. He has to send a money order.
3. Go to the post office, buy some stamps, send a money order, a telegram, inquire about postage rates.
4. Go to the bank, deposit a check and draw out some money.
5. Discuss a friend of yours who has just been put in jail.

Continue conversation. Additional check-up if necessary.

Finder List

ˀamyôuðâ	citizen, fellow countryman
bélauttán	what value, what denomination
cêinân yaitté	sends a telegram
ceˀ lephmaˀ	check
chéindé	weighs
chîdé	lends, borrows (money)
dájàummòu	so that's the reason, for that reason
dílauttán	even this much
hlàdé	is pretty
hlàðâbê	is really pretty, is rather pretty
hmídé	reaches, attains to, overtakes
hmín	ink
hmínˀôu	bottle of ink
kaláundán	pen
khádâin	every time
khâindé	employs, asks to do
khêdán	pencil
kòuhá kóu	one's self
léiyímbyán	airplane
lôdé	is in a hurry
mánéijá	manager
mánní ˀódá pháun	money order form
peitté	is closed, closes
phândé	tries to catch, catches
sábòuðamâ	postman, letter carrier
sáˀeiˀ	envelope
shóu	but you said. . .
shwéimyôu	relatives
tabêdán	one anna denomination
taissí, or *taksí*	taxi
takhù	one unit
tándé	is fit, sufficient
tanèigà	the other day
tazeiˀ	mark made by stamping, a seal
tazeiˀ gâun	postage stamp
téliphóun	telephone
θánjôu yaitté	sends a telegram
θwîndé	puts in

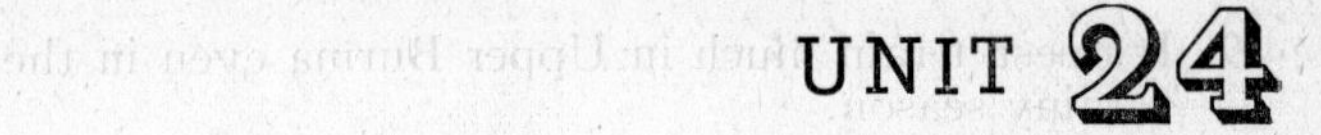

UNIT 24

REVIEW

SECTION A—SENTENCE REVIEW

To the Leader: Begin this review of the work so far by having a session in which you call out at random English sentences from Part III (units 13-17) and ask members of the class to give the Burmese. The members of the class should not prepare in any special way for this. You can take the sentences you ask for from Sections B and C of Unit 18, but take them in random order.

SECTION B—SENTENCE REVIEW

Practice saying out loud the Burmese for the following sentences. Keep at them until you know them all thoroughly. Do not write anything down. This is individual study.

I

1. I don't know what's happening.
2. I don't feel well.
3. I think I have a fever.
4. My hand aches a little too.
5. Did you sleep well last night?
6. My fever was high all night.
7. I want to go to the hospital.
8. What's the matter?
9. I have a cough and a cold in the head.
10. Open your mouth; I'll take your temperature.

II

1. What's your name?
2. My name is ——————, I'm an American.
3. Where are you going?
4. What brings you here?
5. I am very grateful for what you have said.
6. I am on the point of going into the fields—come along with me.
7. I myself will go along and show you everything.
8. As far as I can see, they're having a lot of fun.

9. It doesn't rain much in Upper Burma even in the rainy season.
10. We are very grateful for your explanation.

III

1. Have you had breakfast?
2. We had breakfast in the city this morning.
3. How about dinner—will you eat here?
4. What time did Mr. Po Kyo invite us to dinner?
5. He said to come at six.
6. It's time to go.
7. Come into the living room.
8. Come and sit in this chair.
9. Please have some tea and a cigar before we have dinner.
10. I am delighted to have had the opportunity of having you to dinner.

IV

1. Who is going to cook today?
2. I'll wash these dishes and glasses.
3. Why don't you turn on the light?
4. Does your watch keep good time?
5. If you want light open those doors and windows.
6. You won't be able to turn on the lights because the wire is broken.
7. My shirt button has come off—will you please get me a needle and thread to sew it back on?
8. Please fill the tub with water from the well.
9. There are towels in that cupboard.
10. Is there a bed to sleep on in that room?

V

1. Please give me some paper, a bottle of ink, and a pen; I want to write a letter.
2. Whom do you intend to write?
3. Hasn't the postman brought the mail yet?
4. If you are coming along, hurry up.
5. Be careful.
6. Where can I buy a stamp?
7. I have to go send a telegram too.
8. How much postage do I have to put on this envelope?
9. I still have to go to the bank to draw out some money.
10. When you get the money can you lend me about five rupees?

SECTION C—HOW DO YOU SAY IT?

Quiz by the Group Leader on the sentences in Section B, asking various members of the group to give the Burmese equivalents of the English sentences.

SECTION D—HOW WOULD YOU SAY IT?

Practice the Burmese equivalents of the following sentences until you know them thoroughly. This is individual study.

I

1. I misspoke. 'It slipped out.'
2. I bumped you accidentally.
3. If you want to know—go ahead and ask.
4. Why don't you come along?
5. I don't have a single pice.
6. I don't want to do anything.
7. You will be able to speak Burmese well only if a Burman teaches you.
8. It rained just as I went out yesterday.
9. I knew it was wrong.
10. I don't know what I should do.

II

1. I'm going to change clothes.
2. Wait!
3. I'll probably be able to come along.
4. We'll stop and rest a while.
5. I'll have to change the tire.
6. I know how to do it.
7. I'll have to put it somewhere.
8. I can't say as yet.
9. I allowed him to speak.
10. I'll probably have to go.

III

1. We'll come and eat here.
2. He has finished eating.
3. He enjoyed the meal.
4. He hasn't come down yet.
5. I don't really know where he lives.
6. I said so too.
7. I have been waiting for you a half an hour.
8. My wife is good-natured.
9. Hang your hat on that hook.
10. If I dress this way I'll be able to stand the heat better.

IV

1. What do you want?
2. What's your business?
3. What does it mean?
4. How is it done?
5. He went outside.
6. Aren't you going to get out of the car?
7. What's under the house.
8. I found it in the car.
9. Don't go into his room.
10. He stopped the car beside the house.

V

1. I was under the impression you were going to write your sweetheart.
2. Please weigh this letter and see how much it will cost.
3. If you go to the post office please buy me six 2 anna stamps.
4. He doesn't even know how to do this.
5. Even I don't know.
6. I go to Rangoon every year.
7. Tell everybody.
8. Everybody talks this way.
9. Even this is better.
10. That's very true.

SECTION E—HOW DID YOU SAY IT?

Quiz by the Group Leader on the sentences in Section D, asking various members of the group to give the Burmese equivalents of the English sentences.

SECTION F—CONVERSATION REVIEW

Hold a series of conversations on any of the topics covered so far. All members of the group should have a chance to take part. Here are some suggested topics.

1. Your friend is sick. Discuss his symptoms with him.
2. Go to a hospital and ask questions about the various patients.
3. Discuss farming in Burma.
4. Discuss farming in America.
5. Discuss domestic customs in Burma.
6. Take parts and have dinner in a Burmese house.
7. Discuss the furnishings of your room.
8. You meet an old friend who has gotten married. Ask him about it.
9. You want to send a telegram, send some air mail letters, send a money order. Ask your friend how to do it.
10. Go to a bank to cash a check.

PART FIVE

UNIT 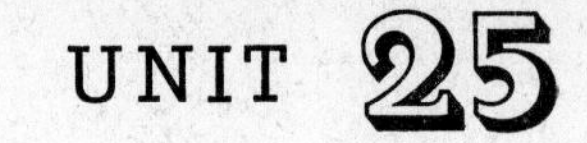

AN EXPEDITION

SECTION A—BASIC SENTENCES

ENGLISH EQUIVALENTS	AIDS TO LISTENING
	máun gódín (Gordon)
Is the road we're on the right one?	*couttòu ˀakhù θwâdè lân hmán-yèlâ*
	máun samiˀ (Smith)
guide	*lâmbyà*
compass needle	*ˀéin hmyáun*
is wrong, is in error	*hmâdé*
Because the compass needle is stuck I can't say whether this is the right road or the wrong one.	*lâmbyà ˀéin hmyáun kaˀ néidè ˀatweˀ, lân hmánðalâ, lân hmâðalâ shóudá mapyôhnáimbû*
	máun gódín
opinion, thought, fancy	*seiˀˀathín*
is confused, befuddled	*myessì lédé*
My opinion is that we have gone astray in the forest and are on the wrong road.	*cúndò seiˀˀathín tôdêhmá couttòu myessì lé, lân hmâ néibí, thíndé*

army	*sitta?*
army encampment	*sitta? sakhân*
south	*táun*
north	*myau*
I don't know whether we should go north or south from here to reach the army camp.	*sitta? sakhânlê dígà néi θwâyín, táumbekkóu θwâyàmalâ, myaupphekkóu θwâyàmalâ, maθìbû*
shortcut	*phyallân*
It will be good if we come across a shortcut.	*phyallân takhù twèiyín, kâumhmábê*

máun sami?

is depressed, dispirited, downcast, dejected	*sei? ŋédé*
Don't be so dejected, my friend.	*dílaullê sei? ŋé manéibánè, kwé θaŋéjîn*
considers, thinks, deliberates	*sînzâdé*
Come on, let's sit down and rest for a little while under that tree and think.	*lá, hóu θippín ?auphmá khanà tháin nâ pî, sînzâjà?ôunzòu*

máun gódín

canteen, flask, water bottle	*yéibû*
I'm thirsty; the water we had along in the canteen is all used up.	*cou? yéi ŋatté, yéibûdêhmá pádè yéilê kóun θwâbí*
stream, large brook	*châun*
I'm going to (go and) drink the water in that stream up ahead.	*hóu šèigà châumhmá yéi θwâ θau??ôummê*

máun sami?

a deep or extensive forest, jungle	*tône?*
every time, whenever (one) meets	*twèidâin*

If you drink water at random every time you come across it in the jungle you'll get sick.	*tôneccîdêhmá yéi twèidâin ʔayân θauyyín, phyâlèimmé*
(As far as that goes) there's still water in my canteen.	*couʔ bûdêhmádò yéi šìðêidé*
If you want to, go ahead and drink a little.	*θaucchín-yín, nênê θaullaiʔ*

máun gódín

strength	*ʔâ*
recuperates, is strong, satisfied	*ʔâ šìdé*
Now that I've had some water I've recuperated a little.	*yéi θauyyàdè ʔatwe, lú nênê ʔâ šì ládé*
Which direction do you think we should follow (in order) to reach the camp?	*ʔakhù bébekkóu θwâyín, sittakkóu pyán yaulèimmé, thínðalê*

máun samiʔ

If we go to the right and keep on, I think we'll get there.	*nyábekkóu tèdè θwâyín, yaullèimmé, thíndé*

máun gódín

path, road	*lânjâun*
Mr. Smith, come here and look: I can see a path.	*máun samiʔ, díhmá lá cìzân, tôlânjâun myín-yàdé*
according to, in accordance with	*ʔatâin*
Don't you think we should follow this road?	*dì lân ʔatâin laiʔ θwâyín, makâumbûlâ*

máun samiʔ

If we follow this road we'll get to a village, I think.	*dí lân ʔatâin laiʔ θwâyín, tôywágóu yaullèimmé, thíndé*

enemy	*yánðú*
However we'll have to be careful about meeting the enemy on the way.	*dábéimè, lâmhmá yánðúnè twèihmá sôuyéin-yàdé*
hides, conceals oneself	*pôundé*
gun, rifle	*θana?*
lies in wait, lurks	*châundé*
shoots	*pyitté*
The Japs hide in trees and snipe.	*jápándéihá θippímbóhmá pôun néi pî, θanannè châun pyitté*

máun gódín

ponders, reflects, considers	*twêidé*
same, implying doubt or uncertainty	*twêi cautté*
Don't be afraid about that, my friend.	*dádéi twêi cau? manéibánè kwé*
till one finds	*matwèi twèi?áun*
We will have to look for the village till we find it.	*ywágóu matwèi twèi?áun, šáyàlèimmé*

[Interval]

máun sami?

dog	*khwêi*
barks	*háundé*
Stop a minute—listen: I hear a dog barking.	*khana? ya? nâ tháunzân: khwêi háunðán câdé*
I think there's a village not far away.	*manî mawêihmá ywá šìlèimmé, thíndé*

máun gódín

That's right—I heard it, too.
houtté, coullê câlaitté

I think we've come near a village.
ywánè nî lábí, thíndé

Hey, there's a village up ahead.
hô, hóu šèihmá ywágalêi twèiyàbí

máun samiʔ

Wait—It isn't a good idea to go into every village you come across without investigating.
néibáʔôun, ywá twèidâinlê ʔayân θwâlòu, makâumbû

edge of the jungle — *tôzaʔ*
a sign, mark, indication — *ʔayeiʔ ʔachí*

Let's sit at the edge of the jungle and wait till we see some sign from the village.
dí tôzakkàbê khanà tháin pî, ywá ʔayeiʔ ʔachígóu sàun cìjàʔôunzòu

máun gódín

It's about half an hour now that we've been sitting and watching.
ʔakhù couttòu tháin cì néidá náyíwellauʔ cá θwâbí

I don't think there'll be any enemy.
yánðú šìlèimmé, mathímbû

headman (of a village) — *θajî*

Come on, we'll go into the village and look for the headman's house.
lá, ywádê wín pî, θajîʔéiŋgóu laiʔ šámé

[They find their camp]

[A few days later]

máun samí?

catches with bait, lures	*hmyâdé*
How many fish did you catch today, Gordon?	*máun gódín, dí nèi ŋâ hmyâlòu, ŋâ bé hnakáun yàðalê*

máun gódín

is at liberty, free, unrestrained	*lutté*
One big one got away; I got three small ones.	*ŋâjî tagáun lu? θwâdé, ŋâgalêi θòuŋgáun yàdé*

máun júnsín

game, flesh of beasts	*?amê*
I'm going hunting in the jungle day after tomorrow.	*θabekkhá tôdêhmá ?amê θwâ pyimmé*
hunter, guide	*mousshôu*
appoints, fixes, sets (a time)	*chêindé*
I made a date with a guide; will you come along?	*mousshôunè chêin thâdé, khímbyâdòu laimmalâ*

máun samí?

You won't be able to go.	*khímbyâdòu maθwâhnáimbû*
order, command	*?amèin*
gives an order	*?amèin chàdé*
The officer has ordered that the camp move tomorrow.	*nepphyíŋgá sitta? pyâumbòu sipbóugà ?amèin chà pîbí*

máun gódín

canvas	*ywetthé*
tent	*ywetthéyóun*

arms, munitions	*lenne?*
mule	*lâ*
carries (on the shoulder)	*thândé*
If we are to move how are we going to carry the tents and other things across the river!	*pyâummé shóuyín, ywetthéyóun lenne? pyissîdéinè lâmyâgóu hóu bekkán yau??áun, bélóu lou?, thân yá θwâmalê*

máun sami?

bridge	*tadâ*
builds, constructs	*shautté*
It'd take a long time to build a bridge.	*tadâ shaummé shóuyín, θei? cálèimmé*
bamboo	*wâ*
raft	*pháun*
boat	*hléi*
The officer said we'd make rafts and boats and cross over.	*wâ pháunnè hléimyânè lou? kûmélòu, sipbóu pyôdé*

máun gódín

In that case, I'll go to the village for bamboo.	*dílóu shóuyín, wâ ?atwe? ywádêgóu θwâmé*

[Interval]

máun sami?

My friend, we want to make a raft to cross the river.	*meisshwéijî, cúndódòu myi? kûbòu pháun loucchíndé*
helps, assists	*kúnyídé*
Please come and help.	*khímbyâdòu tashei? lá kúnyíbá*

	bamá
chops, hews, cuts	*khoutté*
O.K., Mg. Tun and Mg. Mya, you two go and cut some bamboo.	*kâumbábí, máun thûnnè máun myà, khímbyâdòu hnayauʔ wâ θwâ khouppá*
strip of bamboo, used in binding things together	*hnî*
rattan	*céin*
As for the bamboo strips and rattan, they're ready here.	*hnînè céindò díhmá ʔayánð̆ìṇ šìdé*
cart, wagon	*hlê*
carts, carries on a wagon	*hlênè taitté*
Bring the bamboo you've cut on wagon.	*khouʔ pîdè wâgóu hlênè taiʔ yúgè*
[Interval]	
	máun gódín
Where would be a good place to cross?	*bé néiyáhmá phyaʔ kûyín, kâummalê*
	bamá
Near that tree would be a good place to cross.	*hóu θippínnâhmá phyaʔ kûyín, kâunlèimmé*
current is strong, fast	*yéi sîdé*
The current isn't very strong there.	*ʔêdí néiyáhmá yéi θeiʔ masîbû*
	máun thûn
old thing (is old)	*ʔahâun (hâundé)*
sets on fire	*mî šòudé*
Should we burn up the old things you leave behind when you go?	*cáŋgèdè pyissî ʔahâundéigóu khímbyâdòu θwâdè ʔakhá mî šòulaiyyàmalâ*

méijá sami?

Don't burn them. If you do, the Japanese will get to know our camp.	*mî mašòunè, mî šòuyín, couttòu sakhângóu jápándéi θì θwâlèimmé*
hole in the ground	*twîn*
digs	*tûdé*
Dig a hole and cover them with earth.	*twîn tû pî, myéi phòulai?*

SECTION B—WORD STUDY AND REVIEW OF BASIC SENTENCES

1. Word Study

A. Numeral Classifiers

Classifiers are nouns which occur immediately after numerals or *bè hna-* 'how many'. Phrases which consist of a classifier immediately preceded by a numeral or *bè hna-* are *classifier phrases*. Classifier phrases often appear with a preceding noun expression; the noun expression means that which is counted:

lú tayau?	1 person

There are three types of classifiers.

1. A classifier phrase containing a classifier of type 1 can be preceded by various noun expressions.

mêimmà tayau?	1 woman
lúbyóu hnayau?	2 young men
θâðamî θôun-yau?	3 children ('sons and daughters')

2. A classifier phrase containing a classifier of type 2 is preceded only by a noun expression the main word of which is the same as the classifier.

?éin ta?éin	1 house
ywá hnaywá	2 villages
myòu θôummyòu	3 cities
myi? lêimyi?	4 rivers
sáu?ou? ŋâ?ou?	5 books
θippín chauppín	6 trees
shêilei? khúnnalei?	7 cigars
shêidán šittán	8 pipes

3. A classifier phrase whose classifier is of type 3 is never preceded by a noun expression.

hnahni?	2 years
θôunlà	3 months
lêiye?	4 days
ŋânáyí	5 hours
chaummani?	6 minutes

4. Tens, hundreds, and so on, are not followed by a classifier. The numeral ten, *tashé*, occurs both with and without a classifier, but when it is used with a classifier it lacks the prefixed *ta-*.

lú shéyau?	10 people
lú tashé	10 people
myîn lêizé	40 horses
máin tayá	100 miles
?éin tatháun ŋâyá	1500 houses

5. Common classifiers of type 1 are the following:

cha? 'flat things'

phyá hnacha? khîn thâdé	(They've) spread out 2 mats.
pagámbyâ θôunja? pêibá	Give (us) 3 plates.

châun 'long and slender things'

khêdán θôunjâun wégèbá	Please buy 3 pencils.
zûn lêi ŋâjâun yú lágèbá	Please bring 4 or 5 spoons.

káun 'animals'

myîn hnakáun wéjîndé	(I) want to buy 2 horses.
?éimhmá khwê tagáun thâdé	(I) keep 1 dog at home.

khù 'units' often substituted for another classifier

tazei? gâun hnakhù wé pêivá	Please buy 2 stamps for me.

khûn 'words, utterances'

zagâ takhûn hnakhûn pyôjîndé	(I'd) like to have a word with you.

kwîn 'circles, hoops'

yá tagwîn wémé	(I'm) going to buy a plot of land.
lessu? hnakwîn yîzâgóu pêijîndé	(I) want to give my sweetheart 2 rings.
lé tagwînlôun sai? pyôu pîbí	The whole field has been planted.

le? 'tools, weapons'

myephmán hnale? wégèdé	(I) bought 2 pairs of glasses.
θana? θôunle? yúgèdé	(He) brought 3 guns.

lôun 'spherical or cubical things'

θittá θôunlôun thân ládé	(He) comes along carrying 3 boxes.
cúndòhmá ?outthou? hnalôun šìdé	I have two hats.

pâ 'sacred things'

cúndògóu phôunjî tabâ θín pêidé	A certain *pongyi* (Buddhist monk) taught it to me.
phôunjî bè hnapâ myínðalê	How many monks do you see?

phe? 'one of a pair'

chéidau? taphe? côu θwâdé	(He) broke one (of his) legs.
myessí taphe? dán-yá yà θwâdé	One (of his) eyes got hurt.

pín 'trees, hairs, threads'

myîŋgóu côu hnapínnè chíyàdé	The horse had to be tied with 2 ropes.
θippín hnapínzalôuŋgà ?aθî sâ kâundé	The fruit of both trees is good to eat.

sáun 'writings'

lephma? tazáun pêibá	Please give (me) 1 ticket.
sá hnasáun yêilaitté	(He) wrote 2 letters.

sháun 'buildings'

dí myòuhmá phôunjî câun hnasháun šìdé	There are 2 monasteries in this city.
?éin θôunzáun hŋâ thâdé	(They) rented 3 houses.

shú 'pagodas, images of the Buddha'

dí ywáhmá phayâ hnashú šìdé	There are 2 pagodas in this village.

sî 'things ridden'

mótókâ θôunzînè sî ládé	(They) came in 3 cars.
pyissîmyâgóu hlê θôunzînè tai? ládé	(I) brought the things in 3 carts.
shín hnasînè θwâdé	(We) went on 2 (riding) elephants.

sîn 'ships, automobiles, planes; cutting and piercing instruments'

léiyímbyán hnasîn myín-yàdé.	(I) can see 2 planes.
θîmbô hnasîn wín ládé	2 steamers came in.
dâ hnasîn pyau? θwâdé	(We) lost 2 knives.

sóun 'pairs, complete assortments'

dóubígóu chéi?ei? bè hnasóun pêilaiθθalê	How many pairs of socks did you send to the laundry?
?êinjí lóunjí tazóun yú lábá	Bring me an outfit of clothes (a suit).

šîn 'yokes of animals'

nwâ tašîn lessháun yàdé	(I) got a yoke of bullocks as a present.
cwê tašîn pêidé	(They) gave (him) a yoke of buffalo.

thé 'articles of clothing'

chwêigán ?êinjí chautthé wéjíndé	(I) want to buy 6 under-shirts.
lóunjí θôundé chou? néidé	(She) is sewing 3 *longyis*.

?û 'respected persons'

shayá ta?û sá pha? néidé	A certain teacher is reading.
shayáwún bè hna?ûnè kùyàðalê	How many doctors did you have to call in to treat (you)?

yán 'pairs'

cúndòhmá phana? ŋâyán šìdé	I have 5 pairs of shoes.
chéizu? chauyyán pêidé	(I) gave (him) 6 pairs of socks.

yau? 'human beings'

lú ŋâyau? phei? thâdé	(We) invited 5 people.
θâðamî θôun-yau? šìdé	(I) have 3 children.

6. Some nouns appear both in ordinary noun use and as classifiers of type 1. They denote measures and the like.

bíyá tabalîn	a bottle of beer
bíyá takhwe?	a glass of beer
shêilei? tabû	a tin of cigarettes
lé bè hna?éikà	how many acres of land
billaye? tabwê	a game of billiards
zagâ ŋâmyôu	five different languages

7. As indicated in the preceding paragraph, type 1 classifiers determine classes of nouns with which the several classifiers are used. However, the selection of a classifier is not rigidly restricted.

In many expressions *khù* 'unit' occurs with nouns which are also counted by means of another classifier of type 1 or 2.

kalatháin talôun	1 chair
kalatháin takhù	
lephmaʔ tazáun	1 ticket
lephmaʔ takhù	
ʔéin taʔéin	1 house
ʔéin takhù	

Otherwise also, some nouns appear with more than one classifier of type 1.

shín hnakáun	2 elephants
shín hnasî	
shín tašîn	
mótókâ hnasî	2 automobiles
mótókâ hnalôun	
mótókâ hnasîn	

dâ taleʔ	1 knife
dâ tazîn	
dâ tacháun	

In some cases nouns which are counted by means of type 2 classifiers are also counted by means of type 1 classifiers.

ʔéin taʔéin	1 house
ʔéin tasháun	
ʔéin talôun	
sagabóun tabóun	1 story
sagabóun takhù	
tô tadô	1 forest
tô takhù	

2. Covering English and Burmese of Word Study

Give the English equivalents of all Burmese expressions in the *Word Study* and the Burmese for all the English.

3. Review of Basic Sentences

Further oral practice with the first part of the *Basic Sentences*.

1. Review of Basic Sentences (*Cont.*)

Further oral practice with the second part of the *Basic Sentences.*

2. Covering the English of Basic Sentences

Check your knowledge of the meaning of all words and phrases in the *Basic Sentences*. This is individual study.

3. What Would You Say?

Give full answers to the following questions.

1. *cúndòzíhmá paisshán bélau? šìdé shóudá, khímbyâ pyôhnáimmalâ*
2. *cúndò ?eitthêhmá paisshán bélau? šìdé shóudá, pyôhnáimmalâ*
3. *tôdêhmá lân hmâbûðalâ*
4. *lâmbyà ?éinhmyáun myímbûðalâ*
5. *khímbyâ sei??athín dí náyí ?aphôu bélaullê*
6. *dígà néi pî, táumbekkóu θwâyín, bégóu yaummalê*
7. *dí ?anî ?anâhmá sitta? sakhân šìðalâ*
8. *phyallân shóudá, bálê, pyô pyàhnáimmalâ*
9. *shêiyóunzígóu phyallân mašìbûlâ*
10. *sei? ŋé néiðalâ*
11. *hóu θippín?auphmá tháinjínðalâ*
12. *bédòmà masînzâbûlâ*
13. *yéi ŋaθθalâ*
14. *yéibûdêhmá yéi cán-yèlâ*
15. *dí châuŋgà yéigóu ?ayân θaullòu kâumbàmalâ*
16. *?â šìdé shóu . . . dí sabwêgóu tayautthê thânhnáimmalâ*
17. *tôlânjâumhmá mótókâ θwâhnáimmalâ*
18. *tôywádêhmá ?eipphûðalâ*
19. *khímbyâhmá yánðú bé hnayau? šìðalê*
20. *tôdêhmá câ kaiphmá sôuyéinzayá šìðalâ*
21. *jápándéihá θippímbóhmá pôun pî, θanannè châun pyittaθθalâ*
22. *bámyâ twèi pî, dilau? cau? néidálê*
23. *shayáwúŋgóu matwèi twèi?áun, khó láhnáimmalâ*
24. *khwêi bélóu háundé shóudá θìyèlâ*
25. *θìyín, khwêilóu háun pyàhnáimmalâ*
26. *cou? pyôdágóu bá phyillòu nâ matháumbûlê*
27. *nâ tháunzân—hóubekkhâmhmá shayá sá pyà néidá câyàðalâ*
28. *dí néiyágà manî mawêidè néiyáhmá thamînzáin šìlèimmé, thínðalâ*
29. *dí ?anî ?anâhmá shêizáin šìðalâ*
30. *θú bá pyôhmân câlaiθθalâ*
31. *cúndódòunè thamîn ?atúdú sâbòu sàun néihnáimmalâ*
32. *khímbyâ ?atwe? bélau? cájá sàun néiyàmalê*

33. *dí nèi bamázá θín pyà néidá bélauʔ cá θwâbalê*
34. *badùgóu laiʔ šá néiðalê*
35. *ŋâ hmyâjínðalâ*
36. *θanaʔ pyittaθθalâ*
37. *ʔamê laipphûðalâ*
38. *ʔamê θwâ pyicchín-yín, badúnè chêin thàyàmalê*
39. *tadâ shaupphòu θeiʔ cámalâ*
40. *wâpháun louʔ sîbûðalâ*
41. *myikkóu kûyín, bánè kûyàðalê*
42. *wâ makhoupphûbûlâ*
43. *céin kalatháin shóudá bálêlòu θìyèlâ*
44. *myiyyéi θeiʔ sîhmân bélóu pyôhnáimmalê*

SECTION D—LISTENING IN

1. What Did You Say?

With the other members of the group give orally your responses to the previous exercise as the Leader calls for it.

2. Word Study Check-Up

Give the Burmese for all English equivalents in the *Word Study* as the Leader calls for it.

Listening In

1. Hunting.

máun bà: *nepphyíŋgá ʔamê laipphòu mousshôu tayaunnè chêin thâdé*
khímbyâdòu laicchínðalâ

máun séin: *laittò laicchímbayè*
dábéimè cúndó θanaʔ mapyittapphû

máun bà: *dí ʔatweʔ seiʔ mapúbánè*
cúndó khímbyâgóu mataʔ taʔʔáun, θín pêibámé
cúndó pyôdè ʔatâinðá nâ tháun pî, louʔ

máun séin: *tô dí néiyágà θeiʔ wêiðeiðalâ*
θwâbòu phyallân mašìbûlâ

máun bà: *mašìbû*
mapúbánè, kwé
tôzakkóu macágín yaulèimmé

máun séin: *dí tôlânjâun ʔatâin laiʔ θwâyàmalâ*

máun bà: *néibáʔôun, hô, dí θippínʔaunnâhmá tô ʔayeiʔ ʔachígóu pôun cì pî,*
tareisshámmyâgóu châun néijàʔôunzòu

máun séin: *khímbyâ bá ʔacâuŋgóu sînzâ néidálê*

máun bà: *siʔ ʔacâuŋgóu twêi néidé*

máun séin: *siʔ bédò pîmé, thínðalê*

máun bà: cúndò sei??athín ?atâin shóuyín, hnahni?
θôunhni? cá?ôummé
yánðú sittattwéihá myámmyán ?ašôun
pêihmá mahoupphû

máun séin: khímbyâ pyôdá hmâlèimmé
cúndò ?athíndò tahnillaupphê cádòmé

máun bà: hô díhmá θanakkóu khanà kâin thâbá
câgóu myín myínjîn, pyipphòu maméinè

máun séin: cúndó pyittá mahmámbû
câ lu? θwâbí

máun bà: sei? ŋé manéibánè
pyissà shóudò dílóu pò
yéi ŋatté
yéibûdêhmá yéi šìðêiðalâ

máun séin: cúndó θaullaillòu, yéi kóun θwâbí
khímbyâ lóujín-yín hóu châuŋgà yéi kha?
pêimé

máun bà: tôdêhmá twèidâin yéigóu maθaukkâumbû
ywágóu pyán yauttè ?akháhmàbê θaummé

máun séin: ywágóu mapyáŋgín, ŋâ θwâ hmyâyà?áun

máun bà: ládôuŋgà θanakkóu cúndó thân láyàdé
?akhù khímbyâ thâmbá

2. Getting information from the village headman.

kóu sán yà: ywá θajî, khímbyâ khwêi cúndògóu
kaittòmé

ywá θajî: cúndò khwêi háunðá háundatté

kóu sán yà: makaittayyínlê ?â šì pî, caussayá kâundè
khwêibê

ywá θajî: máun bàdòu máun hládòu, pyóbyó šwínswín
šìjàyèlâ

kóu sán yà: hóu tanèigà θúdòu hnayau? ?amê laiyyîn,
lâmbyà ?éin hmyáuŋgàlê ka?, myessìgàlê
lé pî, táun θwâyàmalâ, myau? θwâyàmalâ
maθìlòu, tôdêhmá ?eiyyàdé

ywá θajî: θúdòuzíhmá ywetthéyóun pá θwâyèlâ

kóu sán yà: mapá θwâlòu, θippímbóhmá ?eiyyàdé
sipbóu ?amèin ?aθi? thouttá bá ?acâunlê

ywá θajî: ywádâimhmá sekkúhâun ?awussoummyâgóu
mî mašòubê twîn tû pî, phòu thâyàmélòu
?amèin chàdé

kóu sán yà: cúndódòu wâ tadâ shauttáhmá khímbyâ
?akú ?anyí pêihnáimmalâ

ywá θajî: bé néiyáhmá shaummalòulê

kóu sán yà: yéi θei? sîdè néiyáhmá shaummalòu
?ayíndôuŋgà myikkóu phya? kûmé
shóuyín, hléinè phyisséi, wâ pháunnè
phyisséi, phya? kûyàdé
?akhù tadâ shau? pîyín, dádéinè kûbòu
malóubû

ywá θajî: ké, máun pùdòu hnî loupphòu wâdéi θwâ
khou? pî, hlênè tai? yúgè

SECTION E—CONVERSATION

1. Covering the Burmese of Basic Sentences

With the Burmese covered, practice until you can speak the Burmese for each English sentence without hesitation. This is individual study.

2. Vocabulary Check-Up

Give the Burmese for all English sentences in the *Basic Sentences* as the Leader calls for it.

3. Conversation

Suggested Topics:

1. You are lost in the woods with a companion. Ask whether you are on the right road. Tell him it would be a good idea to find a short-cut. He tells you not to be worried, that he knows the way. Discuss the directions you might go.
2. Discuss with a friend the best way to go through strange country in which there may be enemies.
3. Ask your friend how many fish he caught, where he fished, how he liked it.
4. Discuss the making of a raft to cross a river.
5. Go to see the village headman to get supplies and information.

SECTION F—CONVERSATION (*Cont.*)

Continue conversation. Additional check-up if necessary.

Finder List

ʔâ	strength
ʔahâun (hâundé)	old thing
ʔamê	game, flesh of beasts
ʔamèin	order, command
ʔamèin chàdé	gives an order
ʔâ šìdé	recuperates, is strong
ʔatâin	according to, in accordance with
ʔayeiʔ ʔachí	sign, mark, indication
céin	rattan
chûun	stream, large brook
châundé	lies in wait, lurks
chêindé	appoints, fixes, sets (a time)
ʔéimhmyáun	compass needle
háundé	barks
hâundé	is old
hlê	cart, wagon

hlênè taitté	carts, conveys on a cart
hléi	boat
hmâdé	is wrong, is in error
hmyâdé	catches with bait, lures
hnî	strip of bamboo used in binding things together
khoutté	chops, hews, cuts
khwêi	dog
kúnyídé	helps, assists
lâ	mule
lâmbyà	guide
lânjâun	path, trail, road
lenneʔ	arms, munitions
lutté	is at liberty, free, unrestrained
matwèi twèiʔáun	until one finds
mî šòudé	sets on fire
mousshôu	hunter, guide
myauʔ	north
myessì lédé	is confused, befuddled
pháun	raft
phyallân	short cut
pôundé	hides, conceals oneself
pyitté	shoots
seiʔ ʔathín	opinion, thought, fancy
seiʔ ŋédé	is depressed, dispirited
shautté	builds, constructs
sînzâdé	considers, thinks, deliberates
sittaʔ	army
sittaʔ sakhân	army encampment
tadâ	bridge
táun	south
thândé	carries (on the shoulder)
tôneʔ	deep or extensive forest, jungle
tôzaʔ	edge of the jungle
tûdé	digs
twêi cautté	ponders, considers (implying doubt or uncertainty)
twèidâin	every time or whenever one meets
twêidé	ponders, reflects, considers
twîn	hole in the ground
θajî	headman of a village
θanaʔ	gun, rifle
wâ	bamboo
wâ pháun	bamboo raft
yánðú	enemy
yéibû	canteen, flask
yéi sîdé	current is strong, fast
ywetthé	canvas, sail cloth
ywetthéyóun	tent

UNIT 26

SPORTS

SECTION A—BASIC SENTENCES

ENGLISH EQUIVALENTS	AIDS TO LISTENING
	máun kalaʔ
health	*kóuleʔ câmmáyêi*
What kinds of games do you Burmans play in Burma for your health?	*khímbyâdòu bamá pyéihmá bamá lúmyôumyâ kóuleʔ câmmáyêi ʔatweʔ bélóu kazâmyôugóu kazâðalê*
	kóu sán yà
outside	*ʔapyín*
continually, everlastingly, without cessation	*ʔasín mapyaʔ*
indulges in, complies with	*laiʔ sâdé*
Since we Burmans, men and women and everybody stay outside and always have to be working, we don't need to indulge our health especially.	*couttòu bamá lumyôu yauccâ mêimmà badúmashóu ʔéin ʔapyímhmá néipî, ʔalounnè lennè ʔasín mapyaʔ louʔ káin néiyàdè ʔatweʔ, câmmáyéigóu ʔathû laiʔ sâbòu malóubû*
puts into water to soak, soaks	*yéi séindé*
We're always as healthy as water buffaloes.	*yéi séin cwêmyâlóu ʔamyê câmmá néijàdábê*
is young, in the prime of life	*pyóudé*
young, unmarried man	*lúbyóu*

is old, aged	*ʔóudé*
old man	*lúʔóu*
indiscriminate ('not choosing')	*maywêi*
sometimes	*takhá taléi*
Burmese football (made of rattan)	*chînlôun*
strikes, by a side or back blow	*khatté*
Sometimes men both young and old do play *chinloun* to loosen up.	*lúbyóu lúʔóu maywêi takhá taléi ʔanyâun pyéilauttò chînlôun khaʔ kazâjàdé*

máun kalaʔ

How is *chinloun* played? Please explain it so I can understand.	*chînlôun khatté shóudá, bélóulê, coukkóu nâ léʔáun, pyô pyàbá*

kóu sán yà

ball	*bólôun*
round thing	*ʔalôun (lôundé)*
weaves	*yetté*
Rattan which has been woven by hand into the shape of a round ball is called *chinloun* in Burmese.	*chînlôun shóudá céiŋgóu bólôunlóu ʔalôun phyiʔʔáun, lennè yeʔ thâdágóu bamálóu chînlôun khódé*
is upright, makes erect	*matté*
in an upright posture, perpendicular	*mattaʔ*
is raised up, elevated	*myautté*
tip of the foot	*chéibyâ*
Six men, standing up, play by turns kicking the ball with their feet so that it stays up (in the air).	*yauccâ chauyyauʔ mattaʔ yaʔ pî, chînlôuŋgóu tayauʔ tahlèzí ʔapógóu myauʔ teʔ θwâʔáun, chéibyânè khaʔ kazâjàdé*

máun kala?

Even though you have explained it, I still don't understand it well.	*khímbyâ pyô pyàbéimè, cúndó kâuŋgâun nâ malébû*
a game of Burmese football	*chînwâin*
I want to see a game myself so as to understand it.	*nâ lé?áun, cúndó kóudáin chînwâiŋgóu cìjíndé*

máun bà

Come on, there's a big game over there.	*lá, hóuhmá chînwâinjî šìdé*
surrounds, makes a circle	*wâindé*
People are gathering around and looking.	*lúdwéi wâin cì néijàdé*
We'll go and look too.	*couttóulê θwâ cìmé*

máun kala?

thigh	*páun*
tattoos	*shêi thôudé*
black	*?ane?*
I see tattooing on everybody's thighs.	*yauccâdâin páumhmá shêi ?ane? thôu thâdágóu myíndé*
Why are they tattooed?	*bá phyillòu thôu thâðalê*

máun bà

They are tattooed because they want to be.	*θúdòu thôujínlòu thôu thâdá*
How could I know (about it).	*cou? bélóu θìhnáimmalê*

considers, thinks, figures out — *cán phándé*
with perverted ingenuity — *cánján phámbán*
You are a genius at asking (foolish) questions. — *cánján phámbán mêidè lú*

máun kala?

This is really nice to see. — *cìlòu ?akâunðâbê*

a non-Burman — *bamá mahouttè lú*
is hard, difficult, arduous — *khetté*
I think it would be very difficult for non-Burmans to play this kind of game. — *dí kazâmyôugóu bamá mahouttè lúmyâ kazâmé shóuyín, θei? khellèimmé, thíndé*

Can't women play in a football game? — *chînwâimhmá mêimmàmyâ makazâhnáimbûlâ*

kóu sán yà

propriety, dignity — *?éindayéi*
diamond — *séin*
gold — *šwéi*
Womanly dignity cannot be bought with gold or diamonds — *mêimmàdòu ?éindayéigóu séin šwéi ŋwéi pêilòulê mayàhnáimbû*

together with — *?atú*
appears, comes into view — *pódé*
That's the reason why our Burmese women don't play with boys, showing their knees and thighs. — *dájàun couttòu bamá mêimmàmyâ yauccâgalêimyânè ?atú dû pó páun pó lou? makazâjàbû*

---

engages in rivalry, competes — *pyáindé*
a race, match, contest — *pyáimbwê*
I still want to show you a boat race. — *khímbyâgóu cúndó hléi pyáimbwê pyàjínðeidé*

máun kala?

Where are Mg. Hla and Mg. Ba (the two of them)? *máun hlànè máun bà θúdòu hnayau? béhmálê*

kóu sán yà

They're both gone to the boat race, I think. *θúdòu hnayau? hléi pyáimbwê yau? néibí, thíndé*

máun kala

intermediate space, interstice	*?acâ*
in the middle of a crowd	*lúdwéijâhmá*
a little like (as if)	*lóulóu* (particle *-lóu*)
in the way of catching a glimpse of	*yeikkhanê*
I'm not sure, but I think I caught a glimpse of what looked something like Mg. Hla and Mg. Ba in that crowd.	*hóu lúdwêijâhmá máun hlàlóulóu máun bàlóulóu yeikkhanê myínlaitté*

kóu sán yà

Come on, we'll go and look for them there. *lá, θùdòu hnayaukkóu hóuhmá θwâ šámé*

There they are, Mg. Hla and Mg. Ba. *hóuhmá, máun hlànè máun bà*

máun kala?

boat race, regatta	*hléibwê*
How long have you been at the race, Mg. Ba?	*máun bà, khímbyâdòu hléibwêgóu yau? néidá bélau? cábalê*

máun bà

Not very long.	*θeiʔ macáðeibábû*
Just arrived a moment ago.	*khùdíŋgàbê yautté*

kóu sán yà

festival	*pwê*
Whose boats are competing in the first race?	*pathamà pwêhmá badù hléinè badù hléi pyáimmalê*

máun hlà

name of a village 'one palm tree'	*thân tabín ywá*
name of a boat 'one diamond'	*séin talôun*
name of a village 'garland of *θabyéi* flowers'	*θabyéigôun*
name of a boat 'victory'	*ʔáunzéiyà*
The two boats called 'one diamond' from *Htan ta bin* and 'victory' from *Thabyigon* will probably start the race.	*thân tabîn ywágà séin talôun khódè hléinè θabyéigôun ywágà ʔáunzéiyà khódè hléi hnasîn sá pyáinlèimmé*

máun kalaʔ

bet, wager	*ʔalâun (lâundé)*
Which boat has the more bets?	*bé hléigà ʔalâun myâðalê*

máun bà

new	*ʔaθiʔ (θitté)*
not (even) once	*takháhmà* (or *takhámà*)
The boat called 'one diamond' is new and hasn't yet raced once.	*séin talôun khódè hléigà ʔaθiʔ, takháhmà mapyáimbûðeibû*

last year	*ˀayín hnikkà*
"Victory" is old and has already won two or three races in a meet last year.	*ˀáunzéiyàgà ˀahâun, ˀayín hnikkà hléibwêhmá hnapwê θôumbwê náimbûdé*
stakes a wager, bets	*lâundé*
Even so there are lots of people betting on "one diamond."	*dábéimè, séin talôuŋgóu lâundè lú myâdé*

kóu sán yà

paddles (a canoe or boat)	*hlódé*
signal, blow, stroke	*ˀacheˀ*
one gun shot signal	*θanaˀ tacheˀ*
Listen—they've fired the signal shot for the boats to start paddling.	*nâ tháumbá: hléi sà hlóbòu θanaˀ tacheˀ pyillaippí*
Hey, there the two boats have started off.	*hô, hóumá hléi hnasîn sà thweˀ lábí*

máun kalaˀ

reward, prize	*shù*
Now who will give a prize to the boat that won.	*ˀakhù náin θwâdè hléigóu badúgà shù pêimalê*
What sort of prizes will they get?	*bá shùmyâ yàmalê*

kóu sán yà

umpire, judge, referee	*dáin*
prize money	*shùŋwéi*
metal cup or bowl	*phalâ*
The referees will probably give [them] 50 rupees prize money and one big silver bowl.	*dáin lújîmyâgà shùŋwéi ŋâzénè ŋwéi phalâjî talôun pêilèimmé*

máun kala?

Quite a few people have come to the meet.	*hléi pyáimbwê láđè lú tódó myâđé*
And it's nice to look at.	*cìlòulê kâundé*

kóu sán yà

collective term for boats, oars, tackle, etc.	*hléide?* (*hléi te?*)
There's nothing admirable in the way they row, sitting down and using paddles with their hands.	*dílóu tháin pî, hléi tekkóu lennè káin hló θwâđá chîmûnzayá mahouθθêibábû*
arises gets up	*thàdé*
the Shan people	*šân lúmyôu*
leg	*chéidau?*
The Shans instead of paddling with their hands, stand upright and paddle just with their legs.	*šân lúmyôumyâ lennè mahlóbê, matta? thà, hléi tekkóu chéidaunnèđá hló θwâdé*

máun kala?

In that case why didn't you show me leg paddling when we were in Maymyo?	*dílóu shóuyín, bá phyillòu méi myòuhmá chéidaunnè hléi hlódá coukkóu mapyàđalê*

kóu sán yà

Not in Maymyo—in the Shan States.	*méi myòuhmá mahoupphû, šân pyéihmá*
At first I intended to go there and show it to you.	*cou? ?asàgà, ?êdí néiyágóu yau??áun, θwâ pî, khímbyâgóu pyàmalòubê*

turns around	*hlèdé*
We turned around and came back from Maymyo because you said you wanted to.	*khímbyâ pyánjíndélòu pyôdánè méi myougàbê hlè pyángèyàdé*

SECTION B—WORD STUDY AND REVIEW OF BASIC SENTENCES

1. Word Study

A. Derivation

Noun expressions are derived from verb expressions by means of particles.

1. ʔa-

loutté 'works'	*ʔalouʔ* 'work'
ʔalouʔ loutté	he works, i.e. does as work
ʔaloukkóu θwâmé	I will go to work.
ʔaloukkà pyàn néidé	He is coming back from work.
myâdé 'is many'	*ʔamyâ* 'many'
cêizû ʔamyâjî tímbádé	Thanks very much
θôundé 'uses'	*ʔaθôun* 'use'
ʔaθôun càdé	It is useful
ʔaθôun macàbû	It is not of use.
tódé 'is suitable, sufficient'	*ʔató* 'fairly, quite'
ʔatóbê	It is just right.
ʔato kâundé	It is fairly good.

kóundé 'is done, used up'
ʔakóunlôun θéi θwâbí
ʔakóun θwâbí

ʔakóun 'the whole, all'
They've all died.
Everybody's gone.

thìdé 'touches'
ʔéin ʔathì laikkhè
bé ʔathì lân šaummalê

ʔathì 'up to'
Come along as far as the house.
How far (up to which place) are you going to walk?

θwâdé, ládé 'goes and comes'
dí lâmhmá ʔaθwâ ʔalá myâðalâ

ʔaθwâ ʔalá 'travel'
Is there much travel on this road?

lóudé 'needs, wants'
ʔalóu mašìbû

ʔalóu 'need'
There's no need.

sàdé 'begins, starts'
ʔasàgà bá phyillòu mapyôbûlâ
ʔasà mamyínlaipphû
ʔasà thweʔ néidé

ʔasà 'beginning'
Why didn't (you) say so from the start?
(I) didn't see the beginning.
The end is showing.

sâdé, θautté 'eats, drinks'
ʔasâ ʔaθauʔ páyèlâ

ʔasâ ʔaθauʔ 'food'
Do (you) have food with you?

ʔa- makes abstract nouns from verbs.

2. *ta-*

lwêdé 'errs, is wrong'
talwê loutté

talwê 'wrongly'
(He) does (it) wrong.

chòudé 'is wanting, defective'
tachòu lúdéi nèidâin yéi machôubû
tachòugà dílóu pyôdé, tachòugà hóulóu pyôdé

tachòu 'some'
Some people don't bathe every day.
Some say this and some say that.

lân šautté 'walks' | *lân tašaullôun* 'the whole walk'
lân tašaullôumhmá lú tayauphmà mašìbû | There wasn't a single person along the whole road.

châdé 'divides, separates' | *tachâ* 'other'
tachâmyôu mašìbûlâ | Are there any other kinds?
tachânéiyáhmá θwâ tháimbálâ | Why don't you go sit somewhere else?
tachâ thâlai? | Keep it separate.
tachânéiyáhmá thâlai? | Keep it in a separate place.

sheitté | *tashei?* 'please'
tashei? pyô pyàbá | Please explain.
tamín louttá mahoupphû | I didn't do it on purpose.

ta- is not freely productive and occurs only in a limited number of fairly common words.

3. *-tá, -thá*

loutté 'does, works' | *louttá, loutthá* 'what is done'
θú louttá macaipphû | (I) don't like what he does.

myâdé 'is many' | *myâdá* 'many'
siθθâ dílau? myâdá θíyèlâ | Did (you) know there were this many soldiers?

θôundé 'uses' | *θôundá* 'use'
díhá θôundá mamyínlaipphû | I didn't see him using this.

pyôdé 'says' | *pyôdá* 'What is said'
θú pyôdá câlaiθθalâ | Did (you) hear what he said?
θú pyôdá θabô càdé | (I) like what he said.

myíndé 'sees' — *myíndá* 'what is seen'
mamyímbûbû 'has never seen' — *mamyímbûdá* 'what has never been seen'
mamyímbûdádéigóu myín-yàdé — (I) had a chance to see what (I) had never seen before.

twèidé 'meets, finds' — *matwèibûdá* 'what has never been found'
ʔayíŋgà mamyímbû matwèibûdadéigóu ʔakhùhmàbê myín-yà twèiyàdé — (I) have just had a chance to see what I had never seen before.

-tá (with some speakers *-thá*) makes action nouns from verbs.

4. *-hmá*

θù mêimmà ʔìmmatán wûn nêhmábê	His wife must be very sad.
phyâhmá sôuyéin-yàdé	You have to look out for fever.
lân hmâhmá sôuyéin-yàdé	There's cause for concern about losing one's way.
lân hmâhmá cautté	I am afraid I'll lose my way.
θéihmá macaupphûlâ	Aren't you afraid of dying?
mótókâ taimmìlòu θeíhmágóu macaupphûlâ	Aren't you afraid of dying in an automobile accident?

-hmá makes action nouns from verbs. In most cases the main verb denotes fear or concern.

B. *Weights and Measures*

1. *Distance*

taʔíncí (taʔínsí)	1 inch (English)
talemmaʔ	1 inch (1 thumb)
tathwá	1 hand span (app. 9 inches)
tabéi (-péi)	1 foot (English)
tadáun (-táun) = hnathwá	1 cubit (app. 18 inches)
tagaiʔ	1 yard (English)
talán	1 fathom (English)
tapháláun	1 furlong (English)

tamáin	1 mile (English)
tadáin (-táin)	2½ miles (approx.)

2. Weights

taʔàunzà	1 ounce (English)
hnapáun	2 pounds (English)
tatán	1 ton (English)
tabeiθθá (-peiθθá)	1 viss (3.60 lbs.)
tajaθθâ	1 tical (1/100 of a viss)
tabeiθθá ŋâzé	1½ viss
tabeiθθá ʔaseiʔ	1¼ viss
tadîn (-tîn)	1 basket (bushel)
taʔeiʔ	1 sack, bag = 3 baskets
takhwê	½ basket
tabyí	1/12 basket
tabû (nòuzíbû)	1 tin (empty condensed milk tin)

2. Covering the English and Burmese of Word Study

Give the English equivalents of all Burmese expressions in the *Word Study* and the Burmese for all the English.

3. Review of Basic Sentences

Further oral practice with the first part of the *Basic Sentences*.

SECTION C—REVIEW OF BASIC SENTENCES (*Cont.*)

1. Review of Basic Sentences (*Cont.*)

Further oral practice with the second part of the *Basic Sentences*.

2. Covering the English of Basic Sentences

Check your knowledge of the meaning of all words and phrases in the *Basic Sentences*. This is individual study.

3. What Would You Say?

Give full answers to the following questions:

1. *khímbyâ kóuleʔ cámmáyêi ʔatweʔ bá kazâðalê*
2. *khímbyâ bá kazâmyôu kazâdaθθalê*
3. *khímbyâ tanèilôun ʔapyímhmá bá louʔ néiðalê*
4. *khímbyâ ʔasín mapyaʔ ʔalouʔ louʔ néidá bélauʔ cá θwâdalê*

5. *ʔakhù thà θwâmalâ*
6. *ʔasín mapyaʔ shêileiʔ θauttaθθalâ*
7. *cwêdéi néi kâun-yèlâ*
8. *lúʔóulê chînlôun kazâðalâ*
9. *khímbyâ chînlôun khattayyèlâ*
10. *chînlôun shóudá bálê, θìyèlâ*
11. *chînlôumbwêhmá lú bé hnayauʔ kazâðalê*
12. *hóu ʔašèihmá chînwâimbwêgóu khímbyâ myínðalâ*
13. *wâin cì néidè lúdéihá ʔamyâjîlâ*
14. *cúndódòu θwâ cìyín, kâumbàmalâ*
15. *páumbóhmá shêi thôu thâdá myimbûðalâ*
16. *θúdòu bá phyillòu páumbóhmá shêi thôu thâðalê*
17. *bamá ʔapyín tachà lúmyôu chînlôun kazâdaθθalâ*
18. *chînwâimhmá mêimmà kazâjàðalâ*
19. *mêimmàmyâ séin šweigóu caiθθalâ*
20. *bamá mêimmàmyâ dû pó páun pódágóu caiyyèlâ*
21. *hléi pyáimbwê θwâbûðalâ*
22. *máun bà bé θwâ néiðalê*
23. *náindè hléi bá shù yàðalê*
24. *θúdòugóu díhmá šá twèimalâ*
25. *khímbyâdòu díhmá yauʔ néidá bélauʔ cá θwâbalâ*
26. *khùdíŋgà badú thweʔ θwâðalê*
27. *díhmá badú ʔacîzôunlê*
28. *sá phattòmalâ*
29. *bé hléigà ʔalâun myâðalê*
30. *bé hléinè bé hléi pyáimmalê*
31. *hléi pyáimbwê caiyyèlâ*
32. *hléi pyáimbûðalâ*
33. *dí ʔakhândêhmá câunðâ bé hnayauʔ šìðalê*
34. *hléi hlóbûðalâ*
35. *hlê sîbûðalâ*
36. *khímbyâ páumbóhmá shêi thôu thâðalâ*
37. *khímbyâ pháun sîbûðalâ*
38. *díhá bá khóðalê, khêdán khóðalâ, kaláundán khóðalâ*
39. *ʔakhù bé ʔachéinlê, khímbyâ θìðalâ*
40. *ʔakhù θwâzayá šìðalâ*

SECTION D—LISTENING IN

1. What Did You Say?

With the other members of the group give orally your responses to the previous exercise as the Leader calls for them.

2. Word Study Check-Up

Give the Burmese for all English equivalents in the *Word Study* as the Leader calls for it.

3. Listening In

1. What's that crowd?

máun hlà: *hóuhmá lúdéi pwê cà néiðalóu wâin néijàdé*
bálêlòu θwâ cìyà?áun

máun bà cí: *?athû ?ashân takhù šìhmábê*
lú?óu lúbyóu maywêi wâin cì néijàdé

máun máun: *?atúdú θwâyà?áun*
cúndò ?atwellê khanà sàun néibá?ôun

máun bà cí: *máun máun béhmálê*

máun hlà: *lúdéijâhmá pyau? néibí, thíndé*
θù ?atwe? pú manéibánè
khùdíŋgàbê yeikkhanê myínlaitté
khímbyâ bá phyi? néidé shóudá, myín-yàyèlâ

máun bà cí: *mamyín-yàbû*

máun hlà: *lúgalêi tayaukkóu mótókâ tai? θwâdé*
tai? θwâbéimè, kán kâunlòu du pûn dán-yánè lu? θwâdé

máun bà cí: *bélóu phyi? θwâdélòu, câðalê*

máun hlà: *lúgalêi θù θaŋéjîndéinè lâmbóhmá bólôun kha? hmyau? kazâ néiyîn, mótókâ tai? θwâdélòu, câdé*

máun bà cí: *cánján phámbán lâmbóhmá kazâdattè khalêidéibê*

máun hlà: *myòudêhmá kóule? câmmáyêi ?atwe? kazâbòu néiyámyâhmà mašìbê, dílóu lâmbóhmá kazâjàhmá pò*

2. Do you want to see a game of *chinloun?*

máun máun thûn: *dí ganèi chînlôun kha? kazâdá θwâ cìmé, laiccàmalâ*

máun séin thûn: *khímbyâ néidâinlóulóu θwâ cìdé, thíndé*

máun máun thûn: *?ayín hnikkà nèidâinlóu θwâ cìdé*
?akhùdò ?achéin mašìlòu takhá taléibê θwâ cìhnáindòdé

máun kala?: *chînlôun kha? kazâdá macìbûbû*
?awêigàðá chînwâiŋgóu myímbûdé

máun séin thûn: *dílóu shóuyín, khímbyâ lai? θwâbálâ*

máun kala?: *laittò laicchímbáyè*
dábéimè, máun bà cínè hléi pyáimbwêgóu θwâ cìmélòu, chêin thâdé

máun máun thûn: *hléi pyáimbwê šìhmân maθìlòu, chînlôun kha? kazâdá θwâ cìmélòu, sei? kûdábà*
?akhùdò hléi pyáimbwêgóubê laikkhèmé

3. A visit to a friend.

ʔû tín hlà: *ʔapyímhmá ʔêidé*
ʔathêhmá lá wín tháimbá

ʔû bà sôu: *khímbyâ šwéi phalâjîhá θeiʔ hlàdé*
bédôuŋgà wé thâdálê

ʔû tín hlà: *wédá mahoupphû*
cúndò θâ hléi pyáimbwêhmá náinʔáun hlólòu shùyàdábà
phalâ talôun ʔapyín shùŋwéilê yàðêidé

ʔû bà sôu: *ʔîŋgaleittòuhmádò phalâ ʔapyín tekkóulê shùlóu pêidé*

ʔû tín hlà: *khímbyâ θâgalêigô, bènélê*
câumhmá pyóyèlâ

ʔû bà sôu: *cúndò θâgà sá phapphòu pyîndé*
hóu tanèigà sá matallòu, tanèilôun mattaʔ yaʔ néiyàdé
θù hnamàgalêigàdò θúnè matúbû
ʔéindayéilê šìdé
lóunjílê yettatté

ʔû tín hlà: *khalêidéihá sá maphacchín-yín, phaʔ khâimbòu ʔato khetté*

4. What do you want to bet?

máun hlà: *yéi kûbòu yéi θeiʔ ʔêiðalâ*

máun bà: *θìjín-yín, chéibyânè sân cìbálâ*

máun hlà: *yéi ʔéidé hè*
khímbyâ mathwepphê náyíwellauʔ yéi séinhnáimmalâ

máun bà: *bélauʔ lâummalê*

máun hlà: *khímbyâ ʔasín mapyaʔ ʔalâun laiʔ sâdattè lúbê*
kâumbí, cúndó ŋâjaʔ lâummé
khímbyâ dû páun chéidauʔ ʔakóunlôun mapóbê, yéi séin-yàmé nó
nauʔ hlè cìzân
khímbyâ nauphmá bálê maθibû
mwéi thíndé
myámmyán thà, thweʔ lágè

máun bà: *mwéi thín-yín, θanaʔ tacheʔ pyillaippá*

SECTION E—CONVERSATION

1. Covering the Burmese of Basic Sentences

With the Burmese covered, practice until you can speak the Burmese for each English sentence without hesitation. This is individual study.

2. Vocabulary Check-Up

Give the Burmese for all English sentences in the *Basic Sentences* as the Leader calls for it.

3. Conversation

Suggested Topics:ʔ

1. Discuss with a friend the Burmese game of football. Who plays it? Why? What kind of a ball do they use?
2. Discuss American sports with a friend.
3. Discuss with a friend the Burmese boat race. How do Burmans paddle? How do the Shans paddle? What are the prizes?
4. Pay a visit to a friend. Discuss the weather, your families, and so on.
5. Describe a swimming party. What happened?

SECTION F—CONVERSATION (*Cont.*)

Continue conversation. Additional check-up if necessary.

Finder List

ʔacâ	intermediate space, interstice
ʔacheʔ	signal, blow, stroke
ʔalâun (lâundé)	bet, wager
ʔalôun (lôundé)	round thing
ʔaneʔ (netté)	black
ʔapyín	outside
ʔasín mapyaʔ	continually, without cessation
ʔatú	together with
ʔaθiʔ (θitté)	new
ʔayín hnikkà	last year
bólôun	ball
cánján phámbán	with perverted ingenuity
chéibyâ	tip of the foot
chéidauʔ	leg
chînlôun	cane ball, Burmese football
chînwâin	game of Burmese football

dáin	umpire, judge, referee
ʔéindayéi	propriety, dignity
hlèdé	turns around
hléibwê	boat race, regatta
hléi teʔ (*hléideʔ*)	oars
hlódé	paddles (a canoe or boat)
khatté	strikes by a side or back blow
khetté	is hard, difficult
kóuleʔ câmmáyêi	health
laiʔ sâdé	indulges in, complies with
lâundé	stakes a wager, bets
lóulóu	a little like (as if)
lôundé	is round
lúbyóu	young, unmarried man
lúdwéijâ	middle of a crowd
lúʔóu	old man
matté	is upright, makes erect
mattaʔ	in an upright posture, perpendicular
maywêi	indiscriminate ('not choosing')
myautté	is raised up, elevated
ʔóudé	is old, aged
páun	thigh
phalâ	metal cup, bowl
pódé	appears, comes to light
pwê	festival
pyáimbwê	race, match, contest
pyáindé	engages in rivalry, competes
pyóudé	is young, in the prime of life
séin	diamond
shêi thôudé	tattoos
shù	reward, prize
shùŋwéi	prize money
šân lúmyôu	the Shan people
šwéi	gold
takhá taléi	sometimes
thàdé	arises, gets up
θanaʔ tacheʔ	gunshot signal, one shot
θitté	is new
wâindé	surrounds, makes a circle
yéi séindé	puts into water to soak, soaks
yeikkhanê	in the way of catching a glimpse
yetté	weaves

UNIT 27

GEOGRAPHY

SECTION A—BASIC SENTENCES

ENGLISH EQUIVALENTS	AIDS TO LISTENING
	máun kalaʔ
does a favor, obliges	*cêizû pyùdé*
Mr. San Ya, please do me the favor of telling me something about Burma.	*kóu sán yà, khímbyâdòu cúndògóu tasheiʔ cêizû pyù pî, bamá pyéi ʔacậun pyô pyàbá*
	kóu sán yà
What shall I talk about first?	*bá ʔacâuŋgóu sà pyôyàmalê*
	máun kalaʔ
is large, great	*cé wîndé*
population	*lúʔûyéi*
I want to know how big Burma is and how many people there are.	*baná pyéi bélauʔ cé wîndé, lúʔûyéi bélauʔ myâdé, shóudágóu θìjíndé*
	kóu sán yà
census	*θagáun sayîn*
according to, by	*ʔayà*

approximately	*nî kabâ*
According to the 1941 census there are approximately seventeen million.	*tatháun kôuyà lêizè takhù hniʔ θagáun sayîn ʔayà shóuyín, bamá pyéihmá tashè khunnaθân nî kabâ šìdé*
	máun bà
length	*ʔašéi*
In length it is about 1200 miles.	*ʔašéi máimbâun tatháun hnayálauʔ šìdé*
width	*ʔacé (cédé)*
In width it is 575 miles.	*ʔacé ŋâyà khúnnashè ŋâmáin šìdé*
	máun kalaʔ
is really bigger	*póu cîðâbê*
In that case it's even bigger than England.	*dílóu shòuyín, ʔîŋgaleiʔ pyéideʔ póu cîðâbê*
	kóu sán yà
India	*kalabyéi*
either . . . or	*phyisséi . . . phyisséi*
studies, compares	*sá cìdé*
tiny, very small	*ŋéŋégalêi*
Although it's big, if you compare it with either India or China, Burma is very tiny.	*cî béimè, kalabyéinè phyisséi, tayouʔ pyéinè phyissèi, sá cìlaiyyín, bamá pyéihá ŋéŋégalêibê*
	máun kalaʔ
the west (side)	*ʔanaupphe ʔ*
You told me before that India was to the west of Burma.	*bamá pyéi ʔanaupphephmá kalabyéi šìdélòu khímbyâdòu coukkóu pyôbûdé*

other	*tachâ*
country (nation)	*tâin pyéi*
What countries are there on the other sides?	*tachâbephmá bá tâin pyéi šìðalê*

kóu sán yà

the east (side)	*ʔasèibeʔ*
To the east of Burma is China.	*bamá pyéi ʔašèibephmá tayouʔ pyéi šìdé.*
south-east (side)	*ʔašèi táumbeʔ*
Thai, Siamese	*yôudayâ*
To the south-east is Siam (Thailand.)	*ʔašèi táumbephmá yôudayâ pyéi šìdé*

máun kalaʔ

by land	*kôunjâun*
going and coming, travel	*ʔaθwâ ʔalá*
Is there much travel by land to the countries near Burma?	*bamá pyéinè nîdè tâin pyéimyâgóu kôunjâun ʔaθwâ ʔalá myâðalâ*

kóu sán yà

People don't go to China and India by land because there are big mountains and forests on the way.	*lâmhmá tôjî táunjîmyâ šìdè ʔatweʔ, kalabyéinè tayouʔ pyéigóu kôunjâun maθwâjàbû*
They come and go by steamer.	*θîmbônè θwâjà lájàdé*

máun bà

As for Siam, some traders do go by land.	*yôudayâgóudò tachòu kóunðémyâ kôunjâun θwâjàdé*

máun kalaʔ

outside (of), besides	*ʔapyín*
lives, resides	*néi tháindé*
Besides the Burmese, what nationalities reside in Burma?	*bamá pyéihmá bamá lúmyôu ʔapyín bá lúmyôumyâ néi tháinðalê*

máun bà

nation, country	*náiŋgán*
foreign country	*náiŋgánjâ*
national of a foreign country	*náiŋgánjâðâ*
Speaking of foreigners, there are Indians, Chinese, and English.	*náiŋgánjâðâ shóuyín, kalâ tayouʔ ʔìŋgaleiʔ šìdé*
nationals of one's own country, native	*tâin-yînðâ*
Karen	*kayín*
Kachin	*kachín*
As for citizens, there are Burmans, Shans, Karens, Kachins, and other peoples living in the jungles and mountains.	*tâin-yînðâgàdò, bamá, šân, kayín, kachínnè tachâ tôdé táundêhmá néidè lúmyâ šìdé*

máun kalaʔ

What difference is there between Burmans and Shans?	*bamánè šân bámyâ thûðalê*

kóu sán yà

There isn't much difference. There is a Shan language and a Karen language.	*θeiʔ mathûbábû, šân zagâ kayín zagâ šìdé*

However, most of them know how to speak Burmese.	*šìbéimè, ʔamyâ ʔâ phyìn θúdòu bamá zagâgóu pyôdatté*
religion, (also, language)	*báðá*
Buddhism	*boutdà báðá*
worships	*kôugwédé*
They are Buddhists.	*boutdà báðá kôugwéjàdé*
	máun kalaʔ
believes	*yóundé*
believes implicitly	*yóun cídé*
Are there many Buddhists in Burma?	*bamá pyéihmá boutdà báðá yóun cí kôugwéjàdè lú myâðalâ*
	kóu sán yà
Yes. Ninety percent (90 in 100) are Buddhists.	*houtté, tayáhmá kôuzégà boutdà báðágóu kôugwéjàdé*
Christianity	*khariyyán báðá*
Of the remaining ten percent some are Christians or of other faith.	*cándè tashéhmá tachòu khariyyán báðánè tachâ báðámyâgóulê kôugwéjàdé*
	máun kalaʔ
How many big rivers are there in Burma?	*bamá pyéihmá myiccî bé hnamyiʔ šìðalê*
	kóu sán yà
There are three big rivers, the Irrawaddy, the Salween, and the Sittang.	*ʔéiyáwadí, θánlwín, sittâun, myiccî θoummyiʔ šìdé*

flows down	*sî shîndé*
sea	*pínlé*
ocean	*θamoutdayá*
From the north of Burma they flow to the south, and flow into the sea.	*bamá pyéi myaupphekkà táumbekkóu sî shîn lá pî, pínlê θamoutdayádêgóu sî wín θwâdé*

máun kala?

When we went from Rangoon to Mandalay by steamer, which river did we go on?	*couttòu ?ayín yáŋgóun myòugà mândalêi myòugóu θîmbônè θwâdè ?akhá, bé myitthêgà θwâðalê*

kóu sán yà

By going on the Irrawaddy we even got to Prome.	*?éiyáwadí myitthêgà θwâlòu, pyéi myòudáun yaukkhèðèidé*
remembers	*hmammìdé*
Don't you remember?	*khímbyâ mahmammìbûlâ*

máun kala?

Don't you get to Mandalay if you go by steamer on other rivers?	*dì pyín myitthêgà θîmbônè θwâyín, mândalêi myòugóu mayaupphûlâ*

kóu sán yà

You can't go—You get there only by going on the Irrawaddy.	*maθwâhnáimbû, ?éiyáwadí myitthêgàðá θwâlòu yautté*
is short	*tóudé*
You can't go by the Sittang River because it is short.	*síttâun myikkàlê tóudè ?atwe? maθwâhnáimbû*

is rough	*cândé*
The Salween River flows very rapidly (is very rough)	*θánlwín myiʔ yéi sî ʔímmatán cândé*
stone, rock	*cauʔ*
ledge of rocks, large boulder	*causshâun*
is plentiful, not scarce	*pôdé*
There isn't a great deal of steamer (river boats) travel because of the numerous rocks.	*causshâun pôdè ʔatweʔ, θîmbô θeiʔ ʔaθwâ ʔalá mašìbû*

máun bà

forest (timber)	*θittô*
forest (of bamboo)	*wâdô*
That's right. There are very big forests on both sides of the Sittang and the Salween Rivers	*houtté, ʔêdí sittâun myinnè θánlwín myiʔ hóubeʔ díbephmá ʔímmatán cîdè θittôjî wâdôjî šìdé*
sets afloat	*hmyôdé*
That's the reason (why) it's useful for floating down timber and bamboo made into rafts.	*dájàun θiʔ wâgóu pháun louʔ, hmyô chàbòu kâundé*

máun kalaʔ

How many big bridges are there in Burma?	*bamá pyéihmá tadâjî béhnakhù šìðalê*

kóu sán yà

There are three big ones, the Sittang, the Sagaing and Goteik Bridges.	*sittâun tadâ, sagâin tadâ, goutthei? tadâ, tadâjî θôuŋgù šìdé*

máun bà

builds, erects	*shautté*
The Sittang and Sagaing bridges were built across the Sittang and Irrawaddy Rivers so they could be crossed.	*sittâun tadânè sagâin tadâhá sittâun myinnè ʔéiyáwadí myikkóu kûhnáinʔáun, phyaʔ shauʔ thâdé*

máun kalaʔ

What about the Goteik bridge. Tell me about it.	*goutthei? tadâjî ʔacâun pyôbáʔôun*

kóu sán yà

ravine	*jauʔ*
The Goteik Bridge is a big bridge built so that trains can cross a big ravine between two mountains.	*goutthei? tâdâhá táun hnalôunjâdêhmá šîdè jauccîgóu mîyathâ phyaʔ kûhnáinʔáun, tadâjî shauʔ louʔ thâdé*

máun kalaʔ

steamer dock	*θîmbôzeiʔ*
Are there seaports in Burma?	*bamá pyéihmá θîmbôzeiʔ myòujîmyâ šîðalâ*

kóu sán yà

There are big wharves at Rangoon, Bassein, Moulmein and Akyab where ocean going steamers can dock.	*yángóun myòu, paθéin myòu, mólamyáin myòunè sittwéi myòuhmá pínlé kû θîmbôjîmyâ shaithnáindè θîmbôzeiccîmyâ šîdé*

SECTION B—WORD STUDY AND REVIEW OF BASIC SENTENCES

1. Word Study

A. Derivation (Cont.)

1. -té

šìdé mašìdégóu bèné louʔ θìhnáimmalê	How can (I) know whether there is or not.
šìdé mašìdé shóudá, khímbyâ bèné louʔ pyôhnáinðalê	How can you say whether there is or not.
θú pyôdá hmándé mahmándé shóudá maθìbû	(I) don't know whether what he says is correct or not.
kâundé makâundé shóudá badú pyôhnáinðalê	Is there anyone who can say whether it's good or bad?

-té makes nouns from verbs. Most often this type of noun is used in noun expressions of the type *kâundè lú* (paragraph 2).

2. -tè

díhmá mašìdè lú maθìhnáimbû	People who aren't here can't know.
mahmándè ʔaphyéigóu malóujímbû	(I) don't want answers which aren't right.
makâundè lúdéigóu macaipphû	(I) don't like people who aren't good.

Nouns made from verbs by means of the particle *-té* are used in noun expressions as modifiers with change of tone to *-tè*.

3. -mé

kâummé makâummé bélóu pyôhnáinðalê	How can you tell whether it's going to be good?
θwâmé maθwâmé shóudá mapyôhnáimbû	(I) can't say whether he'll go.

-mé makes nouns from verbs. Most often this type of noun is used in noun expressions of the type *θwâmè ywá* (paragraph 4).

4. *-mè*

ʔakhù θwâmè ywágóu bé ʔachéin yaummalê	What time will we reach the village to which we are now going?
nepphyíŋgá louyyàmè ʔalouʔ bá ʔaloullê	What is the work we have to do tomorrow?
lámè lú badúlê	Who is it that will come?

Nouns made from verbs by means of the particle *-mé* are used in noun expressions as modifiers with change of tone to *-mè*.

5. *-sayá* 'necessity, purpose'

θwâzayá šìdé	I have to go (somewhere).
sôuyéinzayá mašìbû	There's no cause for anxiety.
sâzayá bá šìðalê	What is there to eat?
pyózayá kâundé	It's fun.
sâzayámyâ lóujínðalâ	Do you want some food?
dí twêhmá tháinzayá néiyá mašìbû	There's no place to sit in this car (coach).

-sayá makes nouns of verbs. (See Unit 9).

6. *-phòu* 'possibility or purpose'

lânchânè θwâbòu θeiʔ wêidé	It's too far to go by car.
dí yéigóu θaupphòu cautté	I'm afraid to drink this water.
sá phapphòu pyîndé	It's boring to read.
θwâbòu kâundé	We should go.
θwâbòu ʔachéin càbí	It's time to go.
θwâbòu ʔachéin tóbí	It's about time to go.

θwâbòu lân maθìbû	I don't know the road I'm supposed to take.
ˀeipphòu néiyà béhmalê	Where's a place to sleep?
tháimbòu néiyá mašìbû	There's no place to sit.

-phòu makes nouns of verbs (See Unit 9).

7. *-tâin* 'every time'

yáŋgóun θwâdâin paisshán kóundé	Every time I go to Rangoon I spend money.
thamîn sâdâin hînjóu mapáyín thamîn mawímbû	If I don't have soup whenever I have a meal I don't enjoy it.
khímbyâ ˀéiŋgóu ládâin môu ywádé	Every time I come to your house it rains.
θùgóu twèidâin θú sá phaˀ néidé	Every time I run across him he's reading.

-tâin makes nouns out of verbs. There is also a syllable *-tâin* used in noun expressions in the meaning 'every', *lúdâin* 'everybody' (See Unit 23).

8. *-tôun* 'time when'

bamá pyéihmá néidôuŋggá, thamîn kâuŋgâun sâyàdé	When I lived in Burma, I had good food.
ˀalouˀ louˀ néidôun zagâ mapyônè	Don't talk when you're working.
câun θwâdôuŋgà bámà maθímbû	I didn't learn anything when I went to school.

-tôun makes nouns from verbs. There is a syllable *-tôun* used in noun expressions in the same meaning.

ˀaséidôuŋgà macaipphû	I didn't like it at first.
ŋéŋédôungà khanà khanà phyâdé	I was sick time and again when I was young.
bédôuŋgà bamá zagâ pyôdaθθalà	When did you learn to speak Burmese?
bédôuŋgà ˀéindáun càðalê	When did you get married?

9. *-yóun* 'just so much and no more'

dílau? shêiyóunnè bashímmalê	How will it be clean with just this much washing?
dílau? θauyyóunnè yéi ŋa? pyéimalâ	Will you get rid of your thirst by drinking only so much.
pyôyóunnè keissà mapîbû	The work won't get done by mere talk.
dí ganèi dí ?alou? louyyóunðá lou?	Do only this work today.

-yóun makes nouns from verbs.

2. Covering English and Burmese of Word Study

Give the English equivalents of all Burmese expressions in the *Word Study* and the Burmese for all the English. This is individual study.

3. Review of Basic Sentences

Further oral practice with the first part of the *Basic Sentences*.

SECTION C—CONVERSATION

1. Review of Basic Sentences (*Cont.*)

Further oral practice with the second part of the *Basic Sentences*.

2. Covering the English of Basic Sentences

Check your knowledge of the meaning of all words and phrases in the *Basic Sentences*. This is individual study.

3. What Would You Say?

Give full answers to the following questions.

1. *bamá pyéi shóudá béhmálê*
2. *khímbyâ bá ʔacâuŋgóu pyô néiðalê*
3. *bamá pyéihmá lú bé hnayauʔ šìðalê*
4. *bamá pyéi cîðalâ, ŋéðalâ*
5. *bamá pyéihmá lúbâun tashè khúnnaθân šìdé shóudá hmán-yèlâ*
6. *khímbyâ tâin pyéi šéiðalâ, céðalâ*
7. *khímbyâ tâin pyéihmá lúbâun bé hnayauʔ šìðalê*
8. *bamá pyéi ʔîŋgaleiʔ pyéideʔ cîðalâ*
9. *bamá pyéinè tayouʔ pyéi sá cìhnáinðalâ*
10. *ʔíndìyà pyéihá bamá pyéideʔ ŋéðalâ*
11. *bamá pyéi ʔanaupphephmá bé tâin pyéi šìðalê*
12. *bamá pyéi ʔašèibephmá bé tâin pyéi šìðalê*
13. *khímbyâ tachâ tâin pyéigóu yaupphûðalâ*
14. *yôudayâ pyéi shóudá câbûðalâ*
15. *bamá pyéinè nîdè tâin pyéigóu kôunjâun ʔaθwâ ʔalá myâðalâ*
16. *khímbyâ tâin pyéihmá tô táun myâðalâ*
17. *táun tepphûðalâ*
18. *θîmbô sîbûðalâ*
19. *khímbyâdòu bédôuŋgà lájàðalê*
20. *bamá pyéihmá bamá lúmyôu ʔapyín tachâ lúmyôumyâ šìðalâ*
21. *kalâdéi bégà lájàðalê*
22. *kachîndéi ʔamyâ ʔâ phyìn, béhmá néijàðalê*
23. *bamánè šân bá thúðalê*
24. *khímbyâ šân zagâ nâ léðalâ*
25. *šândéi bamá zagâ pyôdaθθalâ*
26. *khímbyâ bóutdà báðálâ*
27. *khímbyâ bá báðágóu kôugwéðalê*
28. *bamá pyéihmá boutdà báðágóu yóun cídè lú myâðalâ*
29. *tayáhmá bé hnayauʔ boutdà báðágóu kôugwéðalê*
30. *bámá pyéihmá myiccî bé hnamyiʔ šìðalê*
31. *myittéi myaupphekkà sà pî, bébekkóu sî θwâðalê*
32. *mândalêigóu θwâyín, bé myikkà θwâyàðalê*
33. *khímbyâ cúndògóu hmammìðalâ*
34. *myiccî θôummyitthêhmá bé myiʔ ʔatóuzôunlê*
35. *bamá pyéihmá tadâjî bé hnakhù šìðalê*
36. *goutthéiʔ tadâjîhá bágóu phyaʔ shauʔ thâðalê*
37. *sagâin tadâgô, bágóu phyaʔ shauʔ thâðalê*
38. *sagâin tadâbóhmá mîyathâ θwâhnáinðalâ*
39. *bamá pyéihmá θînbôzeiʔ myòujîmyâ šìðalâ*
40. *khímbyâ thamîn sâjínðalâ*

SECTION D—LISTENING IN

1. What Did You Say?

With the other members of the group give orally your responses to the previous exercise as the Leader calls for them.

2. Word Study Check-Up

Give the Burmese for all English equivalents in the *Word Study* as the Leader calls for it.

3. Listening In

1. Buying fruit.

máun tín: *khímbyâhmá paisshán bélau? páðalê*

máun có: *ŋâja? nîkabâ pálèimmé, thíndé*

máun tín: *cúndògóu cêizû pyù pî, θôunjallau? chîhnáimmalâ*

máun có: *hô díhmá θôunja? bá wéjínlòulê*

máun tín: *θiθθî wéjíndé léimmóðî phyisséi, hŋapyôðî phyisséi, wémélòu*

máun có: *?akhù léimmóðî pôdé léimmóðîbê wébálâ*

máun tín: *?akâummyôu léimmóðî pyàbá*

sháin šín: *hô díhmá kalabyéigà léimmóðî*

máun tín: *dádéi ŋéŋégalêidéibê tachâ léimmóðî ?acî mašìbûlâ*

sháin šín: *hô díhmá yôudayâ pyéigà thwettè léimmóðî hóu kalabyéi léimmóðînè sâ cìbá*

máun có: *khímbyâ dí léimmóðîmyâgóu caiyyèlâ*

máun tín: *kâunðábê dí ?amyôu ?apyín tachâmyôu mašìyín, dágóubê wédòmé*

sháin šín: *tachâmyôu mašìbû bé hnalôun yúmalê*

máun tín: *shélôun pêibá*

2. Where are you from?

máun bà: *khímbyâdòu tâin-yînðânè matúbû náiŋgánjâðâ thíndé bé tâin pyéigàlê*

máun kala?: *cúndódòu ?améiyìkán pyéiðâ ?akhùbê θîmbôzeikkà myòudêgóu wín ládé*

máun wílyán: *θîmbô shaittá nau? càlòu, nau? macàyín, manèigà yau? pîðâ*

máun bà:	*pínlé θamoutdayádéigóu θîmbônè kû sî ládá bélauʔ cáðalê*
máun wílyán:	*θôunlàlauʔ cádé*
máun bà:	*θôunlàdáun cádé ʔayíndôuŋgà talànè yauthnáindágóu hmammìyèlâ*
máun kalaʔ:	*hmammìbádé*
máun bà:	*khímbyâdòu lúʔûyéi bé hnayauʔ šìðalê*
máun kalaʔ:	*nausshôun θagáun sayîn ʔayà shóuyín lúbâun shè θôuŋgadéilauʔ šìdé*
máun bà:	*khímbyâdòu tâin pyéihmá lúdéi bá báðágóu yóun cíjàðalê*
máun kalaʔ:	*khariyyán báðágóu yóun cíjàdé khímbyâdòu tâin pyéihmágô, bá báðágóu kôugwéjàðalê*
máun bà:	*boutdà báðágóu kôugwéjàdé*
máun wílyán:	*khímbyâ ʔaméiyìkán pyéihmá néi tháimbûðalâ*
máun bà:	*ʔaméiyìkán pyéigóu takháhmà mayaupphûbû*

3. Out in the country.

máun séin:	*dí myikkóu kûbòu yéi θeiʔ sîdé, thínðalâ douttóu tachâuŋgóu hmyô chà cìyín, θìlèimmé*
kóu sán yà:	*dí myiʔ ʔímmatán masî shîn-yínlê makûhnáimbû ʔašèi nâhmá chaussháun myâdé dí néiyáhmá kûbòu célê θeiʔ cédé kôunjâun ʔanauʔ myaupphekkóu θwâyín, yaucchíndè néiyágóu yaullèimmé*
máun hlà:	*kâumbí ʔanauʔ myaupphekkóu θwâjàzòu hóu tapakkà khímbyâdòu bé θwâjàðalê*
kóu sán yà:	*jauccî takhùgóu phyaʔ kûhnáinʔáun shauʔ néidè tadâgóu θwâ cìjàdé*
máun séin:	*lân cân ʔâ cîlòu cúndò chéidauʔ ná lábí khanà nâyàʔáun*

SECTION E—CONVERSATION

1. Covering the Burmese of Basic Sentences

With the Burmese covered, practice until you can speak the Burmese for each English sentence without hesitation. This is individual study.

2. Vocabulary Check-Up

Give the Burmese for all English sentences in the *Basic Sentences* as the Leader calls for it.

3. Conversation

Suggested Topics:

1. Ask a friend questions about Burma: its size, its population, its neighbors, routes of travel, number of foreigners, languages spoken, religion, natural features.
2. Discuss with a friend travel in Burma: rivers, roads, bridges, railways, steamship lines.
3. Go to a market and buy supplies.

SECTION F—CONVERSATION (*Cont.*)

Continue conversation. Additional check-up if necessary.

Finder List

ʔalá (ládé)	a coming
ʔanauʔ	west
ʔapyín	outside of, besides
ʔašéi	length
ʔasèi	east
ʔasèi táumbeʔ	south-east (side)
ʔaθwâ ʔalá (θwâdé ládé)	travel, coming and going
ʔayà	according to
báðá	religion, language
boutdà báðá	Buddhism
cândé	is rough
cauʔ	stone, rock
causshâun	ledge of rocks, large boulder
cé wîndé	is large, great
cêizû pyùdé	does a favor, obliges
hmammìdé	remembers
hmyôdé	sets afloat
jauʔ	ravine

kachín	Kachin
kalabyéi	India
kayín	Karen
khariyyán báðá	Christianity
kôugwédé	worships
kôunjâun	by land
lúˀûyéi	population
náiŋgán	nation, country
náiŋgánjâ	foreign country
náiŋgánjâðâ	national of a foreign country
nî kabâ	approximately
ŋéŋégalêi	tiny, very small
phyisséi . . . phyisséi	either . . . or
pínlé	sea
pôdé	is plentiful, not scarce
póu cíðâ	is really bigger
sá cìdé	studies, compares
shautté	builds, erects
sî shîndé	flows down
tachâ	other
tâin pyéi	country
tâin-yînðâ	national of one's own country
tóudé	is short
θagáun sayîn	census
θamoutdayá	ocean
θìmbôzeiˀ	steamer dock
θittô	forest (timber)
wâdô	forest (bamboo)
yôudayâ	Thai, Siamese
yóundé	believes
yóun cídé	believes implicitly

INDUSTRY

SECTION A—BASIC SENTENCES

ENGLISH EQUIVALENTS	AIDS TO LISTENING
	kóu sán yà
knowledge, art, science	*pyínnyá*
craft, manual art	*lephmù pyínnyá*
wonders	*ʔàndé*
exposition, exhibition	*ʔàmbwê*
loads, places upon	*tíndé*
exhibits, shows	*tín pyàdé*
I want to go see the arts and craft exhibition at the Jubilee Hall—coming along?	*úbalíhô yóunjîhmá bamá pyéigà thwettè lephmù pyínnyá pyissîmyâ ʔámbwê tín pyà néidágóu θwâ cìjíndé, laimmalâ*
	máun hlâ
Yes, I'll come along.	*laimmé*
What time in the evening are you going?	*nyànéi bé ʔachéin θwâmalê*

kóu sán yà

last, final	*nausshôun*
Tonight is the last night.	*dí nèinyà nausshôunnyàbê*
early	*sôzô (sôdé)*
It would be a good idea to go early.	*sôzô θwâyín, kâunlèimmé*

[They go to the exhibition]

máun bà

Shall we go inside and look or look around outside first?	*ʔayín yóundêgóu wín cìmalâ, ʔapyímhmá cìmalâ*

kóu sán yà

First we'll go in and look around.	*pathamà ʔathêgóu wín cìmé*

máun kala?

What is there special inside?	*ʔathêhmá ʔathû ʔashân bámyâ šiðalê*

kóu sán yà

painter	*pají shayá*
paints	*pají yêidé*
pulls, draws, hauls	*shwêdé*
has drawn, sketched	*yêi shwê thâdé*
picture	*kâ*
carver, sculptor	*pabù shayá*
carves, engraves, sculptures	*thùdé*

tusk, fang, eye tooth	*ʔaswé*
ivory	*shínzwé*
wood	*θiθθâ*
seed, seed grain	*myôuzèi*
There are examples of the work of painters and of carvers in ivory and wood, and in addition there are all kinds of seed grain for planting.	*pají shayámyâ yêi shwê thâdè kâ, pabù shayámyâ thù thâdè shínzwénè θiθθâ ʔaloummyâ ʔapyín, saiʔ pyôubòu myôuzèi ʔamyôumyôu šìdé*

máun kalaʔ

is clever (also, is suitable, sufficient)	*tódé*
I have heard that Burmese carvers are very clever.	*bamá pabù shayámyâ ʔímmatán tódélòu câbûdé*
Therefore I'd like to go see it (their work) first.	*dájàun ʔêdágóu pathamà θwâ cìjíndé*

máun bà

O.K., let's go in and start on this side.	*kâumbábí, díbekkà sà wín cìjàzòu*

máun kalaʔ

representation, figure, image	*ʔayouʔ*
The carving by hand of figures in ivory is quite praiseworthy.	*shínzwégóu ʔayouʔ phyiʔʔáun, lennè thù thâdágóu tódó chîmûnzayá kâundé*

máun hlà

loom	*yekkânzín*
silk cloth	*pôu thé*
Where are the women weaving silk by hand on the looms?	*mêimmàmyâ yekkânzímhmá pôu thémyâgóu lennè yeʔ néidá béhmálê*

kóu sán yà

suspends from the shoulder	*lwédé*
bag that hangs from the shoulder	*lwéˀeiˀ*
goes around	*patté*
circuit, a round	*ˀapaˀ*
If you want to see all kinds of Mandalay silk lounjis and bags you'll have to make a complete circle of the building.	*mândalêi pôulóunjínè lwéˀeiˀ ˀamyôumyôugóu cìjín-yín, yóunjîgóu tabaˀ paˀ cìyàlèimmé*

máun bà

glazed pot or jar	*sìnˀôu*
Come on, I'm going to see them making jars and dishes by hand out of clay.	*lá, hóu šèihmá myéigóu lennè sìnˀôu ˀôu khwemmyâ phyiˀˀáun, louˀ néidágóu θwâ cìmé*

máun hlà

up to now, already, still	*ˀakhùdetthì*
place	*ˀayaˀ*
In some parts of Burma we Burmans still use these earthen utensils for cooking our meals.	*couttòu bamá lúmyôumyâ ˀakhùdetthì, dí myéiˀôumyânèbê tachòu ˀayaphmá thamîn hîmmyâ cheˀ sâjàdôun šiðèidé*
definitely, with precision	*θéiðéi chájá (θéijádé)*
Observe carefully how the pots are made.	*ˀôu phyiˀˀáun, bélóu louyyàdé shóudá θéiðéi chájá cì*

máun kalaˀ

wonders, is amazed, surprised	*ˀànˀôdé*
It's quite surprising the way they make pots by hand.	*lennè ˀôu phyiˀˀáun, louttá tódó ˀànôbòu kâundé*
What else is there to see?	*bámyâ cìzayá šiðèiðalê*

máun bà

umbrella
thî

is pretty
hlàdé

There are still the umbrellas that are made in Burma—they're very pretty.
bamá pyéihmá louttè thîmyâ šìðêidé, ʔìmmatán hlàdé

The umbrellas are made out of bamboo by hand.
wâgóu thî phyiʔʔáun, lennè loutté

Usually they're called Bassein umbrellas because they're made in the city of Bassein.
ʔamyâʔâ phyìn, thîmyâgóu paθéin myòuhmá loullòu, paθéin thîlòu khódé

máun kalaʔ

Where are they? Come along and show me.
ʔêdá béhmálê, coukkóu laiʔ pyàbá

máun hlà

It's outside, near the building. Come on, we'll go and see (it).
yóun ʔapyìnnâhmá šìdé, lá, θwâ cìmé

máun kalaʔ

They're very pretty to look at. Why is the color of the umbrellas red?
cìlòu θeiʔ hlàdé, bá phyillòu thî ʔayáun nìðalê

kóu sán yà

is tight, as water-tight
lóundé

water-proof, rain-proof
môu lóundé

soaks, steeps
séindé

They're a reddish color because they have to be soaked in oil to make them water-proof.
môu lóunʔáun, shí séin pî, louyyàdè ʔatweʔ, ʔayáun nênê nìdé

máun kala?

plan, design, pattern, form	*póun*
I want six good looking umbrellas to give my sweetheart and friends as presents when I go back to America.	*cúndó ?améiyìkán pyéigóu pyán θwádè ?akhá, yîzânè meisshwéigóu lessháun pêibòu póun hlàdè thî kâuŋgâun chaulle? lóujíndé*
You pick them out for me.	*khímbyâ ywêi pêibá*

kóu sán yà

These six umbrellas are very pretty. Do you like them?	*dí thî chaulle? θei? hlàdé, khímbyâ caiyyèlâ*

máun kala?

Yes, I like them. How much apiece?	*caippádé, tale? belaullê*

sháin šìn

They sell for 3½ rupees apiece.	*thî talekkóu θôunjakkhwêzí yâundé*

máun kala?

price	*?aphôu*
Here's the money for the umbrellas.	*díhmá thî phôuŋwéi*
I know about handicrafts from your explanation; now tell me about manufacturing.	*khímbyâdòu coukkóu lephmù pyínnyá ?acâun pyô pyàlòu θìbábí, sennè louttágóu pyôbá?ôun*

máun bà

We don't have big factories which can make all sorts of things the way you do in your country.	*khímbyâdòu tâin pyéilóu ?amyôumyôu phyi??áun, louthnáindè seyyóunjîmyâdò mašìbû*

There are rice mills, timber mills, oil refineries and all sorts of little factories.	*sabâzeʔ, θisseʔ, yéinánzennèʔamyôumyôu seyyóuŋgalêimyâ šìdé*

máun kalaʔ

teak	*cûnðiʔ*
Is it true that there's a lot of teak in Burma?	*bamá pyéihmá cûnðiʔ θeiʔ myâdé shóudá houyyèlâ*

kóu sán yà

saw	*hlwà*
saw mill	*hlwàzeʔ*
That's right. When they have cut up the wood in big saw mills in Rangoon and Moulmein they send it to other countries.	*houppádé, yáŋgóun myòunè mólamyáimhmá šìdè hlwàzeyyóunjîmyâgà θimmyâgóu sennè khwê seiʔ pîdè ʔakhá, dì pyín náiŋgámmyâgóu pòudé*
world	*kabá*
Teak from Burma is the best in the world.	*kabábóhmá bamá pyéigà thwettè cûnðiʔ ʔakâunzôumbê*
floor	*cân*
Other countries buy lots of it to make decks for ships.	*θîmbôhmá cân khîmbòu ʔatweʔ, dì pyín náiŋgáŋgà ʔamyâjî wéjàdé*
crushes, grinds	*ceitté*
In all of Burma rice husking mills are the most plentiful.	*bamá pyéi tabyéilôumhmá sabâ ceisseʔ ʔamyâzôumbê*

máun kalaʔ

husked rice	*shán*
What do they do with the husked rice after husking the paddy with machinery?	*sabâgóu sennè ceillòu shán phyittè ʔakhá, shàŋgóu bá louθθalê*

máun bà

All over Burma we don't eat bread. — *couttòu bamá pyéi tabyéilôumhmá páummòuŋgóu masâbû*

We cook and eat husked rice made into all sorts of things besides the rice (boiled) we eat at breakfast and at dinner. — *manessá nyàzá thamîn ʔapyín sháŋgóu ʔamyôumyôu louʔ cheʔ sâjàdé*

kóu sán yà

The surplus rice and paddy which cannot be consumed in Burma is available for sale in large quantities to other countries. — *bamá pyéigà thwettè shán sabâmyâgóu bamá pyéihmá sâlòu makóundè ʔapyín, dì pyín náingámmyâgóu ʔamyâjî yâun-yàðéidé*

máun kalaʔ

Where (from what city) does petroleum come from in Burma? — *bamá pyéihmá bé myòugà yéinán thweθθalê*

máun bà

It comes from the cities of Yenangyaung, Kyauk, and Yenangyat. — *yéinánjâun, chauʔ, yéinánjeʔ myòugà ládé*

máun kalaʔ

exports — *tín pòudé*

How about the oil, is it exported and sold to other countries? — *yéinámmyâgóugô, dì pyín náiŋgámmyâgóu tín pòu yâunðalâ*

kóu sán yà

Yes, oil also is exported to other countries. — *houtté, yéináŋgóulê dì pyín náiŋgáŋgóu yâundé*

máun kalaˀ

metals extracted from ore	*θattù*
Are there other minerals besides petroleum? [that come out of the ground]	*yéinán ˀapyín myéigà thwettè θattùmyâ šìðèiðalâ*

kóu sán yà

lead	*khê*
tin	*θámbyú*
zinc	*θuˀ*
ruby	*badamyâ*
jade ('green stone')	*caussêin*
district, state, county	*né*
Besides lead, silver, tin and zinc, rubies and jade are found in great quantities in the Mogok district.	*khê, ŋwéi, θámbyú, θuˀ ˀapyín badamyânè caussêimmyâgóulê môugouˀ néhmá ˀamyâjî thwetté*

máun kalaˀ

is of worth, precious, valuable	*ˀaphôu tándé*
There's really quite a lot of valuable products produced in your country.	*khímbyâdòu tâin pyéihmá tódó ˀaphôu tándè pyissîmyâ thweθθâbê*
finger ring	*lessuˀ*
one (of circular things)	*tagwîn*
I want to buy a ruby ring.	*cúndó badamyâ lessuˀ tagwîn wéjíndé*

SECTION B—WORD STUDY AND REVIEW OF BASIC SENTENCES

1. Word Study

Derivation (*Cont.*)

Doubled Verbs:

Doubled verbs are noun expressions which consist of two verb members.

1. The verb members may be the same verb repeated.

kâundé 'is good'	
kâuŋgâun loutté	(He) works well.
hnêidé 'is slow'	
hnêihnêi pyôbá	Speak slowly.
tódé 'is sufficient'	
tódó kâundé	(It) is fairly good.
nêdé 'is few, little'	
nênê ŋédé	(He) is a little young.
túdé 'is the same'	
túdúbê	Just the same
tèdé 'is straight'	
tèdèhmá šìdé	(It's) straight ahead.
tèdè θwâ	Go straight.
myándé 'is fast'	
myammyán louppá	Do (it) quickly.
sôdé 'is early'	
sôzô thàbá	Get up early.
ˀêidé 'is cool'	
ˀêiˀêi louˀ néidé	(He) is taking his time.

2. The verb members may be the parts of a dissyllabic verb repeated.

θéijádé 'is precise'	
θéiðéi chájá mapyôhnáimbû	(I) can't say precisely.
θéiðéi chájá loutté	(He) does (it) with great efficiency.
thûzândé 'is strange, extraordinary'	
thûdû shânzâmbê	(It) *is* strange.

3. The verb members may be a negated verb repeated.

cádé 'is long in time'	
macámacá ládé	(He) comes often.

4. The verb members may be two different negated verbs.

nîdé 'is near' *wêidé* 'is far'	
manîmawêihmá šìdé	(It) is not far.

ládé 'comes' *chîndé* 'approaches'
θú malámachîn cúndó I'll wait until he comes.
sàun néimé

yatté 'stops' *nâdé* 'stops to rest'
mayaʔ manâ without stopping

5. The expression may be a verb followed by a rhyming syllable.

kàndé 'marks across, intersects'
kànlàn mathânè Don't put it crosswise.

6. The expression may be a verb followed by two rhyming syllables.

nídé 'is red'
ní tídí reddish

sêindé 'is green'
sêin têindêin greenish

hloutté 'shakes'
hlouʔ touttouʔ shaky

7. The verb members may be a negated verb followed by the same verb with prefixed *ta-*. The first member, if tone I, changes to tone III.

pyèidé 'is full'
mapyèi tabyèi 'is not quite full'

sêindé 'is green'
masêin tazêin 'almost green'

myíndé 'sees'
mamyìn tamyín 'almost visible'

houtté 'is true'
mahouʔ tahouʔ Don't say things which
mapyônè aren't definite.

8. Doubled verbs are often preceded by *khaʔ* 'rather, somewhat.'

khapphyêibyêi rather slowly
khammyámmyán rather quickly
khaccîjî rather big
khaŋŋéŋé rather young
khawwêiwêi rather far

1. Review of Basic Sentences (*Cont.*)

Further oral practice with the second part of the *Basic Sentences*.

2. Covering the English of Basic Sentences

Check your knowledge of the meaning of all words and phrases in the *Basic Sentences*. This is individual study.

3. What Would You Say?

Give full answers to the following questions.

1. *lephmù pyínnyá ʔàmbwêgóu khímbyâ laimmalâ*
2. *ʔàmbwê bédò phwìmmalê*
3. *dí ganèi nausshôun nèilâ*
4. *sôzô θwâyín, kâummalâ, nauʔ cà θwâyín, kâummalâ*
5. *pathamà ʔapyímhmá lé cìmalâ, ʔayín ʔathêhmá lé cìmalâ*
6. *lé macìjímbûlâ*
7. *ʔakhù šauʔ lé cìjínðalâ*
8. *tareisshán-yóumhmá tareisshán ʔathû ʔashân šìðalâ*
9. *khímbyâ pají shayámyâgóu θìðalâ*
10. *bá ʔayouʔ shwê néiðalê*
11. *bamá pabù shayámyâ tódé shóudá hmán-yèlâ*
12. *hóugóu bá phyillòu θwâjínðalê*
13. *díbekkà wínlòu yàmalâ*
14. *khímbyâ shínzwégóu ʔayouʔ thù thâdá myímbûðalâ*
15. *mândalêi lóunjí shóudá pôu lóunjílâ*
16. *khímbyâ ʔôu khwemmyâgóu lennè louttá myímbûðalâ*
17. *thamîŋgóu myéiʔôunè cheʔ sâbûðalâ*
18. *khímbyâ bágóu ʔànʔô chîmûn néidálê*
19. *loussayá bámyâ šìðêiðalê*
20. *cìzayá bámyâ šìðêiðalê*
21. *bamá pyéigà thwettè thîmyâ hlàðalâ*
22. *thîmyâgóu bé myòuhmá louθθalê*
23. *mótókâ yóun bé nâhmálê*
24. *yauccâ thînè mêimmà thî thûðalâ*
25. *khímbyâ thînè cúndò thî túðalâ*
26. *khímbyâ ʔaméiyìkán pyéigóu bédò pyámmalê*
27. *khímbyâ cúndò ʔatweʔ ywêi pêihnáimmalâ*
28. *léimmóðî talóun tajaʔ shóuyín, zêi macîbûlâ*
29. *thî ʔatweʔ paisshán pêi pîbalâ*
30. *shánzennè θisseʔ béhmálê*
31. *bamá pyéihmá cúnðiʔ myâdé shóudá houyyèlâ*
32. *cúnðiʔ ʔakâunzôun θillâ*
33. *cúnðikkóu béhmá ʔaθôun pyùðalê*
34. *khímbyâ páummòun masâbûlâ*
35. *bamá pyéihmá bé myòugà yéinán thweθθalê*
36. *ʔaméiyìkán pyéihmá dasshí tagálán bélaullê*
37. *bamá pyéigà bá θattùmyâ thweθθalê*
38. *badamyâ bégà thweθθalê*
39. *khímbyâ bé pyéiðâlê*
40. *khímbyâ bé myòuhmá néiðalê*

SECTION D—LISTENING IN

1. What Did You Say?

With the other members of the group give orally your responses to the previous exercise as the Leader calls for them.

2. Word Study Check-Up

Give the Burmese for all English equivalents in the *Word Study* as the Leader calls for it.

3. Listening In

1. Repairing the house.

ʔû bà séin: *môu ywámélóulóu phyiʔ néidé ʔéindêgà thî hnaleʔ thoukkhè, máun pù*

máun pù: *díhmá póun ʔamyôumyôu thîmyâ šìdé béhágóu lóujínðalê*

ʔû bà séin: *ʔamèi ʔaphôudán thîgóudò mayúgènè*

máun pù: *ʔakhù bé θwâmalòulê, ʔaphéi*

ʔû bà séin: *hlwàzephmá hmá thâdè cûnðittéigóu bélóu phyaʔ seiʔ néiðalêlòu, θwâ cìyàʔôummé*

dó hlà: *ʔakhùdetthì θwâ macìðêibûlâ*

ʔû bà séin: *ʔalouʔ myâ néilòu, dí nèihmàbê θwâbòu ʔachéin ʔâdé*

máun pù: *bá ʔatweʔ cúnðiθθâmyâgóu hmá thâðalê, phéibéi (= ʔaphéi)*

ʔû bà séin: *ʔéimhmá cân ʔaθiʔ khîmbòu hmá thâdé*

máun pù: *cúnðiθθâhá ʔaphôu cîdé, mahoupphûlâ*

ʔû bà séin: *ʔaphôu cîbéimè, cájá khándé*

máun pù: *mótókâ yóuŋgóu mapyímbûlâ*

ʔû bà séin: *pyímmé*

máun pù: *θámbyúnè pyímmalâ, θunnè pyímmalâ*

ʔû bà séin: *θámbyúnè pyímmé*

2. Arts and Crafts Exhibition.

máun myà: *phayâ ʔayoukkóu shînzwégà θéiðéi chájá thù thâlòu ʔalún chîmûn ʔànʔôzayâ kâundé*

máun séin: *bé pabù shayá thù thâdè ʔayoullê*

máun myà: *pabù shayá kóu séin thûn thù thâdè ʔayouʔ*

máun séin: *ʔêdí ʔayoukkóu lephmù pyínnyá ʔàmbwêhmá tín pyàbòu kâundé*

máun myà: *ʔêdágóu tín mapyàbû*
hô díhmá pají shayá máun tín shwê thâdè ʔayoukkâgóudò tín pyàmé

máun séin: *dí hni? ?àmbwê sôzô phwìmmélòu câdé houyyèlâ*
sôzô phwìmmé shóuyín, ?awêi néiyakkà lúdéi θúdòu louttè lwé?eimmyâgóu tín pyàhnáimhmá mahoupphû

máun myà: *dábéimè, hnittâinlóu yekkânzímmyânè pôu thé ?amyôumyôu ?àmbwêhmá šìlèimmé*

3. How are things?

máun θín: *khímbyâ badamyâ lessu? ?ató hlàdé bé pyéigà thwettè badamyâlê*

máun ní: *bamá pyéigà thwettè badamyâ*

máun θín: *dájàummòu dílau? hlâdágóu kabábóhmá bamá pyéigà thwettè badamyâdéihá ?ahlàzôumbê*

máun ní: *khímbyâ caussêin lessullê hlàðâbê*

máun θín: *khímbyâ sabâ ceisse? bènélê pei? thâdé shóu*

máun ní: *houtté, shánlôundéihá ceiyyîn, kwêlòu sekkóu pyímbòu pei? thâdé*

máun θín: *máun séin bélóulê, câumhmá pyóyèlâ*

máun ní: *θei? mapyóbû, thíndé*
θù shayá θùgóu hóu tanèigà θaŋéjîndéinè câuŋgóu taba? pa? pyêi kâindágóu macaipphû

máun θín: *?akhù cúndòhmá sìn?ôu talôun wézayá šìðêidé θwâlaippá?ôummé*

SECTION E—CONVERSATION

1. Covering the English of Basic Sentences

With the Burmese covered, practice until you can speak the Burmese for each English sentence without hesitation. This is individual study.

2. Vocabulary Check-Up

Give the Burmese for all English sentences in the *Basic Sentences* as the Leader calls for it.

3. Conversation

Suggested Topics:

1. Ask a friend questions about an arts and crafts exhibition in Burma.
2. Ask a friend questions about an exhibition in America.
3. Discuss the industries of Burma.
4. Discuss the industries of America.
5. Go to a market and buy presents for your friends in America.

SECTION F—CONVERSATION (*Cont.*)

Continue conversation. Additional check-up if necessary.

Finder List

ʔakhùdetthì	up to now, already, still
ʔàmbwê	exposition, exhibition
ʔàndé	wonders
ʔànʔôdé	wonders, is amazed
ʔapaʔ (patté)	circuit, a round; a week
ʔaphôu	price
ʔaphôu tándé	is of worth, precious, valuable
ʔaswé	tusk, fang, eyetooth
ʔayaʔ	place
ʔayouʔ	representation, figure, image
badamyâ	ruby
cân	floor
caussêin	jade
ceitté	crushes, grinds
cûnðiʔ	teak
hlàdé	is pretty
hlwà	saw

hlwàze?	saw mill
kâ	picture
kabá	world
khê	lead
lephmù pyínnyá	craft, manual art
lessu?	finger ring
lóundé	is tight, as watertight
lwédé	suspends from the shoulder
lwé?ei?	bag that hangs from the shoulder
môu lóundé	water-proof, rain-proof
myôuzèi	seed, seedgrain
nausshôun	last, final
né	district, state, county
pabù shayá	carver, sculptor
pají shayá	painter
pají yêidé	paints
pôu thé (*pôu ?athé*)	silk cloth
póun	plan, design, pattern, form
patté	goes around
pyínnyá	knowledge, art, science
séindé	soaks, steeps
shán	husked rice
shínzwé	ivory
shwêdé	pulls, draws, hauls
sìn?ôu	glazed pot or jar
sôzô (*sôdé*)	early
tagwîn	one (of circular rings)
thî	umbrella
thùdé	carves, engraves, sculptures
tíndé	leads, places upon
tín pòudé	exports
tín pyàdé	exhibits, shows
tódé	is clever (also, suitable, sufficient)
θámbyú	tin
θattù	metals extracted from ore
θéiðéi chájá	definitely, with precision
θiθθâ	wood
θu?	zinc
yêi shwê thâdé	has drawn, painted, sketched
yekkân	weaving
yekkânzín	loom

UNIT 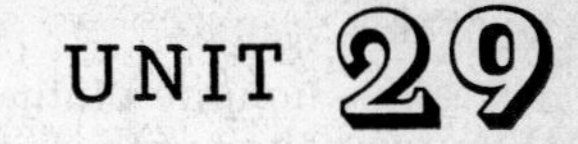

GOVERNMENT

SECTION A—BASIC SENTENCES

ENGLISH EQUIVALENTS	AIDS TO LISTENING
	máun θín
newspaper	*θadînzá*
"The Sun" (name of a paper)	*θúrìyà*
Is the paper you're reading now "The Sun"?	*ʔakhù phaʔ néidè θadînzáhá, θúrìyà θadînzálâ*
	máun bà cí
Burmese	*myámmá (=bamá)*
"The New Light of Burma" (name of a newspaper)	*myámmá ʔalîn*
No, I'm reading The New Light of Burma.	*mahoupphû, myámmá ʔalîn θadînzágóu phaʔ néidé*
Why? What is it you want to know?	*khímbyâ bá ʔacâuŋgóu θìjínlòulê*
	máun θín
plays at certain games of chance	*thôudé*
lottery	*thí*
"The Burma State Lottery"	*θêin thí*
I asked because I wanted to know whether the number of the lottery ticket I bought was in the paper or not.	*θadînzádêhmá cúndó thôu thâdè θêin thí lephmaʔ námbaʔ páðalâ mapábûlâ shóudágóu θìjínlòu, mêidábá*

máun bà cí

alias, nom de plume	*ʔateiʔ*
What was the number of your ticket and the name you put down?	*khímbyâ thí lephmaʔ namba? bá námballê, ʔateiʔ bélóu yêi thâðalê*

máun θín

897524	*šiθθêin kôuðâun khúnnathàun ŋâyà hnashè lêigù*
lion	*cínðèi*
My lottery ticket number is 897524, and my alias was put down as "Big Lion."	*cúndò thí lephmaʔ námbaʔ šiθθêin kôuðâun khúnnathàun ŋâyà hnashè lêigù, ʔateiʔ cínðèijîlòu yêi thâdé*

máun bà cí

The first figures of your ticket are all there.	*khímbyâ lephmaʔ šèigà námbaʔ ʔakóun pádé*
useless, to no purpose	*ʔalagâ*
Nevertheless, it's worthless	*pábéimè ʔalagâbê*
numeral, numerical figure	*ganân*
errs, goes wrong	*lwêdé*
The last number being a three, you missed by one figure.	*naukkà lêiganânhá θôun phyiʔ pî, talôumbê lwê θwâdé*

máun wílyán

You've been talking about a lottery.	*khímbyâdòu ʔakhù thí ʔacâun pyô néidé*
What is this Burma State Lottery?	*bélóu θêin thílê*

máun θín

government — *ˀasôuyà*
revenue accruing from assessments — *ˀakhún*
tax receipts — *ˀakhúndóŋwéi*

The government, wanting to increase its revenue has set up the Burma State Lottery and is selling tickets at two rupees. — *asôuyàgà ˀakhúndóŋwéi póu lóujíndè ˀatweˀ, θêin thí shóu pî, lephmaˀ tazáuŋgóu ŋwéi hnacannè yâun néidé*

máun wílyán

How much money does the winner of the Burma State Lottery get? — *θêin thí pathamà pauttè lú shùŋwéi bélauˀ yàðalê*

máun bà cí

Because they give a hundred thousand rupees to the winner, it is given the name "hundred thousand" (in Burmese) — *pathamà thí pauttè lúgóu shùŋwéi taθêin pêidè ˀatweˀ, θêin thílòu khódé*

máun wílyán

From what other sources do they get revenue besides the state lottery? — *θêin thí ˀapyín, bélóu néiyámyôugà ˀakhúndóŋwéimyâ yàðèiðalê*

máun θín

head tax, poll tax — *lúgún*
land revenue, property tax — *légún*

Besides the revenue from the lottery, all sorts of taxes, personal taxes, property taxes, have to be paid. — *θêin thígà yàdè ˀakhúndóŋwéi ˀapyín, lúgún légún ˀamyôumyôu ˀakhún pêiyàdé máun wílyán*

picks up, collects	*kautté*
How are the taxes collected in country villages?	*tôywáhmá ʔakhúndóŋwéimyâgóu bélóu kauθθalê*

máun θín

Once a year you have to go to the headman's house and pay it.	*tahniʔ takhá ywá θajî ʔéiŋgóu θwâ pêiyàdé*

máun bà cí

one step, one stage	*tashìn*
township officer	*myòuʔouʔ*
The headman has to send it on to the township officer.	*θajîgà tashìn myòuʔousshígóu pòuyàdé*
subdivisional officer	*wúndauʔ*
district commissioner	*ʔayêibáin*
From the township officer on to the subdivisional officer, and from the sub-divisional officer it is sent on to the district commissioner.	*myòu ʔoukkà tashìn wúndauʔ, wúndaukkà tashìn ʔayêibáinzígóu pòudé*
slowly, gradually	*taphyêibyêi*
treasury	*ŋwéidaiʔ*
It goes on by stages from the District Commissioner and is gradually deposited in the Treasury.	*ʔayêibáingà tashìn taphyêibyêi ʔasôuyà ŋwéidaitthêgôu θwînlaitté*

máun wílyán

comes to an end, is finished	*shôundé*
decides, settles, adjudicates	*shôun phyatté*
Who decides how and where the money in the treasury is to be used?	*ʔasôuyà bándaitthêgà ŋwéigóu bé néiyáhmá bélóu θôun-yàmé shóudá, badúgà shôun phyaθθalê*

máun θín

finance minister	*bándáyêi wúnjîjou?*
The finance minister decides.	*bándáyêi wúnjîjoukkà shôun phyatté*

máun séin thûn

parliament	*hluttó*
elects	*tín hmyautté*
lot, ballot	*mê*
votes	*mê ywêi kautte*
Have you heard when the voting will take place to elect the members of parliament?	*hluttóhmá lújî tín hmyaupphòu bédò mê ywêi kaummélòu câðalê*

máun θín

is proclaimed publicly, spreads as news, promulgates	*cónyádé*
It was advertised only yesterday in the papers that three months from now there'll be an election.	*nau? θôunlà cáyín, mê ywêi kaummélòu, manèigàbê θadînzádêhmá thè cónyálaitté*

máun wílyán

person of rank, member of parliament	*?ama?*
How many members are there in the Burmese parliament?	*myámmá pyéi hluttóhmá ?ama? bé hnayau? šìðalê*

máun bà cí

senate, upper house	*?athe? hluttó*
There are thirty-six members in all in the senate.	*?athe? hluttóhmá ?amappâun θôuŋzè chauyyau? šìdé*

house of representatives, lower house	*ʔauʔ hluttó*
There are one hundred and thirty-two in the house of representatives.	*ʔauʔ hluttóhmá tayà θôunzè hnayauʔ šìdé*

máun θín

party	*pátí*
governor	*bayíŋgán*
has charge of, rules, manages	*ʔouʔ chouttè*
premier	*nân-yîn wúnjîjouʔ*
position, office	*ʔayá*
puts out of the way, gives away	*hlwêdé*
disposes of, transfers to another	*hlwê ʔatté*
The head of the party which gets the most votes in the election is called by the governor and given the post of premier to run the country.	*mê ywêi kaullòu ʔauʔ hluttóhmá mê ʔamyâzôun yàdè pátígà lújîgóu bayíŋgàŋgà khó pî, tâin pyéi ʔouʔ chouppòu nân-yîn wúnjîjouʔ ʔayá hlwê ʔallaitté*

máun wílyán

appoints to an office	*khànde*
And how about the other ministerial offices—who makes the appointments?	*wúnjîjoummyâ loupphóu ʔayámyâgóugô, badúgà khànðalê*

máun θín

leader	*gâunzáun (gâun sháundé)*
has jurisdiction, responsibility	*sháindé*
pertaining to jurisdiction, responsibility	*sháin-yá*
each to his own work	*sháin-yá sháin-yá ʔalouʔ*
The premier calls the leaders of the party and assigns ministers each to his respective position.	*nân-yîn wúnjîjoukkàbê pátígà gâunzáun lújîdwéigóu khó pî, sháin-yá sháin-yá ʔalounnè loupphòu wúnjîjouʔ khàndé*

máun bà cí

dacoit, bandit	*damyà*
business, affair, case in law	*ʔahmù*
case of dacoity, robbery	*damyàhmù*
catches, arrests	*phândé*
jail	*gaʔ*
has control over	*choutté*
places in confinement, in custody	*chouʔ thâdé*
It says in the paper that Mr. Pyu was arrested by the police for dacoity and put in jail.	*máun phyúgóu damyàhmùnè paleiʔ phân θwâ pî, gatthêhmá chouʔ thâdélòu θadînzádêhmá pádé*

máun θín

attack (as a band of dacoits)	*taitté*
Where did the dacoity take place?	*béhmá taittè damyàhmùlê*

máun bà cí

broker	*pwêzâ*
It's the holdup that took place at the broker's house in Lammadaw.	*lâmmadógà pwêzâʔéin taiʔ θwâdè damyàhmùbê*

máun wílyán

law	*tayâ*
judge	*tayâ θajî*
examines, investigates	*sitté*
examines, investigates	*sisshêidé*
Which judge is going to try the case?	*dí damyàhmùgóu bé tayâ θajî sisshêimalê*

máun θín

criminal offense — *yázawuʔ*
judge of criminal court — *yázawuʔ tayâ θajî*
session — *sheššín*
Probably Judge U Sein Daing of the criminal court or Judge U Ba Kya of the session court will try. — *yázawuʔ tayâ θajî ʔû shéin dáin phyisséi, sheššín tayâ θajî ʔû bà câ phyisséi, sisshêilèimmé*

---

máun wílyán

How about the war news, what does it say? — *siʔ θadîŋgô, bélóu páðalê*

the Allies — *mahà meittòu*
Are the Allies winning? — *mahà meittòu náin néiðalâ*

máun bà cí

French — *pyinθiʔ*
Russian — *yúšà*
army, ground forces — *kôundaʔ*
fights against, attacks — *taiʔ khaitté*
Yes. Since the French soldiers and soldiers of the Russian armies are victoriously fighting to defeat the German forces, the Germans will lose before long. — *houtté, pyinθiʔ siθθânè yúšà kôundaʔ siθθâmyâgàlê jámaní sittakkóu ʔamyê náinʔáun, taiʔ khaiʔ néidè ʔatweʔ, macágín jámaní šôunlèimmé*

máun θín

air force — *léidaʔ*
bomb — *bôun*
drops bombs, bombs — *bôun cêdé*

Planes of the American Air Force are constantly bombing Germany and Japan.	*ʔaméiyìkán léidakkà léiyímbyámmyâgàlê jápánnè jámanígóu ʔamyê θwâ bôun cê néidé*

máun wílyán

navy	*yéidaʔ*
What is there about the Japanese Navy?	*jápán yéidaʔ ʔacâuŋgô, bélóu páðalê*

máun bà cí

causes to sink, sinks	*hnitté*
submerges, causes to sink	*hmyoutté*
destroys by sinking	*hniʔ hmyoutté*
is extinct,	*pyoutté*
Since the American warships have been sinking the ships of the Japanese Navy they are about done for.	*ʔaméiyìkán siʔ θîmbômyâgà jápán yéidakkóu taiʔ khaiʔ hniʔ hmyoullaittè ʔatweʔ, jápán yéidaʔ pyouttòmé.*

SECTION B—WORD STUDY AND REVIEW OF BASIC SENTENCES

1. Word Study

A. *Derivation* (Continued)

Doubled Nouns

Doubled nouns are noun expressions which consist of two noun members.

1. The noun members may be the same noun repeated.

When the noun members are derived nouns in *ʔa-* or *ta-*, the prefix of the second member is dropped.

ʔamyôu 'race, people'
ʔamyôumyôu 'various or all races'
ʔasà 'start, beginning'
ʔayá 'thing'
ʔasàzà ʔayáyá 'in all respects'
taphyêibyêi 'slowly'
talwêlwê 'wrongly'

2. When the nouns are independent nouns, which do not have prefixed *ʔa-* or *ta-*, *ʔa-* is prefixed to the prior member.

   myòu 'city'
   ʔamyòumyòu 'cities in general'
   ywá 'village'
   ʔaywaywá 'villages in general'

3. The noun members may be parts of a dissyllabic noun with a modifier accompanying each part.

   seilleʔ 'mind' *ʔêidé* 'is cool'
   seiʔʔêi leʔʔêi 'relaxed'
   seiʔʔêi leʔʔêi shóuðalóu taphyêibyêi θwâmé (I) will go slowly, relaxed, as the saying is

4. The noun members may be two different nouns.

   ʔanî 'near' *ʔanâ* 'near'
   ʔanî ʔanâhmá šìdé (it) is near
   ʔalouʔ 'work' *ʔakáin* 'work'
   θù ʔalouʔ ʔakáin zagabyán his profession (is that of) interpreter

5. The noun members may be a noun repeated with *ta-* prefixed to the first member. The prefixed *ta-* is the numeral *tiʔ*, and the members of this type of doubled noun are classifiers.

   takhùgù 'one thing or another'
   tayauyyauʔ 'one person or another'
   tanèinèi 'one day or another'

6. The noun members may be nouns with prefixed *ta-*. The members of this type are classifiers.

   takhá taléi 'from time to time'
   takhá takhá 'from time to time'
   tajéin takhá 'this once'
   tayaussí tayaussí 'individually'

7. Doubled nouns with distributive force are used in questions requiring an enumeration.

khímbyâ θaŋéjîn badú badúlê 'Who are your friends?'
hóu ʔalán bá ʔayáun bá ʔayáunlê 'What color is that flag?'

2. Covering English and Burmese of Word Study

Give the English equivalents of all Burmese expressions in the *Word Study* and the Burmese for all the English. This is individual study.

3. Review of Basic Sentences

Further oral practice with the first part of the *Basic Sentences*.

1. Review of Basic Sentences (*Cont.*)

Further oral practice with the second part of the *Basic Sentences.*

2. Covering the English of Basic Sentences

Check your knowledge of the meaning of all words and phrases in the *Basic Sentences*. This is individual study.

3. What Would You Say?

Give full answers to the following questions.

1. *khímbyâ bá θadînzagóu pha? néiðalê*
2. *θadînzádêhmá ?athû θadîn bá páðalê*
3. *khímbyâ thí thôubûðalâ*
4. *θêin thí shóudá bálê*
5. *θêin thí pathamà shù pauttè lú ŋwéi bélau? yàðalê*
6. *?améiyìkán pyéihmá ?asôuyàgóu ?akhúndó ?amyâjî pêiyàðalâ*
7. *?asôuyà ŋwéigóu béhmá θôun-yàmé shóudá badúgà shôun phyaθθalê*
8. *mê ywêi kauttáhmá khímbyâ mê thèbûðalâ*
9. *?améiyìkán pyéihmá tahni? bé hnakhá mê ywêi kauθθalê*
10. *nau? ?apaphmá bé nèi mê ywêimélòu câðalê*
11. *myámmá pyéi hluttóhmá ?amaccî bé hnayau? šìðalê*
12. *?athe? hluttóhmágô ?ama? bé hnayau? šìðalê*
13. *bayíŋgánnè nân-yín wúnjíjou? badúgà ?ayá cîðalê*
14. *?akhù nân-yîn wúnjíjoukkóu khímbyâ caiyyèlâ*
15. *macaiyyín, bá phyillòu macaiθθalê*
16. *wúnjíjoummyâgóu badùgà khànðalê*
17. *máun phyúgóu paleittwéi bájàun phân θwâðalê*
18. *θùgóu badú phân chou? thâðalê*
19. *damyàmyâgóu phammìðalâ*
20. *dí damyàhmùgóu badú sisshêimalê*
21. *damyàmyâ lu? θwâjàðalâ*
22. *kabábóhmá bé náiŋgáŋgà yéida? ?acîzôunlê*
23. *jámaní ?ašôun pêidá bé hnahni? cá θwâbalê*
24. *?améiyìkán pyéigóu bèdò pyámmalê*
25. *khímbyâ ?éindáun càbalê*
26. *khímbyâ θàðamî bé hnayau? šìðalê*
27. *khímbyâ bé báðágóu kôugwéðalê*
28. *?éinðá béhmálê*
29. *khímbyâ wûn sháðalâ*
30. *ŋâjattán sekkú ?ânhnáimmalâ*
31. *shéja? ?âmbòu šìðalâ*
32. *ŋwéi tashé lêzayá šìyèlâ*
33. *yéi kû θwâmalòulâ*
34. *phayâbóhmá phana? masîyàbûlâ*

35. *thamînzáin béhmálê*
36. *khímbyâ hléi hlóbòu taθθalâ*
37. *cúndódòunè myîmbwêgóu laimmalâ*
38. *khímbyâ myámmá pyéihmá bé hnahni? néimalòulê*
39. *bayíŋgán ?éin dí néiyágà θei? wêiðalâ*
40. *cúndó yéi kûjíndé, béhmá kûhnáimmalê*
41. *ŋâ hmyâbòu néiyágâummyâ šìðalâ*
42. *taissínè θwâyín, tamáiŋgóu bélaussí pêiyàmalê*
43. *hóu tanèigà léiyimbyán pye? càdé shóudá béhmálê*
44. *khímbyâ ?amèizígóu nèidâin sá yêiðalâ*
45. *khímbyàhmá mîji? páðalâ*
46. *θadînzá tazáun bélaullê*
47. *mótókâ dasshí tagálán bélaullê*
48. *khímbyâ pyóbwêzâ θwâmalòulâ*
49. *bamó shóudá bélau? wêiðalê*
50. *?êinjímyâ béhmá chouthnáimmalê*
51. *khímbyâ shêilei? θauttaθθalâ*
52. *télíphóun bélóu sheyyàðalê*
53. *?aye? tabalîn béhmá wélòu yàmalê*
54. *khímbyâ néilòu kâun-yèlâ*

SECTION D—LISTENING IN

1. What Did You Say?

With the other members of the group give orally your responses to the previous exercise as the Leader calls for them.

2. Word Study Check-Up

Give the Burmese for all English equivalents in the *Word Study* as the Leader calls for it.

3. Listening In

1. War and reconstruction.

máun myà séin: *yúšá kôunda? siθθâmyâ taphekkà, ?améiyìkán ?îŋgaleinnè pyinθi? siθθâmyâ nau? taphekkà néi pî, jámanígóu wâin taittò, jámaní ?ašôun pêiyàdá pò*

máun hlà myìn: *dájàunjîbê mahouppábû mahà mei? léidakkà ?amyê θwâ bôun cêlòu dílau? myámmyán ?ašôun pêidá*

máun sán nyóu: *jámaní yéidakkóu mahà meittòugà ?asín mapya? tai? kai? hni? hmyoullòu θúdòu ?ašôun mapêigíŋgàdáun, pyoummélóulóu phyi? néidé*

màun hlà myìn: *?akhù jápáŋgóulê jámanílóu ?ašôun pêi?áun, tai? kaiyyàmé* *máun myà séin:* *myammà θadîn ˀacâun bélóu câðalê*

máun hlà myìn: *manéigàbê θadînzádêhmá jápámmyâ myámmá pyéigà thweˀ pyêi θwâjàbílòu phallaitté*

máun sán nyóu: *ˀêdílóu shóuyín, myámmá pyéi ˀasôuyàgà tâin pyéigóu ˀousshoubòu ŋwéi lóudé shóu pî, θêin thígóu macágín pyán phwìnlèimmé*

máun myà séin: *dí takhádò ˀalîn-yáun ˀateinnè thôumé thí pauyyín, ˀakhúndó pêizayá šìdádéigóu pêihnáimmé*

máun sán nyóu: *khímbyâ thí pauppéimè légún lúgún ˀakhún ˀamyôumyôugóu pêi lóuyín, bámà cándòhmá mahoupphû*

máun hlà myìn: *ˀasouyàgàlê bá ˀatweˀ mashóu ˀakauˀ kauˀ néidábê*

máun sán nyóu: *ŋwéi mašìbê maˀousshôuhnáimbû dájàummòu hóu tanéigàbê bándáyêi wúnjíjoukkà ˀasôuyà ŋwéidaiphmá nwéi mašìlòuˀakhún ˀapòu kaupphòu shôun payatté*
dílóu ˀakhún ˀamyôumyôu kauˀ pîdòbê ŋwéidaikkóu taphyêibyêi phyèiyàmé

máun hlà myìn: *ˀasôuyàhmá ŋwéi mašìyín, ˀayájîdéigóu ˀayágà pyoullaittá pò*

máun sán nyóu: *ˀêdílóulê maphyipphû*
ˀayêibáindòu seššín tayâ θajîdòu myòuˀouttòu mašìyín, tabyéilôumhmá damyà hmùdé
póu pî pó pauˀ lálèimmé

máun hlà myìn: *damyàdéigóu phân pî, gatthêhmá chouˀ thâbòu paleittéi šìðâbê*

máun sán nyòu: *paleittéi šìbéimè, paleinnè sháin-yá gâunzáun lújîmyâ mašìyín, ˀalagâbê*

máun hlà myìn: *ˀakóunlôuŋgóu phyouyàmélòu cúndógà mashóubábû*
tachòu tayâ θajîmyâgóulê ˀahmù si?
shêibòu thâðeidá pò

2. Politics.

máun hlà: *bayíŋgáŋgà badùgóu nân-yîn wúnjíjouˀ ˀayá kàmmélòu shôun pyaθθalê*

máun mê: *nân-yîn wún ˀayágóu cínðèi pátígà ˀû phôu θêimbógóu hlwê ˀammélòu câdé*

máun hlà: *hóu tanèigà ˀatheˀ hluttógà ˀamaccî tayauˀ θéi shôun θwâdé*
θù néiyáhmá badùgóu khàmmalêlòu câðalê

máun mê: *ʔakhù maθìðèibû ʔauʔ hluttógà ʔamattéi mê ywêi kauʔ pî, khàndè ʔakhá θìyàlèimmé*

máun hlà: *badùgóu khàmmalê shóudá cúndó bélóu θìhnáimmalê*

máun mê: *θadînzádêhmá cónyálèimmé macónyábû shóuyíndò, cúndó sá tazáun máun pùgóu pêi khâinlaimmé θúgà khímbyâzígóu tashìn pêilèimmé*

máun hlà: *cêizû ʔamyâjî tímbádé ʔakhù cúndó pwêzâzígóu θwâzayá šìðèidé θwâlaiʔʔôummé nó*

SECTION E—CONVERSATION

1. Covering the Burmese of Basic Sentences

With the Burmese covered, practice until you can speak the Burmese for each English sentence without hesitation. This is individual study.

2. Vocabulary Check-Up

Give the Burmese for all English sentences in the *Basic Sentences* as the Leader calls for it.

3. Conversation

Suggested Topics:

1. Discuss the Burma State Lottery.
2. Discuss tax collection in Burma.
3. Discuss tax collection in America.
4. Discuss the last days of the war.
5. Discuss what will happen in the future.

Continue conversation. Additional check-up if necessary.

ʔahmù business, affair, case in law
ʔakhún taxes, revenues accruing from assessments
ʔakhúndóŋwéi tax receipts
ʔalagâ useless, in vain, to no purpose; for nothing
ʔamaʔ person of rank, member of parliament
ʔasôuyà government
ʔateiʔ alias, nom-de-plume
ʔatheʔ hluttó senate, upper house
ʔauʔ hluttó house of representatives, lower house
ʔayá position, office
ʔayêibáin district commissioner
bándáyêi wúnjîjouʔ finance minister
bayíŋgán governor
bôun bomb
bôun cêdé drops bombs, bombs
chouttê has control over
chouʔ thâdé places in confinement, in custody
cíndèi lion
cónydádé is proclaimed publicly, spreads (as news)
damyà dacoit, bandit
damyàhmù case of dacoity, banditry
gaʔ jail
ganân numeral, numeral figure
gâun sháundé leads, heads
gâunzáun leader
hluttó parliament
hlwêdé puts out of the way, gives away
hlwê ʔatté disposes of, gives to another
hmyoutté submerges, causes to sink
hnashé twenty
hniʔ hmyoutté destroys by sinking
hnitté causes to sink, sinks
kautté picks up, collects
khàndé appoints to an office
kôundaʔ army, infantry
légún land revenue, property tax
léidaʔ air force
lúgún head tax, poll tax
lwêdé errs, goes wrong
mahà meittòu the Allies

mê	lot, ballot
mê ywêi kautté	votes
myámmá (= *bamá*)	Burmese
myámmá ʔalîn	"The New Light of Burma" (name of a newspaper)
myòuʔouʔ	township officer
nân-yîn wúnjîjouʔ	premier
ŋwéidaiʔ	treasury
ʔouʔ choutté	has charge of, rules, manages
pátí	party
phândé	catches, tries to catch
pwêzâ	broker
pyínθiʔ	French
pyoutté	is extinct
sháindé	has jurisdiction
sháin-yá	jurisdiction
sháin-yá sháin-yá ʔalouʔ	each to his own work
sheššín	session
shôundé	comes to an end, is finished
shôun phyatté	decides, settles, adjudicates
sisshêidé	examines, investigates
sitté	examines, investigates
taitté	attacks, as a band of dacoits
taiʔ khaitté	fights against, attacks
taphyêibyêi	slowly, gradually
tashìn	one step, one stage
tayâ	law
tayâ θajî	judge
tháun	1,000
thí	lottery
thôudé	plays at certain games of chance
tín hmyautté	elects
θadînzá	newspaper
θâun	10,000
θêin	100,000
θêin thí	The Burma State Lottery
θúrìyà	'The Sun' (name of a newspaper)
wúndauʔ	sub-divisional officer
yá	100
yázawuʔ	criminal case
yázawuʔ tayâ θajî	judge of the criminal court
yéidaʔ	navy
yúšà	Russian

UNIT 30

REVIEW

SECTION A—SENTENCE REVIEW

To the Leader: Begin this review of the work so far by having a session in which you call out at random English sentences from Part IV. (Units 19-23) and ask members of the class to give the Burmese. The members of the class should not prepare in any special way for this. You can take the sentences you ask for from Sections B and C of Unit 24, but take them in random order.

SECTION B—SENTENCE REVIEW

Practice saying out loud the Burmese for the following sentences. Keep at them until you know them all thoroughly. Do not write anything down. This is individual study.

I

1. Is the road we're on the right one?
2. I can't say whether this is the right road or the wrong one.
3. My opinion is that we have gone astray and are on the wrong road.
4. I don't know whether we should go north or south from here.
5. Don't be so dejected.
6. Let's sit down under that tree for a little while and think.
7. Don't you think we should follow this road?
8. We will have to look for the village until we find it.
9. I think there's a village not far away.
10. We want to make a raft to cross the river.

II

1. What kinds of games do you Burmans play in Burma?
2. Please explain so I can understand.

3. Even though you have explained I still don't understand it very well.
4. I want to see a game myself so that I can understand.
5. People are gathering around and looking.
6. Why are they tattooed?
7. This is really nice to see.
8. At first I intended to go there and show it to you.
9. I just arrived a moment ago.
10. How could I know (about it)?

III

1. Please do me the favor of telling me something about Burma.
2. What shall I talk about first?
3. What difference is there between Burmans and Shans?
4. There isn't much difference.
5. Most of them speak Burmese.
6. Ninety percent of them are Buddhists.
7. Don't you remember?
8. How many big rivers are there in Burma?
9. From the north of Burma they flow to the south, and flow into the sea.
10. They come and go by steamer.

IV

1. What time in the evening are you going?
2. Tonight is the last night.
3. It would be a good idea to go early.
4. It's quite surprising the way they make pots by hand.
5. What else is there to see?
6. Teak from Burma is the best in the world.
7. Oil also is exported to other countries.
8. What is there special inside?
9. First we'll go in and look around.
10. Shall we go inside and look, or look around outside first.

V

1. What is it you want to know?
2. Which judge is going to try the case?
3. How much money does the winner of the Burma State Lottery get?
4. How are the taxes collected in country villages?
5. The head man has to send it on to the township officer.
6. It goes on by stages from the District Commissioner and is gradually deposited in the Treasury.
7. There are thirty-six members in all in the senate.
8. There are one hundred and thirty-two in the house of representatives.
9. It says in the paper that Mr. Pyu was arrested by the police for dacoity and put in jail.
10. Where did the dacoity take place?

SECTION C—HOW DO YOU SAY IT?

Quiz by the Group Leader on the sentences in Section B, asking various members of the group to give the Burmese equivalents of the English sentences.

SECTION D—HOW WOULD YOU SAY IT?

Practice the Burmese equivalents of the following sentences until you know them thoroughly. This is individual study.

I

1. Please bring 4 or 5 spoons.
2. I'd like to have a word with you.
3. He broke one of his legs.
4. We invited 5 people.
5. Have you ever been lost in the jungle?
6. Will it take long to build a bridge?
7. Do you know how to shoot a gun?
8. Now you carry it.
9. I'll drink only when I get back to the village.
10. Let's go fishing before we go back to the village.

II

1. Is there much travel on this road?
2. Why didn't you say so from the start?
3. Come along as far as the house.
4. Some say this and some say that.
5. Why don't you go sit somewhere else?
6. I didn't do it on purpose.
7. I am afraid I'll lose my way.
8. How much will you bet?
9. Keep it in a separate place.
10. I didn't do it on purpose.

III

1. I don't know whether what he says is correct or not.
2. How can you tell whether it's going to be good?
3. What time will we reach the village to which we are now going?
4. I am afraid to drink this water.
5. Where's a place to sleep?
6. Every time I go to Rangoon it's raining.
7. Don't talk when you're working.
8. When did you learn to speak Burmese?
9. The work won't get done by mere talk.
10. It's time to go.

IV

1. When does the exhibition open?
2. Will it be a good idea to go early or late?
3. Aren't you going to fix the garage?
4. Are you going to fix it with tin or zinc?
5. The most beautiful rubies in the world come from Burma.
6. How is Mg. Sein? Is he happy in school?
7. Although it is expensive, it will last a long time.
8. Bring out a couple of umbrellas from the house.
9. I've been busy and only today do I have time to go.
10. Teak is expensive isn't it?

V

1. I want to make a phone call.
2. Is there any special news in the paper?
3. How many times a year do they have elections in America?
4. How much each will we have to pay if we go by taxi?
5. Come along and show me.
6. What news do you hear about Burma?
7. There was a hold-up that took place at a broker's house in Lammadaw.
8. From what other sources do they get revenue besides the State Lottery?
9. Really quite a lot of valuable products are produced in your country.
10. I'll have to be going now.

SECTION E—HOW DID YOU SAY IT?

Quiz by the Group Leader on the sentences in Section D, asking various members of the group to give the Burmese equivalents of the English sentences.

SECTION F—CONVERSATION REVIEW

Hold a series of conversations on any of the topics covered so far. All members of the group should have a chance to take part. Review all the topics suggested in Units 6, 12, 18, and 24.

ENGLISH-BURMESE WORD LIST

English	Burmese
abrades	*pûndé*
accident	*matò tashà*
accompanies	*pádé; laitté*
according to	*ˀayà*
according to, in accordance with	*ˀatâin*
account	*ˀatweˀ; sayîn*
ache	*ˀakaiˀ; ˀaná; ˀanyâun*
aches (*also* bites)	*kaitté*
aches, ear	*nâ kaitté*
aches, tooth	*θwâ kaitté*
address	*néiyaˀ*
adheres to, is attached to (flatwise)	*katté*
adjudicates	*shôun phyatté*
adult (big person)	*lújî*
advances	*tetté*
affair	*ˀayêi; ˀahmù*
afraid, is; fears	*cautté*
afternoon	*nyànéi*
age	*ˀaθeˀ*
agrees	*θabô túdé*
air force	*léidaˀ*
airplane	*léiyímbyán*
air-pump	*léi thôundán*
alias	*ˀateiˀ*
all	*ˀâlôun; ˀakóunlôun; ˀakóun*
all kinds	*ˀamyôuzóun*
Allies, the	*mahà meittòu*
already	*ˀakhùdetthì*
altogether	*ˀâlôumbâun*
always	*ˀamyê; ˀasín mapyaˀ*
amazing, is	*ˀànˀôdé*
American	*ˀaméiyìkán*
amputates	*phyaˀ kùdé*
angry, is	*seiˀ shôudé*
animal	*tareisshán*
anna, one	*tabê*
anna denomination, one	*tabêdán*
answers (a question)	*phyéidé*
anybody	*badú mashóu*
any time	*bé ˀakhá mashóu*
aperture	*ˀapauˀ*
appearance	*ˀashín*
appears	*pódé*
appeases	*pyéidé*
appoints (a time or place)	*chêindé*
appoints to an office	*khàndé*

approves	*θabô càdé*
approximately	*nî kabâ*
arduous	*khetté; pímbândé*
arises	*thàdé*
arm	*leʔ*
arms (munitions)	*lenneʔ*
army	*sittaʔ*
army (infantry)	*kôundaʔ*
army encampment	*sittaʔ sakhân*
arranges (for)	*símándé*
arrests	*phândé*
arrives	*yautté*
arrival	*ʔayauʔ*
art	*pyínnyá*
article	*pyissî*
articles	*pyissîdéi*
ascends	*tetté*
asks	*mêidé*
asks for	*tâundé*
assists	*kú-nyídé*
assortment, complete	*ʔasóun*
attacks	*taiʔ khaitté*
attacks, as a band of dacoits	*taitté*
attains to	*hmìdé*
attention	*θadì*
aunt	*ʔadó*
auto jack	*mótókâ hmyauʔ jeʔ*
auto tools	*mótókâ pyissî*
automobile	*mótókâ*
avoids	*šáundé*
bag	*ʔeiʔ*
bag that hangs from the shoulder	*lwéʔeiʔ*
ball	*bólôun*
ballot	*mê*
bamboo	*wâ*
bamboo raft	*wâ pháun*
bandit	*damyà*
bank	*bándaiʔ*
bank of a river, lake, sea	*kân*
barber	*shabín hnyaθθamâ*
barber shop	*shabín hnyassháin*
barks	*háundé*
barrel	*sí*
bathroom	*yéi chôugân*
bath, takes a; bathes	*yéi chôudé*
beard	*moussheiʔ*
bears (carries)	*sháundé*
bears, is born	*mwêidé*
bed	*ʔeiyyá, ʔeipphòu néiyá*
bed sheet	*ʔeiyyágîn*

before *šèi, ˀayín, ˀayíŋgà*
befuddled *myessì lédé*
beef *ˀamêðâ*
beer *bíyá*
beginning *ˀasà*
begins *sàdé*
behalf *ˀatweˀ*
behind *naukkà*
behind, falls *nauˀ càdé*
behind, from *naukkà*
behind a thing, the space *nauˀ*
believes *yóundé*
believes implicitly *yóun cídé*
belly *wûn*
bend *ˀakauˀ; ˀakwèi*
bends around *kwèidé*
besides, beside *ˀapyín*
besides (this) *dì pyín*
best *ˀakâunzôun*
bet *ˀalâun*
bets *lâundé*
beyond, is or goes *lúndé*
big, is *cîdé*
bird *hŋeˀ*
bite *ˀakaiˀ*
black *ˀaneˀ; ˀamê*
blanket *sáun*
blood *θwêi*
blow (stroke) *ˀacheˀ*
blows *hmoutté*
blows up with air *léi thôudé*
blue *ˀapyá*
blurred, is *hmóundé*
boat *hléi*
body *kóu*
boils *pyoutté*
book *sáˀouˀ*
booth *yóun*
bomb *bôun*
bombs *bôun cêdé*
bored, is *pyîndé*
boredom *ˀapyîn*
borrows, lends, rents, hires *hŋâdé*
borrows (money) *chîdé*
bottle *palîn*
bottle of ink *hmínˀôu*
boulder, large *chausshâun*
bowl, anything of similar shape *khweˀ*
bowl, round *pagánlôun*
box *θittá*
box *bû*
breakfast *manessá*
bread *páummòun*

breaks (crosswise)	*côudé*
brightness	*ˀayáun, ˀalîn, ˀalîn-yáun*
brick building	*taiˀ*
bridge	*tadâ, θadâ*
brings	*yúdé*
brings up, rears	*mwêidé*
broker	*pwêzâ*
brothers and sisters	*nyíˀakóu máunhnamà*
brook, large	*châun*
brother (of a woman)	*máun*
brother, older	*ˀakóu*
brother, younger	*nyí*
brown	*ˀanyóu*
bruises	*pûndé*
Buddhism	*boutdà báðá*
buffalo	*cwê*
building	*ˀasháun*
building (for work or business)	*yóun*
builds	*shautté*
bull	*nwâ*
Burmese	*myámmá, bamá*
Burma, Lower	*ˀauˀ bamá pyéi*
Burma, Upper	*ˀatheˀ bamá pyéi*
Burma State Lottery	*θêin thí*
Burmese people	*bamá lúmyôu; myammá lúmyôu*
burns (a hole)	*mî pautté*
business	*keissà*
business	*ˀayêi; ˀahmù; keissà*
busy, is	*ˀayêi cîdé; ˀalouˀ myâdé*
butter	*thôbaˀ*
button	*céðî*
buys	*wédé*
calculates	*twetté*
calls	*khódé*
cane ball	*chînlôun*
canteen	*yéibû*
canvas	*ywetthé*
cap	*ˀoutthouˀ*
capital	*ˀayîn*
car	*yathâ*
car, forward	*šèidwê*
car, rear	*nauttwê*
card game	*phêwâin*
cards, playing	*phê*
careful, is	*θadì thâdé*
carpet	*kózô*
carriage (horse)	*myîn-yathâ*
carriage	*yathâ*
carries	*sháundé*
carries (on the shoulder)	*thândé*

carries from one place to another	*θédé*
cart	*hlê*
carts	*hlênè taitté*
carver	*pabù shayá*
carves	*thùdé*
case in law	*ˀahmù*
cases, in most	*ˀamyâ ˀâ phyìn*
cask	*sí*
catch, tries to	*phândé*
catches (with bait)	*hmyâdé*
cause	*ˀacâun*
census	*θagáun sayîn*
chair	*kalatháin*
change, pays; changes (money)	*ˀândé*
changes	*lêdé*
changes (place)	*pyâundé*
charge, has of	*ˀouˀ choutté*
check (bank)	*ceˀ lephmaˀ*
cheetah	*caθiˀ*
child, youngster (little)	*khalêi*
chilies	*ŋayouˀ*
Chinese	*tayouˀ*
chooses	*ywêidé*
chops	*khoutté*
Christianity	*khariyyán báðá*
cigar	*shêileiˀ*
cigarette	*sígareˀ*
circuit	*ˀapaˀ*
circumstance	*ˀacâun*
citizen	*ˀamyôuðâ*
city	*myòu*
class	*ˀatân*
clean, is	*síndé*
clever, is	*tódé*
climbs	*tetté*
clock, wall	*táin kaˀ náyí*
closed, is; closes	*peitté*
cloth, piece of	*ˀathé, ˀawusshouˀ*
clothing store	*ˀawussháin*
coat	*ˀêinjí*
coffee	*káphí*
cold, has a (in the nose)	*hná sîdé*
cold season	*shâun ˀakhá: shâun ˀùdù*
collects into one	*pâundé*
color	*ˀayáun; ˀashín*
column	*táin*
come on!	*kê*
comes	*ládé*
comes in	*wín ládé*
comfortable	*θeθθádé*
comfortable and easy in mind, feels	*seiˀ chàdé*

coming, a	*ˀalá*
command	*ˀamèin*
compares	*sá cìdé*
compares	*tâindé*
compass needle	*ˀéin hmyáun, ˀéimhmyáun*
competes	*pyáindé*
complete, is	*sóundé*
complies with	*laiˀ sâdé*
compute	*twetté*
conceals oneself	*pôundé*
concerned, is a	*sôuyéindé*
conducts (to a person or place)	*pòudé*
confinement, places in	*chouˀ thâdé*
confused, is	*myessì lédé*
connects	*shetté*
considers, thinks	*twêidé; sînzâdé*
considers (implying doubt or uncertainty)	*twêi caitté*
considers, is of the opinion	*θabô thâdé*
container	*pôun*
contest	*pyáimbwê*
continually	*ˀasín mapyaˀ*
control over, has	*choutté*
conveys	*pòudé*
conveys (on a cart)	*hlênè taitté*
cooks	*chetté; cheˀ pyoutté*
cool, is	*ˀêidé*
cool of the day	*néiˀêi*
coolie	*kúlí*
cool(ness)	*ˀêiˀêi*
cord	*côu*
corn	*pyâumbû*
corner	*ˀakwèi*
correct, is	*hmándé*
costs	*càdé*
cot, couch, bedstead	*kadín*
cotton	*wágûn*
coughs, has a cough	*châun shôudé*
country	*pyéi; náiŋgán; né; tâin pyéi*
of course	*pò*
court (-house)	*yôun*
covers up, incloses	*ŋóundé*
covers (as with a blanket)	*chóundé*
cow	*nwâ*
crab	*ganân*
craft, manual art	*lephmù pyínnyà*
cries out	*ˀódé*
criminal case	*yázawuˀ*
crook (in a road)	*ˀakauˀ*
crooked, not straight	*kautté*

crushes	*ceitté*
cup	*pagánlôun*
cup, anything of similar shape	*khweʔ*
cup or bowl, metal	*phalâ*
cupboard	*bídóu*
current is strong	*yéi sîdé*
curry	*hîn*
curry, beef	*ʔamêðâhîn*
curry, fish	*ŋâhîn*
curry, pork	*weθθâhîn*
curve	*ʔakwèi*
curved, is	*kwèidé*
custody, places in	*chouʔ thâdé*
custom	*thôunzán*
cut, is	*pyatté*
cuts	*khoutté*
cuts (as with scissors)	*hnyatté*
cuts lengthwise	*seitté*
dacoit	*damyà*
dacoity, case of	*damyàhmù*
dark, is	*hmáundé; netté*
daughter	*θamî*
day (from sunrise to sunset)	*nèi*
day, 24 hour	*yeʔ*
day after tomorrow	*θabekkhá*
dead, is	*θéidé*
decides	*shôun phyatté*
decimal	*dàθamà*
deep, is	*netté*
definitely	*θéiðéi chájá*
dejected, is	*seiʔ ŋédé*
demands	*tâundé*
denomination, what?	*bélauttán*
departs	*thwetté*
depressed, is	*seiʔ ŋédé*
descends	*shîndé*
design	*póun*
desire	*ʔalóu*
destroyed, is	*pyetté; pyessîdé*
destroys by sinking	*hniʔ hmyoutté*
determines	*θabô thâdé*
deterred by fear of offending, is	*ʔâ nádé*
diamond	*séin*
dies	*θéi shôundé; shôundé; θéidé*
difference	*ʔathû*
different, is	*thûdé*
difficult, is	*khetté*
dignity	*ʔéindayéi*
digs	*tûdé*
dim (as the eye), is	*hmóundé*

dinner *nyàzá*
dips up *khatté*
disappears *pyautté*
disapproves *nyîndé*
disease *yôgá; ʔaná;*
dish *pagámbyâ*
dispirited, is *seiʔ ŋédé*
disposes of *hlwê ʔatté*
disposition *θabô*
disputes *nyîndé*
distance between 2 places *khayî*
distant, is *wêidé*
district *né; néiyaʔ*
district commissioner *ʔayêibáin*
diverse, is *thûdé*
divides into two parts *khwêdé*
doctor *shayá*
does *loutté*
does thoroughly, completely *hnàndé*
dog *khwêi*
done, is *kóundé*
door *tagabauʔ*
down, goes *shîndé*
downcast, is *seiʔ ŋédé*
drawer *ʔánzwê; shwêʔán*
drawn, sketched, has *yéi shwê thâdé*
draws, sketches *shwêdé*
draws water *khatté*
dresses (verb) *wutté*
drinks *θautté*
drives (a vehicle) *mâundé*
drives against *taitté*
drug *shêi*
drum (container) *sí*
dysentery, has *wûn kaitté*

each to his own work *sháin-yá sháin-yá ʔalouʔ*
ear *nâ*
early *sôzô (sôdé)*
earth *myéi*
eats *sâdé*
easily, without haste *phyêibyêi (phyêidé)*
east, the *ʔašèi*
either . . . or *phyisséi . . . phyisséi*
elated, is *wûn myautté*
electric light *dammî*
elects *tín hmyautté*
elephant *shín*
elevated, is *myautté*
employs, asks to do *khâindé*

encloses *ŋóundé*
enclosure *chán*
end, comes to an *shôundé*
enemy *yánδú*
engine *se?*
English *?îŋgalei?*
engraves *thùdé*
enjoyment *pyóbyó šwínšwín*
enjoys *méindé*
enjoys oneself *pyódé*
enters *wín ládé*
envelope *sá?ei?*
erect, makes *matté*
erects *saitté*
erects (a building) *shautté*
error, is in *hmâdé*
errs *lwêdé*
estimates *tâindé*
even number, an *?asóun*
everlastingly *?asín mapya?*
every time *khádâin*
examines *sitté; sisshêidé*
exceeds *póudé; lúndé*
excess *?apóu*
excess, is in *póudé*
exchanges *lêdé*
excuse me *katòbáyè*
exhibition *?àmbwê*
exhibition building *pyàdai?*
exhibits *tín pyàdé*
exists *šìdé*
expects, anticipates, looks forward to *hmyódé*
explains *pyô pyàdé*
exports *tín pòudé*
exposition *?àmbwê*
expression *shóudé*
extinct, is *pyoutté*
eye glasses *myephmán*
eye (human) *myessì*
eye (of a needle) *?appau?*

face *myethná*
fact *?acâun*
fact that it is cold *?êihmân*
fairly *tódó*
falls *càdé*
fancy, notion *sei??athín*
fang *?aswé*
farmer *táunδú; léδamâ; yáδamâ*
fashion, this *dílóu*
fashion, what? *bélóu*
fast, is *myándé*
fast, is (of a current) *yéi sîdé*
father *?aphéi; phéibéi*

fatigued	*pímbândé*
favor, does a	*cêizû pyùdé*
fears	*cautté*
fee, entrance	*wíŋgà*
feeds	*cwêidé*
feels	*sândé*
fellow countryman	*ˀamyôuðâ*
fence	*chán*
festival	*pwê*
feverish, is; fever, has a	*phyâdé*
fever medicine	*ˀaphyâ phyasshêi; phyâzêi*
few, is	*nêdé*
fights against	*taiˀ khaitté*
figure	*ˀayouˀ; ganân*
figure, numerical	*ganân*
figures out	*seiˀ kûdé*
fills up partially or entirely (as a pit)	*phòudé*
final	*nausshôun*
finance minister	*bándáyêi wúnjîjouˀ*
finds	*twèidé*
finished, is	*shôundé*
finishes	*pîdé*
fire	*mî*
fireplace	*mîbóu*
fire, sets on	*mî šòudé*
first	*ˀayín; pathamà*
first class	*pathamàdân*
fish	*ŋâ*
fit, is	*tándé*
five	*ŋâ*
fixes	*tatté, pyíndé*
fixes (a time)	*chêindé*
flask	*yéibû*
flesh of beasts	*ˀamê*
floor	*cân*
flower	*pân*
flows down	*sî shîndé*
follows	*laitté*
food and drink	*ˀasâ ˀaθauˀ*
foot (measure)	*péi*
foot	*chéi*
foot, tip of the	*chéibyâ*
foot of the mountain	*táun chéiyîn*
football, Burmese	*chînlôun*
football, game of Burmese	*chînwâin*
foreign country	*náiŋgánjâ*
forest	*tô*
forest (bamboo)	*wâdô*
forest (timber)	*θittô*
forest or jungle, deep or extensive	*tôneˀ*
forgets	*meidé*

fork *khayîn*
form *sáyweʔ*
form *póun; ʔashín; ʔayouʔ*
formerly *ʔayíŋgà*
for sure *ʔahmán*
four *lêi*
flashlight *lethneiʔ dammî*
free *leitté*
free, is *ʔâdé; lutté*
free, is unoccupied *ʔâdé*
French *pyínθiʔ*
friend *θaŋéjîn; meisshwéi*
friend, my *kwé*
friend, school *câun néibeʔ θaŋéjîn*
fries *códé*
front, in front of *šèi*
fruit *θiθθî*
fun, is; 'is good for being happy' *pyózaya kâundé*
future, in the *naukkòu*

gains on *tetté*
gallon *gálán*
game (meat) *ʔamê*
game, plays a *kazâdé*
garden, flower *pânján*
garment *ʔawuʔ; ʔathé*
gasoline *dasshí*
generally *ʔamyâ ʔâ phyìn*
genuine *ʔasiʔ*
gets *yàdé*
gets up *thàdé*
gift *lessuʔ*
gives *pêidé*
gives away *hlwêdé*
gives medicine *kùdé*
glad, is *pyódé*
glass *phán*
glass, window *hmán*
glass, drinking *pháŋgweʔ*
glimpse, in the way of catching a *yeikkhanê*
goes *θwâdé*
goes around *patté*
going and coming *ʔaθwâ ʔalá*
gold *šwéi*
good, is *kâundé*
good and the bad, the *ʔacôu ʔacâun*
government *ʔasôuyà*
governor *bayíŋgán*
gradual, is *phyêidé*
gradually *taphyêibyêi*
great, is *cé wîndé; cîdé*
green *ʔasêin*
grinds *ceitté*

ground	*myéi*
guest	*ʔêðé*
guide	*mousshôu; lâmbyà*
gun, rifle	*θanaʔ*
hair of the head	*shabín*
half, one	*taweʔ*
halves	*khwêdé*
hammer	*tú*
hand	*leʔ*
hand at cards	*ʔéin*
handkerchief	*lekkáin pawá*
happens	*phyitté*
happiness	*pyóbyó šínšwín*
hard, is	*khetté, khêdé*
hardened, is	*khêdé*
harrows	*thúndé*
hat	*ʔoutthouʔ*
hauls	*shwêdé*
he, she, it	*θú*
head	*gâun*
headdress	*gâumbâun*
headman of a village	*θajî*
heads (leads)	*gâun sháundé*
health	*kóuleʔ câmmáyêi*
health, state of	*májâun chájâun*
healthy	*mámá chájá; májádé*
hears	*câdé*
hearth	*mîbóu*
heat	*ʔapú*
helps	*kúdé; kú-nyídé*
hews	*khoutté*
Hey!	*hèi*
hides	*pôundé*
high, is	*myíndé*
hits	*taitté*
holds, takes hold of	*káindé*
hole	*ʔapauʔ*
hole, makes a, in or through	*phautté*
hole in the ground	*twîn*
hook	*jeiʔ*
hooks	*cheitté*
horn	*hûn*
horse	*myîn*
hospital	*shêiyóun*
hot, is	*púdé*
hot, feels	*ʔaitté*
hot tasting, is	*satté*
hot season	*nwéi ʔùdù*
hotel	*hóté*
hour	*náyí*
half an hour	*náyíweʔ*
house	*ʔéin*

house of representatives	*ʔauʔ hluttó*
how?	*bènélê: bélóulê*
how	*bélóu*
how much	*bélauʔ*
hundred	*yá*
hundred thousand	*θêin*
hundred rupee note	*tayádán sekkú*
hungry, is	*shádé; wûn shádé*
hunter	*mousshôu*
hurry, is in a	*lôdé; ʔayêi cîdé*
husband	*lín*
I	*cúndó; couʔ*
I (woman speaking)	*cummà*
immediately	*checchîn; youʔ tayeʔ*
inch	*lemmà*
India	*kalabyéi; ʔíndìyà* (also *ʔíndrìyà*)
Indian	*kalâ*
indication	*ʔayeiʔʔachí*
indiscriminate (not choosing)	*maywêi*
indulges in	*laiʔ sâdé*
infantry	*kôundaʔ*
ingenuity, with perverted	*cánján phámbán*

ink	*hmín*
instructions, gives	*hmádé; hmá thâdé*
instructs	*hmádé; θíndé*
intends	*cán sídé*
interested, is	*seiʔ pádé*
interior	*ʔathê*
intermediate space	*ʔacâ*
interpreter	*zagabyán*
interstice	*ʔacâ*
investigates	*sitté; sisshêidé*
invites	*pheitté*
iron	*mîbú; θán*
ivory	*shínzwé*
iron, flat	*mîbú*
irons	*mîbú taitté*
irrigated rice field	*lé*
is it so?	*houllâ* (=*houθθalâ*)
new, is new	*θitté*
it	*θú*
jacket	*ʔêinjí*
jade	*caussêin*
jail	*gaʔ*
Japan	*jápán*
jar	*ʔôu*
joins	*shetté*
journey	*khayî*
joyful, is	*šwíndé*

Jubilee Hall	*júbalíhô*
Jubilee Hall building	*júbalíhô yóunjî*
judge	*tayâ θajî; dáin*
judge of the criminal court	*yázawuʔ tayâ θajî*
jungle	*tô*
jungle, edge of the	*tôzaʔ*
jurisdiction	*sháin-yá*
jurisdiction, has	*sháindé*
just now	*khùdíŋgàbê*
Kachin	*kachín*
Karen	*kayín*
kind of people	*lúmyôu*
kitchen	*mîbóugân; mîbóujáun*
knee	*dû*
knife	*dâ*
knowledge	*pyínnyá*
knows	*θìdé*
laces, shoe	*phanaccôu*
lack	*ʔalóu*
lacking, is	*lóudé*
land, by	*kôunjâun*
landlord	*ʔéinšín; ʔèin šín*
land, a cultivated piece of (not irrigated)	*yá*
land revenue	*légún*
language	*zagâ; báðá*
large, is	*cîdé; cé wîndé*
last	*nausshôun*
late, is	*nauʔ càdé*
later (on)	*nauʔ, naukkóu*
launderer	*dóubí*
lavatory	*ʔéinðá*
law	*tayâ*
laziness	*ʔapyîn*
lazy, is	*pyîndé*
lead	*khê*
leader	*gâunzáun*
leads	*gâun sháundé*
leaf	*yweʔ*
learns	*θíndé*
leaves	*thâdé; thwetté*
leaves, before it	*mathwekkhín*
left, is	*cándé*
leg	*chéi; chéidauʔ*
lends (money)	*chîdé*
lends (property)	*hŋâdé*
length	*ʔašéi*
leopard	*caθiʔ*
letter-carrier	*sábòuðamâ*
liberty, is at	*lutté*
lies (at full length)	*hlêdé*
lies (in wait)	*châundé*

light	*ʔalîn*
light, is	*lîndé*
light, comes to	*pódé*
like this	*dílóu*
likes	*θabô càdé; caitté*
lives	*néidé*
living room	*ʔêgân*
lion	*cínðèi*
list	*sayîn*
little	*nênê (nêdé)*
little, is	*ŋédé*
little bit	*tasheiʔ*
living, makes a	*louʔ káin sâ θautté*
loads	*tíndé*
lodges	*têdé*
long (time)	*cájá*
long (distance), is	*šéidé*
long (in time), is	*cádé*
looks after, (takes care of)	*cì šùdé*
looks (at)	*cìdé*
looks attentively	*cì šùdé*
loom	*yekkânzîn*
loose, is	*cháundé*
loosens	*phyoutté; pyéidé; phyéidé*
loses	*šôundé*
lost, is	*pyautté*
lot	*mê*
lottery	*thí*
loud (of a voice)	*cédé*
loud, fairly	*khaccéjé*
loudly, loudness	*céjé*
lower floor	*ʔautthaʔ*
lower house	*ʔauʔ hluttó*
lower part	*ʔauʔ*
luck	*kán*
lucky, is; has good luck	*kán kâundé*
lures (with bait)	*hmyâdé*
lurks	*châundé*
malaria, jungle-fever	*hŋepphyâ*
Malay	*pašû*
man	*yauccâ*
man, old	*lúʔóu*
man, young, unmarried	*lúbyóu*
manager	*mánéijá*
manages	*ʔouʔ choutté*
Mandalay (City of)	*mândalêi*
mango	*θayeθθî*
manner	*thôunzán*
manual art	*lephmù pyínnyá*
many, is	*myâdé*
many	*ʔamyâ*

many, not; is few	*nêdé*
mark	*ˀayeiˀˀachí*
mark made by stamping a seal	*tazeiˀ*
market	*zêi*
married, gets; marries	*ˀéindáun càdé*
mat	*phyá*
match	*pyáimbwê*
match	*mîjiˀ*
mattress	*mwèiyá*
meal, gives a	*cwêidé*
meal, evening	*nyàzá*
meal, morning	*manessá*
meaning	*ˀadeipbé*
measures	*tâindé*
medicine	*shêi*
medicine, takes	*shêi sâdé*
meets	*twèidé*
member of parliament	*ˀamaˀ; ˀamaccî*
mends	*phádé*
mental relief	*seiˀˀêi*
metal	*θán*
metals extracted from ore	*θattù*
midday	*nèilé*
mile	*máin*
milk	*nwândù*
mind, presence of	*θadì*
mine	*cundò; couˀ*
minute	*maniˀ*
mirror	*hmán*
Miss, Mrs.	*mà; dó*
Mister	*máun; kóu; ˀû*
moderate, is	*θeθθádé; phyêidé*
moment, instant	*khanà*
money	*paisshán; ŋwéi*
money order form	*mánní ˀódá pháun*
monkey	*myauˀ*
monkey wrench	*ganân lemmà*
morning	*maneˀ*
mountain	*táun*
mouth	*là*
monthly rent	*làgà*
more haste, worse speed	*ˀayín lóu, ˀahnêi phyiˀ*
more than	*ˀatheˀ*
mosquito	*chín*
mosquito netting	*chíndáun*
mother	*ˀaméi*
motor	*seˀ*
mouth	*bazaˀ*
moves	*pyâundé*
movie	*youššímbwê*
mows	*yeitté*

Mrs., Miss	*mà; dó*
much, is	*myâdé*
much not	*nênê* (*nêdé*)
mud	*šùn*
mud puddle	*šùmbweʔ*
mule	*lâ*
munitions	*lenneʔ*
my	*couʔ*, *cúndò*
my (woman speaking)	*cummà*
name	*námé*
nation	*náiŋgán; lúmyôu*
national of a foreign country	*náiŋgánjâðâ*
national of one's own country; native	*tâin-yînðâ*
native of a city	*myòuðâ*
native of a country	*pyéiðâ*
nature	*θabô*
navy	*yéidaʔ*
near, is	*nîdé*
neck	*lébîn*
need	*ʔalóu*
needed, is; needs	*lóudé*
needle	*ʔaʔ*
new (thing)	*ʔaθiʔ*
newspaper	*θadînzá*
New Light of Burma (name of a paper)	*myámmá ʔalîn*
New York	*nú yauʔ; nyû yauʔ*
night	*nyà*
night, last	*nyàgà*
night meal	*nyàzá*
nine	*kôu*
noise	*ʔaθán*
noise, horn	*hûn hmouθθán*
nom de plume	*ʔateiʔ*
noon	*nèilé*
north	*myauʔ*
nose	*hná* (*hnakhâun*)
nothing, for	*ʔalagâ*
now	*ʔakhù; ʔagù*
now, right	*ʔakhùhmàbê*
now, up to	*ʔakhùdetthì*
nothing	*bámà; báhmà*
nowhere, to	*bégóumà; bégóuhmà*
number	*námbaʔ*
numeral	*ganân*
oars	*hléideʔ; hléi teʔ*
object, thing	*pyissî*
obliges	*cêizû pyùdé*
obtains	*yàdé*
ocean	*θamoutdayá*

occupation	*ʔalouʔ ʔakáin*
office	*ʔayá*
army officer	*sipbóu*
often	*macámacá*
oil	*shí*
oil, motor	*sesshí*
old, is	*ʔóudé; hâundé*
old fellow	*kwé*
old (thing)	*ʔahâun*
once	*takhauʔ*
one's self	*kòuhá kóu*
oneself	*kóudáin*
onion	*ceθθún*
only once	*takhùðá*
opener	*phaussayá*
opening	*ʔapauʔ*
opens	*phwìndé; hàdé; pautté*
opinion	*seiʔ ʔathín*
opinion, arrives at an	*θabô yàde*
order	*ʔamèin*
order, gives an	*ʔaméin chàdé; hmá thâdé*
order, puts in	*pyíndé*
orders	*símándé; ʔamèin chàdé; hmá thâdé*
other	*dì pyín; tachâ*
outside (of)	*ʔapyín*
overtakes	*hmídé*
ox	*nwâ*
pack	*bû*
paddle (of a canoe or boat)	*hléideʔ; hléi teʔ*
paddy	*sabâ*
pagoda	*phayâ*
pain, is in	*nádé*
pain	*ʔaná; ʔakaiʔ*
painted	*yéi shwê thâdé*
painter	*pají shayá*
paints	*pají yêidé*
pair	*ʔasóun*
palace	*nândó*
pan	*déʔôu; ʔôu*
pants	*bâumbí*
paper	*sekkú*
parents	*mìbàmyâ*
park	*pânján*
parliament	*hluttó*
party	*pátí*
patches	*phádé*
path	*lânjâun*
patient	*lúná*
pattern	*póun*
peanuts	*myéibê*
pen	*kaláundán*

pencil	*khệdán*
peppers	*ŋayouʔ*
performs work	*louʔ káindé*
perpendicular	*mattaʔ*
person	*lú*
person, sick	*lúná*
person of rank	*ʔamaʔ; ʔamaccî*
photograph	*dappóun*
photograph, takes a	*dappóun yaitté*
picks up, collects	*kautté*
picnic	*pyóbwêzá*
picture	*kâ*
pie, one	*tabáin*
pierced, is; pierces	*pautté*
pillow	*gâunʔóun*
pillow slip	*gâun ʔôunzuʔ*
pit	*twîn*
place	*néiyá; ʔayá*
place to sleep	*ʔeipphòu néiyá*
places	*thâdé*
places upon	*tíndé*
plan	*póun*
plans	*seiʔ kûdé*
plants	*pyôudé; saiʔ káindé; saiʔ pyôudé; saitté*
plate, flat	*pagámbyâ*
platform	*phalepphâun*
plays	*kazâdé*
plays (at certain games of chance)	*thôudé*
please	*tasheiʔ*
plentiful, is	*pôdé*
pliers, tongs	*hnyaʔ*
ploughs	*thúndé*
pocket	*ʔeiʔ*
pocket knife	*mâunjadâ*
points out	*pyàdé*
policeman	*pyátá*
ponders	*twêi cautté; twêidé*
population	*lúʔ ûyéi*
pork	*weθθâ*
porter's fee	*kúlígà*
position	*ʔayá*
post	*táin*
postman	*sábòuðamâ*
post office	*sádaiʔ*
pot	*ʔôu*
pot, glazed	*sìnʔôu*
pot, large iron	*déʔôu*
praises	*chîmûndé*
precedent	*thôunzán*
precious, is	*ʔaphôu tándé*
precision, with	*θéiðéi chájá*
premier	*nân-yîn wúnjîjouʔ*
presses	*mîbú taitté*
prescription	*shêizá*

present (gift)	*lessuʔ*
pretty, is	*hlàdé*
pretty, fairly	*tódó*
price	*zêi; ʔaphôu*
prior time	*ʔayín*
prize	*shù*
prize money	*shùŋwéi*
proclaimed, publicly	*có-nyádé*
Prome (City of Prome)	*pyéi myòu*
promulgates	*có-nyádé*
property tax	*légún*
proprietor	*sháinšín (shàin šín)*
propriety	*ʔéindayéi*
pulls	*shwêdé*
pulse, feels the	*θwêi sândé*
pungent	*satté*
puts	*thâdé*
puts down	*chàdé*
puts in	*tatté; θwîndé; thèdé*
puts into, through	*sutté*
puts on (a turban)	*pâundé*
puts on (around)	*sutté*
puts out of the way	*hlwêdé*
quarter	*maʔ; ʔaseiʔ; tamaʔ; néiyaʔ*
quinine	*kwínáin*

race	*pyáimbwê*
race, boat	*hléibwê*
raft	*pháun*
rag	*ʔawussouʔ*
railroad train	*mîyathâ*
railway car	*twê*
rains (it)	*môu ywádé*
rainy season	*môu ʔakhá*
raised up, is	*myautté*
raises up, elevates (flatters)	*hmyautté*
Rangoon	*yáŋgóun*
rashly	*ʔayân*
rattan	*céin*
ravine	*jauʔ*
reaches (attains to)	*hmídé*
reads	*phatté*
ready	*ʔashínðìn*
real	*ʔasiʔ*
reaps	*yeitté*
reason, for that	*dájàun*
reason, so that's the	*dájàummòu*
recovers	*θeθθádé*
recuperates	*ʔâ šì ládé*
red, is	*nídé*
red, (color)	*ʔaní*
referee	*dáin*
reflects	*twêidé*

regatta	*hléibwê*
register	*sayîn*
rejoices	*šwíndé; wûn myautté; wûn θádé*
relatives	*shwéimyôu*
religion	*báðá*
relish	*chóu chín*
relishes	*méindé*
remains	*néidé; yatté; cándé*
remains for a while	*têdé*
remembers	*hmammìdé*
rent (torn)	*soutté*
repair	*pyíndé*
reporter, newspaper	*θadîndau?*
representation	*?ayou?*
resolves	*θabô thâdé*
restaurant	*thamînzáin*
rest station	*tê sakhân*
rests	*nâdé*
returns	*pyándé*
reward	*shù*
rice, cooked	*thamîn*
rice, husked	*shán*
rickshaw	*lánchâ*
rides	*sîdé*
right	*?ahmán*
right away	*checchîn*
right side	*nyábe?*
right, that's	*houtté; houkkè*
rivalry, engages in	*pyáindé*
river	*myi?*
road	*lânjâun; lân*
road one travels often	*θwâ néijà lá néijà lân*
roams	*lédé*
robbery (case of)	*damyàhmù*
rock	*cau?*
rocks, ledge of	*causshául*
room	*?akhân*
rope	*côu*
rough, is	*cândé*
round, is	*lôundé*
round (thing)	*?alôun*
rubber tube	*yóbá cu?*
ruby	*badamyâ*
rug	*kózô*
ruined, is	*pyetté; pyessîdé*
rules, governs	*?ou? choutté*
runs	*pyêidé*
rupee one	*taja?*
Russian	*yúšà*
sack	*?ei?*
sailcloth	*ywetthé*
sailor	*θîmbôðâ*
salad	*leθθou?*

salary	*làgà*
sand	*θê*
savory	*chóu chín*
saw	*hlwà*
saw mill	*hlwàzeˀ*
says	*pyôdé; shóudé*
saying goes, as the	*shóuðalóu*
said, but you	*shóu*
scar	*dán-yá; ˀaná*
scatters	*cêdé*
school	*câun*
science	*pyínnyá*
scrapes	*pûndé*
scream, a	*ˀóðán*
screams	*ˀódé*
screw	*weˀˀú*
screw driver	*weˀˀúhlè*
sculptor	*pabù shayá*
sculptures	*thùdé*
sea	*pínlé*
searches for	*šádé*
season of the year	*ˀùdù*
second	*dùtìyà*
second class	*dùtìyàdân*
seed	*myôuzèi*
sees	*myíndé*
selects	*ywêidé*
sells	*yâundé*
senate	*ˀatheˀ hluttó*
sesasum	*hnân*
session	*sheššín*
sets	*saitté*
sets afloat	*hmyôdé*
sets (a time)	*chêindé*
sets out	*saiˀ pyôudé*
sets up, in an upright position	*tháundé*
settled, in opinion, is	*θabô càdé*
settles	*shôun phyatté*
sews (up)	*choutté*
shade, shadow; hint	*ˀayeiˀ*
shallow, is	*téindé*
Shan people, the	*šân lúmyôu*
shaves	*yeitté*
she, he, it	*θú*
shed	*yóun*
sheet of paper	*sáyweˀ*
shirt	*ˀêinjí; šaˀˀêinjí; šaˀ*
short-sleeved shirt	*šallettóu*
shoe	*phanaˀ*
shoemaker	*phanaˀ chouθθamâ*
shoots	*pyitté*
shop	*sháin*
short, is	*tóudé*

short cut — *phyallân*
shorts — *bâumbídóu; chwêigán bâumbí*
shout, a — *ˀóðán*
shows — *pyàdé; tín pyàdé*
shrimp (salad) — *bazún (leθθouˀ)*
shuns — *šáundé*
shut in (as in the mouth) — *ŋóundé*
Siamese — *yôudayâ*
side — *pheˀ; nabêi*
side, that — *hóu bekkân*
sign — *ˀayeiˀ; ˀayeiˀ ˀachí*
sign post — *hmattáin*
signal — *ˀacheˀ*
signal, gunshot — *θanaˀ tacheˀ*
silk — *pôu*
silk cloth — *pôu thé*
silver — *ŋwéi*
sings a song — *tachîn shóudé*
sink, causes to; sinks — *hnitté*
sir — *ˀû; khímbyá*
sir (woman speaking) — *šín*
sister, older — *ˀamà*
sister, younger — *nyímà*
sits — *tháindé*
six — *chauˀ*
sketched, has — *yéi shwê thâdé*
skilled person, in some work — *θamâ*
skirt worn by both men and women — *lóunjí*
sleeps well — *ˀeillòu pyódé; ˀeiˀ pyódé*
slow, is — *phyêidé*
slowly — *hnêihnêi (hnêidé); phyêibyêi (phyêidé) taphyêibyêi; ˀêiˀêi shêizêi*
slowly and accurately — *phyêibyêi hmámhmán*
slowness — *ˀahnêi*
small, is — *ŋédé*
smokes — *θautté*
snake — *mwéi*
snow — *hnîŋgê*
soaks — *séindé; yéi séindé*
soap — *shappyá*
soak, puts into water to — *yéi séindé*
sock — *chéizuˀ; chéiˀeiˀ*
soil — *myéi*
soldier — *siθθâ*
some — *tachòu*
sometimes — *takhá taléi*
son — *θâ*
song — *tachîn*
sons and daughters — *θâ θamî (θâðamî)*

sore	*ʔaná; dán-yá*
sound (noise)	*ʔaθán*
sound of shouting	*ʔóðán*
sound of speech	*pyôðán*
soup	*hînjóu*
sour, is	*chíndé*
south	*táun*
southeast (side)	*ʔašèi táum(beʔ)*
sows	*cêdé*
spare	*ʔapóu*
speaks	*pyôdé; shóudé*
spectacles	*myephmán*
speech	*zagâ*
speed	*myámmyán*
splits	*seitté; khwêdé*
spoon	*zûn*
spread (bed), sheet	*ʔeiyyágîn*
spreads	*khîndé*
spreads (as news)	*có-nyádé*
sleeps	*ʔeitté*
slices	*hlîdé*
stage, one	*tashìn*
stakes a wager	*lâundé*
stamp, postage	*tazeiʔ gâun*
stands	*yatté*
start	*ʔasà*
starts	*sàdé*
state	*né*
station	*sakhân*
station, railroad	*mîyathâ búdáyóun*
steamer	*θîmbô*
steamer dock	*θîmbôzeiʔ*
steeps	*séindé*
stick	*douʔ*
stiffness	*ʔanyâun*
stock in trade	*ʔayîn*
stocking	*chéizuʔ; chéiʔeiʔ*
stone	*cauʔ*
stops	*yatté*
stops to rest	*nâdé*
store	*sháin*
story	*wutthù*
straight, is	*phyàundé; tèdé*
straight	*tèdè*
straight ahead	*šèi tèdè*
strange, is	*thûnzândé*
strange (things)	*ʔathûdû shânzân; ʔatthû ʔashân*
stream	*châun*
street	*lân*
street car	*dayyathâ*
strength	*ʔâ*
strikes (against)	*taitté*
strikes (as a clock)	*thôudé*
strikes, by a side or back blow	*khatté*

string *côu*
strip of bamboo, used in binding things together *hnî*
stripe *ˀasîn*
stroke *ˀacheˀ*
strong, is *ˀâ šìdé*
student *câunðâ*
studies *sá cìdé; θíndé*
sub-divisional officer *wúndauˀ*
submerges, causes to sink *hmyoutté*
sufficient, is *tándé; tódé; lóunlautté; lautté*
suitable, is *tódé*
sun *néi*
Sun, The; name of a newspaper *θúrìyà*
sunlight *néiyáun*
surgery, does *khwê seiˀ phyaˀ kùdé*
surprise, interjection denoting *ˀamélêi*
surprised *ˀàndé; ˀànˀôdé*
surrounds *wâindé*
suspends from the shoulder *lwédé*
sweat *chwêi*
sweet, is *chóudé*
sweetheart *yîzâ*
swims *yéi kûdé*

table *sabwê*
tailor *ˀacchouθθamâ*
takes, receives, accepts, experiences *khándé*
takes off *chutté*
takes out *thoutté*
tall *myìndé*
tattoos *shêi thôudé*
tax, head; tax, poll *lúgún*
tax receipts *ˀakhún; ˀakhúndóŋwéi*
taxes *ˀakhún*
taxi *tassí* or [*taksí*]
tea *lapheyyéi*
teacher *shayá*
teaches *θíndé*
teak *cûnðiˀ*
tears *shoutté*
telegram, sends a *cêinân yaitté; θánjôu yaitté*
telephone *télíphóun*
telephone call, makes a *télíphóun shetté*
temperature (body) *ˀapú chéin*
ten- *shé-*
ten thousand *θâun*
tent *ywetthéyóun*

Thai	*yôudayâ*
thank you	*cêizû tímbádé*
that	*hóu*
thermometer	*ˀapúdâin*
thigh	*páun*
thing	*pyissî*
thinks	*sînzâdé; thíndé; cán sídé*
third	*tatìyà*
third class	*tatìyàdân*
thirsty, is	*yéi ŋatté*
this	*dí*
this (that has been mentioned)	*ˀêdí; ˀêdá*
this (thing)	*díhá; dá*
this much	*dílauˀ*
this much, even	*dílauttáun*
thought	*seiˀˀathín*
thousand	*tháun*
thread	*ˀacchí*
thread, spool of	*ˀacchílôun*
three	*θôun*
throws about	*cêdé*
throws down	*chàdé*
throws down (from an erect position)	*hlêdé*
throws into or upon	*phòudé*
thrusts at	*thôudé*
thumb	*lemmà*
ticket	*lephmaˀ*
tiger	*câ*
tight, is	*lóundé*
time	*ˀachéin; ˀakhauˀ; ˀakhá*
time and again	*khanà khanà*
time of arrival	*yaukkhá*
time of swimming	*kûgá*
tin	*θámbyú*
tin can	*θámbôun*
tiny	*ŋéŋégalêi*
tired, is; tiresome, is	*pímbândé*
to, up	*ˀathì*
tobacco	*shêi*
today	*dí nèi; díganèi; ganèi*
toilet	*ˀéinðá*
tomorrow	*nepphán (= nepphyíŋgá)*
too (much)	*θeiˀ; θeillê*
tooth	*θwâ*
tooth (eye)	*ˀaswé*
torn, is	*soutté*
touches	*thìdé*
towel, face	*myethnaθouppawá*
township officer	*myòu ˀouˀ*
transfers to another	*hlwê ˀatté*
transplants (rice)	*kauˀ saitté*
travel	*ˀaθwâ ˀalá*
traveller	*khayîðé*

travels	*khayî θwâdé*
treasury	*ŋwéidaiʔ*
treats (medically)	*kùdé*
tree	*θippín; ʔapín;*
tries	*sândé*
trolley	*dayyathâ*
trouble, goes to a lot of	*pímbân khándé*
trousers	*bâumbí*
tub	*síbâin*
tumbler (water glass)	*pháŋgweʔ*
turban	*gâumbâun*
turns around	*hlèdé; lédé*
tusk	*ʔaswé*
twelve annas	*θôummaʔ*
twenty	*hnashé*
two	*hniʔ*
umbrella	*thî*
umpire	*dáin; dáin lújî*
uncle	*ʔû*
underpants	*chwêigán bâumbí*
undershirt	*chwêigán ʔêinjí*
understands	*nâ lédé*
unfolds	*phyéidé*
unhurriedly	*phyêibyêi; taphyêibyêi; ʔêiʔei shêizêi*
unites	*shetté*
unloosed (by severing of some part), is	*pyoutté*
unoccupied, is	*ʔâdé*
unrestrained	*lutté*
unrolls	*phyéidé*
unties	*pyéidé; phyoutté*
unusual	*thûzândé*
unusual (things)	*ʔathûdû shânzân*
upper floor	*ʔapódaʔ*
upper house	*ʔatheʔ hluttó*
upper part	*ʔapó*
upright, is	*matté*
upright posture, in an	*mattaʔ*
urgent, is	*ʔayêi cîdé*
used up, is	*kóundé*
useless	*ʔalagâ; ʔaθôun macàbû*
uses	*θôundé*
vacant	*ʔâdé*
valuable, is	*ʔaphôu tándé*
value, what	*bélauttán*
very (much)	*θeiʔ; ʔímmatán*
village	*ywá*
village, country	*tôywá*
violent, is	*pyîndé*

violent wind *léibyîn*
visitor *ˀêðé*
votes *mê ywêi kautté*

wage *làgà*
wager *ˀalâun*
wagon *hlê*
waits *sàundé*
walks *lân šautté*
walks around *šauˀ lédé*
wanders *lédé*
want *ˀalóu*
wanting, is *lóudé*
washes with water *shêidé*
washes (clothes, hair) *šódé*
watch, timepiece *náyí*
watch, pocket *ˀeiˀ sháun náyí*
water *yéi*
water, cold *yéiˀêi*
water, drinking *θauyyéi*
water, shallow *yéidéin*
water, warm *yéinwêi*
waterfall *yéi tagûn*
watertight, is *lóundé*
way, custom *thôunzán*
we *couttòu; cúndódòu; dòu*
wears (clothes, etc.) *wutté*
wears (shoes) *sîdé*
weaves *yetté*
weaving *yekkân*
weeks *ˀapaˀ*
weighs *chéindé*
well *yéidwîn; kâuŋgâun*
well, is *májádé; mádé*
well being *majâun chájâun*
well, state of being *mámá chájá*
what *bá*
what (indefinite) *bámyâ*
wheel *bêin*
when *bédò*
which *bé*
whiskey *ˀayeˀ*
white *phyúdé*
who *badú; baðú; béðú*
whole, the *ˀakóun*
wife *mêimmà*
wind *léi*
window *padîmbauˀ*
wine *θabyiyyéi*
winnings *ˀanáin*
wins *náindé*
wide, is *cédé*
wire, electric *daccôu*
with, is *pádé*
with, together *ˀatú; ˀatúdú*

woman	*mêimmà*
woman transplanter (of paddy)	*kauˀ saimmà*
wonders	*ˀànˀôdé; ˀanáin*
wood	*θiθθâ*
word	*zagâ*
work	*ˀalouˀ*
works	*loutté; louˀ káindé*
work and eat	*louˀ káin sâ θautté*
world	*kabá*
worried	*sôuyéindé*
worships	*kôugwédé*
wound	*dán-yá; ˀaná*
wraps around	*patté*

wrist watch	*leppaˀ náyí*
writes	*yêidé*
writing, a	*sá*
wrong, is; goes wrong	*lwêdé*
year	*hniˀ*
yellow	*wádé*
yesterday	*manèigà*
you	*khímbyâ*
young, is	*pyóudé*
zinc	*θuˀ*
zoo	*tareisshán-yóun*

BURMESE-ENGLISH WORD LIST

UNITS 1–30

ʔâ	strength
ʔaʔ	needle
ʔacâ	intermediate space, interstice
ʔacâun	circumstance, cause, fact
ʔacchí	thread
ʔacchílôun	spool of thread
ʔacchouθθamâ	tailor
ʔacheʔ	signal, blow, stroke
ʔachéin	time
ʔacôu ʔacâun	the good and the bad
ʔâdé	is free, unoccupied, vacant
ʔadeipbé	meaning
ʔadó	aunt
ʔahâun	old thing
ʔahmán	right, for sure
ʔahmù	business, affair, case in law
ʔahnêi (hnêidé)	slowness
ʔaitté	feels hot
ʔakaiʔ (kaitté)	ache; bite
ʔakauʔ (kautté)	crook, bend
ʔakâunzôun	best
ʔakâunzôumbê	the very best
ʔakhá	time
ʔakhân	room
ʔakhù	now
ʔakhùdetthì	up to now, already, still
ʔakhùdò	as for now
ʔakhùhmàbê	right now
ʔakhún	revenue accruing from assessments, taxes
ʔakhúndóŋwéi	tax receipts
ʔakóu	older brother
ʔákóun	the whole, all
ʔakwèi (kwèidé)	curve, corner, bend
ʔalá (ládé)	a coming
ʔalagâ	useless, to no purpose; for nothing
ʔalâun (lâundé)	bet, wager
ʔalîn (lîndé)	light
ʔalóu	want, lack, desire, need
ʔalouʔ (loutté)	work
ʔalouʔ ʔakáin	occupation
ʔalôun (lôundé)	round thing
ʔâlôun	all
ʔâlôumbâun	altogether

ʔamà	older sister
ʔamaʔ	person of rank, member of parliament
ʔàmbwê	exposition, exhibition
ʔamê	game, flesh of beasts
ʔamêðâ	beef
ʔamêðâhîn	beef curry
ʔaméi	mother
ʔamèin	order, command
ʔamèin chàdé	gives an order
ʔaméiyìkán	American
ʔamélêi	interjection denoting surprise
ʔamyâ	much, many
ʔamyâ ʔâ phyìn	in most cases, generally
ʔamyê	always
ʔamyôuðâ	citizens, fellow countryman
ʔamyôuzóun	all kinds
ʔâ nádé	is deterred by fear of offending
ʔaná (nádé)	pain, disease, sore
ʔanáin (náindé)	winnings
ʔanauʔ	the west
ʔândé	pays change
ʔàndé	wonders
ʔaneʔ (netté)	black
ʔaní (nídé)	red color
ʔànʔôdé	wonders, is amazing, surprised
ʔanyâun	ache, stiffness
ʔanyóu (nyóudé)	brown
ʔánzwê	drawer
ʔapaʔ	circuit, a round
ʔapauʔ	opening, aperture, hole
ʔaphéi	father
ʔaphôu	price
ʔaphôu tándé	is of worth, precious, valuable
ʔaphyâ phyâjîn	as soon as one gets sick
ʔaphyâ phyasshêi (ʔaphyâzêi)	fever medicine
ʔaphyâzêi (ʔaphyâ phyasshêi)	fever medicine
ʔaphyú	white
ʔapín	tree
ʔapó	upper part
ʔapódaʔ	upper floor
ʔapóu (póudé)	excess, spare
ʔappauʔ	eye of a needle
ʔapú (púdé)	heat
ʔapú chéin	temperature
ʔapúdâin	thermometer
ʔapyá (pyádé)	blue
ʔapyín	outside, outside (of), besides
ʔapyîn (pyîndé)	boredom, laziness
ʔasà (sàdé)	beginning, start
ʔasâ ʔaθauʔ (sâdé θautté)	food and drink

ʔasháun (sháundé).	building
ʔashínðìn	ready
ʔasiʔ (sitté)	real, genuine
ʔasîn	stripe
ʔaseiʔ	a quarter, twenty-five
ʔasêin (sêindé)	green
ʔashín	color, appearance, form
ʔasín mapyaʔ	continually, everlastingly, without cessation
ʔasóun (sóundé)	complete assortment, a pair, an even number
ʔasôuyà	government
ʔaswé	tusk, fang, eyetooth
ʔašéi (šéidé)	length
ʔašèi	the east
ʔašèi táumbeʔ	south-east (side)
ʔâ šìdé	recuperates
ʔatâin	according to, in accordance with
ʔatân	class
ʔateiʔ	alias, nom de plume
ʔathê	interior, inner part
ʔatheʔ	more than, in comparison, upper part
ʔatheʔ bamá pyéi	Upper Burma
ʔatheʔ hluttó	senate, upper house
ʔathì (thìdé)	up to
ʔathû (thûdé)	difference
ʔathû ʔashân (thûzândé)	something special, strange
ʔathûdû shânzân	strange, unusual things
ʔatú (túdé)	together with
ʔatúdú	similar, same, together with
ʔatweʔ (twetté)	account, behalf, (because)
ʔaθán	sound, noise
ʔaθeʔ	age
ʔaθî	fruit
ʔaθiʔ (θitté)	new
ʔaθôun (θôundé)	use
ʔaθwâ ʔalá (θwâdé ládé)	going and coming, travel
ʔauʔ	lower part, space under
ʔáuʔ bamá pyéi	Lower Burma
ʔauʔ hluttó	house of representatives, lower house
ʔautthaʔ	lower floor
ʔawá (wádé)	yellow
ʔawuʔ (wutté)	garment
ʔawussháin	clothing store
ʔawussouʔ	piece of cloth, rag
ʔayá	position, office
ʔayà	according to
ʔayaʔ	place
ʔayân	rashly
ʔayauʔ (yautté)	arrival
ʔayáun	color, brightness

ʔayeʔ	whiskey
ʔayeiʔ	shade, shadow
ʔayêi	business, affair
ʔayeiʔʔachí	sign, mark, indication
ʔayêibáin	district commissioner
ʔayêi cîdé	is busy, is in a hurry, is urgent
ʔayín	first, prior time
ʔayín hnikkà	last year
ʔayín lóu ʔahnêi phyiʔ	more haste worse speed
ʔayín lóudé	is in a hurry, is urgent
ʔâyín	if free, unoccupied
ʔayíŋgà	formerly
ʔayîn	capital, stock in trade
ʔayouʔ	representation, figure, wage
bá	what
badamyâ	ruby
badú (baðú)	who
badú mashóu	anybody
bámà	nothing
bamálóu	Burmese fashion
bamá lúmyôudòu	the Burmese people
bámyâ	what (indefinite)
bándaiʔ	bank
bándáyêi wúnjîjouʔ	finance minister
bá phyillòulê	why?
báðá	religion, language
bâumbí	pants, trousers
bâumbídóu	shorts
bayíŋgán	governor
bazaʔ	mouth
bazún leθθouʔ	shrimp salad
bé	which
bé ʔakhá mashóu	any time
bé . . . mashóu	any at all
bédò	when
bégóumà	to nowhere
bêin	wheel
bélauʔ	how much
bélauttán	what value, what denomination
bélóu	how, what fashion
bènélê	how?
bídóu	cupboard
bíyá	beer
bólôun	ball
bôun	bomb
bôun cêdé	drops bombs, bombs
boutdà báðá	Buddhism
búdáyóun	station
bû	pack, box
câ	tiger
cádé	is long in time
câdé	hears

càdé falls
càdé costs, comes to
caitté likes
cájá long (time)
cân floor
cándé remains, is left
cândé is rough
cánján phámbán with perverted ingenuity
cán sídé thinks, intends
caθiˀ leopard, cheetah
cauˀ stone, rock
câun school
câunðâ student
câun néibeˀ θaŋéjîn school friend
caussêin jade
causshúun ledge of rocks, large boulder
cautté fears, is afraid
cédé is wide, loud (of a voice)
cêdé scatters, throws about, sows
céin rattan
cêinân yaitté sends a telegram
ceitté crushes, grinds
cêizû pyùdé does a favor, obliges
cêizû tímbádé thank you
céjé loudness, loudly
ceˀ lephmaˀ check
ceθθún onions
céðî button

ceˀˀù egg (hen's)
cé wîndé is large, great
chàdé puts down, throws down
chán fence, enclosure
chândé is cold
chauˀ 6
châun stream, large brook
cháundé is loose, not tight
châundé lies in wait, lurks
châun shôudé coughs, has a cough
checchîn right away, immediately
chéi foot, leg
chéibyâ tip of the foot
chéidauˀ leg
chéiˀeiˀ sock
chéindé weighs
chêindé appoints, fixes, sets (a time)
cheitté hooks, catches on a hook
chéizuˀ (=*chéiˀeiˀ*) sock, stocking
cheˀ pyoutté (= *chetté*) cooks
chettá cooking
chetté cooks
chîdé lends, borrows (money)
chîmûndé praises
chín mosquito
chíndé is sour
chíndáun mosquito netting

chînlôun Burmese football (made of rattan), cane ball
chînwâin a game of Burmese football
chóu chín relish, savory
chóudé is sweet
chôudé (= *yéi chôudé*) bathes
chóundé covers (as with a blanket)
choutté sews, sews up
choutté has control over
chou? thâdé places in confinement, in custody
chutté takes off
chwêi sweat
chwêigán bâumbí underpants, shorts
chwêigán ?êinjí undershirt
cîdé is big
cìdé looks, looks at
cínðèi lion
cì šùdé looks attentively, looks after
códé fries
có-nyádé is proclaimed publicly, spreads (as news), promulgates
côu rope, cord, string
cou? I, mine
côudé breaks (crosswise)
couttòu 'we'
cúmmà I, my (woman speaking)
cúndó I
cûnðì? teak
cwê buffalo
cwêidé gives a meal, feeds

dá this (thing)
dâ knife
daccôu electric wire
dádò as for that
dáin umpire, judge, referee
dajàun for that reason
dájàummòu so that's the reason
dammî electric light
damyà dacoit, bandit
damyàhmù case of dacoitry, robbery
dán-yá wound, scar
dappóun photograph
dappóun yaitté takes a photograph
dasshí gasoline
dàθamà decimal
dayyathâ street car, trolley
dé?ôu large iron pot, pan
dí this
díhá this (thing)
dilau? this much
dilauttáun even this much
dílóu like this, this fashion

dìlóu shóuyínlê	even if that is the case
dí nèi	today
dì pyín	other, besides this
dó	aunt
dou?	stick
dòu bamá	we Burmans
dóubí	launderer
dû	knee
dùtìyà	second
dùtìyàdân	2nd class
?êdí	this (that has been mentioned)
?êðé	visitor, guest
?êgân	living room ('guest room')
?ei?	pocket, bag, sack
?êidé	is cool
?êi?êi	cool
?êi?êi shêizêi	slowly, unhurriedly
?êihmân	the fact that it is cold
?eillòu pyódé (*?ei? pyódé*)	sleeps well
?éimhmyáun	compass needle
?éin	house
?éin	a hand at cards
?éindáun càdé	marries, gets married
?éindayéi	propriety, dignity
?éinðá	toilet, lavatory
?êinjí	coat, jacket, shirt
?èinšín (or, *?éinšín*)	landlord
?eipphòu néiyá	place to sleep, bed
?ei? sháun náyí	pocket watch
?eitté	sleeps
?eiyyá	bed, sleeping place
?eiyyágîn	bed sheet, spread
ga?	jail
gálán	gallon
ganân	crab
ganân	numeral, numerical figure
ganân lemmà	monkey wrench
ganèi (= *dí ganéi*)	today
gâumbâun	headdress, turban
gâun	head
gâun?ôun	pillow
gâun?ôunzu?	pillow slip
gâun sháundé	leads, heads
gâunzáun	leader
hàdé	opens
háundé	barks
hâundé	is old
hè	Hey!
hîn	curry
hînðî hîn-ywe?	vegetables
hînjóu	soup

hlàdé	is pretty
hlàðâbê	is really pretty
hlèdé	turns around
hlê	cart, wagon
hlênè taitté	carts, conveys on a cart
hlêdé	lies at full length; throws down from an erect position
hléi	boat
hléibwê	boat race, regatta
hléide? (*hléi te?*)	oars
hlîdé	slices
hlódé	paddles (a canoe or boat)
hluttó	parliament
hlwà	saw
hlwàze?	saw mill
hlwêdé	puts out of the way, gives away
hlwê ?atté	disposes of, transfers to another
hmádé	instructs, gives instructions
hmâdé	is wrong, is in error
hmammìdé	remembers
hmán	window glass, mirror
hmándé	is correct
hmá thâdé	orders, gives orders or instructions
hmattáin	sign post
hmáundé	is dark
hmídé	reaches, attains to, overtakes
hmín	ink
hmín?ôu	bottle of ink
hmóundé	is dim (as the eye), is blurred
hmoutté	blows
hmyâdé	catches with bait, lures
hmyautté	raises up, elevates, (flatters)
hmyódé	looks forward to, expects, anticipates
hmyôdé	sets afloat
hmyoutté	submerges, causes to sink
hná (*hnakhâun*)	nose
hnân	sesamum
hnàndé	does thoroughly, completely
hnapa?	two weeks
hnashé	20
hnashè ŋâ	25
hná sîdé	has a cold in the nose
hnayá	200
hnaye?	two days
hnêihnêi (*hnêidé*)	slowly
hni?	2
hni?	year
hnî	strip of bamboo, used in binding things together
hnîŋgê	snow
hnitté	causes to sink, sinks

hni? hmyoutté	destroys by sinking	*kachín*	Kachin
hnya?	pliers, tongs	*kadín*	cot, couch, bedstead
hnyatté	cuts (as with scissors)	*káindé*	holds, takes hold of
hŋâdé	borrows, lends, rents, hires	*kaitté*	aches (also, bites)
hŋe?	bird	*kalâ*	Indian
hŋepphyâ	malaria, jungle-fever	*kalabyéi*	India
hóté	hotel	*kalatháin*	chair
hóu	that	*kaláundán*	pen
hóu bekkân	that side	*kán*	luck
houkkè	that's right	*kân*	bank of a river, lake, sea
houllâ (= *houθθalâ*)	is it so?	*kán kâundé*	is lucky, has good luck
houtté	that's right	*káphí*	coffee
hûn	horn	*katòbáyè*	excuse me
hûn hmouθθán	horn noise	*katté*	adheres to, is attached to (flatwise)
?ímmatán	very (much)	*kâundé*	is good
?índìyà (also *?índrìyà*)	India	*kâuŋgâun*	well
?îŋgalei?	English	*kau? saimmà*	woman transplanter (of paddy)
		kau? saitté	transplants (rice)
jápán	Japan	*kautté*	is crooked, not straight
jau?	ravine	*kautté*	picks up, collects
jei?	hook	*kayín*	Karen
júbalíhô	Jubilee Hall	*kazâdé*	plays
júbalíhô yóunjî	the Jubilee Hall building	*kê*	come on
		keissà	business
kâ	picture	*khaccéjé*	fairly loud
kabá	world	*khádâin*	every time

khâindé employs, asks to do
khalêi child, youngster (little)
khanà moment, instant
khanà khanà time and again
khánde takes, receives, accepts, experiences
khàndé appoints to an office
khariyyán báðá Christianity
khatté dips up, draws water
khatté strikes, by a side or back blow
khayî distance between 2 places, journey
khayîðé traveller
khayî θwâdé travels
khayîn fork
khê lead
khêdán pencil
khêdé is hard, hardened
khetté is hard, difficult, arduous
khímbyá sir
khímbyâ you
khîndé spreads
khódé calls
khoutté chops, hews, cuts
khwêi dog
khùdíŋgàbê just now
khwe? cup, bowl, anything of similar shape
khwêdé halves, divides into two parts, splits
khwê sei? phya? kùdé does surgery
kóu mister
kóu body
kóudáin oneself
kôu 9
kôugwédé worships
kòuhá kóu one's self
kóule? câmmáyêi health
kôunáyí mattîn 8:45
kôunda? army, infantry
kóundé is done, is used up
kôunjâun by land
kózô rug, carpet
kúdé helps
kûdé see *sei? kûdé, yéi kûdé*
kùdé treats (medically), gives medicine
kûgá time of swimming
kúlí coolie
kúlígà porter's fee
kú-nyídé helps, assists
kwé old fellow, my friend

kwèidé	bends around, is curved
kwínáin	quinine
là	month
lâ	mule
ládé	comes, came
làgà	monthly rent (or salary)
lai? sâdé	indulges in, complies with
laitté	follows, accompanies
lâmbyà	guide
lân	road, street
lânjâun	path, road
lân šautté	walks
lánchâ	rickshaw
lándán	London
lapheyyéi	tea
lâundé	stakes a wager, bets
lautté	is sufficient
lé	irrigated rice field
le?	hand, arm
lébîn	neck
lédé	wanders, roams, turns around
lêdé	changes, exchanges
légún	land revenue, property tax
léðamâ	farmer
léi	wind
lêi	4
léibyîn	violent wind
léida?	air force
léi thôudán	air-pump
léi thôudé	blows up with air
léiyímbyán	airplane
lekkáin pawá	handkerchief
lemmà	thumb, inch
lenne?	arms, munitions
lephma?	ticket
lephmù pyínnyá	craft, manual art
leppa? náyí	wrist watch
lessháun	present, gift
lessu?	ring
lethnei? dammî	flashlight
leθθou?	salad
lín	husband
lîndé	is light
lôdé	is in a hurry
lóudé	is lacking, wanting, needed
lou? káindé	works, performs work
lou? káin sâ θautté	work and eat, make a living
lóulóu	a little like (as if)
lóundé	is tight, as watertight
lôundé	is round
lóunjí	skirt worn by both men and women
lóunlautté	is sufficient
loutté	works, does

lú	person
lúbyóu	young, unmarried man
lúdwéijâ	the middle of a crowd
lúgún	head tax, poll tax
lújî	adult (big person)
lúmyôu	nation, kind of people
lúná	patient, sick person
lúndé	is or goes beyond, exceeds
lú?óu	old man
lutté	is at liberty, free, unrestrained
lú?ûyéi	population
lwédé	suspends from the shoulder
lwêdé	errs, goes wrong
lwé?ei?	bag that hangs from the shoulder
mà	Mrs. Miss
ma?	quarter
mádé	to be well
mahà meittòu	the Allies
májádé	is well, healthy
majâun chájâun	well being, state of health
mámá chájá	state of being well, healthy
macágín	before long
macámacá	often
máin	mile
manâbê	without resting
mândalêi	(City of) Mandalay
mane?	morning
manèigà	yesterday
mánéijá	manager
manessá	morning meal, 'breakfast'
mani?	minute
manîmawêi	not very far, near
mánní ?ódá pháun	money order form
mapyaukkhín	before it disappears, is lost
mathwekkhín	before it leaves
matò tashà	accident
matté	is upright, makes erect
matta?	in an upright posture, perpendicular
matwèi twèi?áun	until one finds
máun	Mister, brother
mâundé	drives (a vehicle)
mâunjadâ	pocket knife
maywêi	indiscriminate ('not choosing')
mê	lot, ballot
mêidé	asks
mèidé	forgets
mêimmà	woman, wife
méindé	relishes, enjoys
meisshwéi	friend
mê ywêi kautté	votes
mî	fire

mìbàmyâ parents
mîbóu fireplace, hearth
mîbóugân kitchen
mîbóujáun (= *mîbóugân*) kitchen
mîbú iron, flat iron
mîbú taitté irons, presses
mîji? match
mî pautté burns (a hole)
mî šòudé sets on fire
mîyathâ railroad train
mótókâ automobile
mótókâ hmyau? je? auto jack
mótókâ pyissî auto tools
môu ?akhá the rainy season
môu lóundé water-proof, rain proof
môu ?ùdù the rainy season
môu ywádé (it) rains
mousshei? beard
mousshôu hunter, guide
mwéi snake
mwêidé bears, brings up
mwèiyá mattress
myâdé is much, is many
myámmá (= ***bamá***) Burmese
myámmá ?alîn Name of a paper "The New Light of Burma"
myámmyán speed
myándé is fast
myau? monkey
myau? north
myautté is raised up, elevated
myéi earth, ground, soil
myéibê peanuts
myephmán eye glasses, spectacles
myessì eye (human)
myessì lédé is confused, befuddled
myethná face
myethnaθouppawá face towel
myi? river
myîn horse
myíndé sees
myìndé is high, tall
myîn-yathâ carriage
myòu city
myòu ?ou? township officer
myòuðâ native of a city
myôuzèi seed, seed grain

nabêi side
nâ ear
nádé is in pain
náiŋgán nation, country
náiŋgánjâ foreign country
náiŋgánjâðâ national of a foreign country
nâ kaitté ear aches

nâ lédé	understands
nâdé	stops to rest, rests
náindé	wins
námbaʔ	number
námé	name
nândó	palace
nân-yîn wúnjîjouʔ	premier
nauʔ	the space behind a thing
nauʔ	later (on)
nauʔ càdé	falls behind, is late
naukkà	behind, from behind
naukkóu	in the future
nausshôun	last, final
nauttwê	rear car
náyí	watch, hour
náyíweʔ	half an hour
né	district, state, country
nêdé	is few, not many
néi	sun
nèi	day (from sunrise to sunset)
néidé	lives, remains
néiʔêi	cool of the day
nèilé	noon, midday
néiyá	place
néiyaʔ	district, address
néiyáun	sunlight
nênê (*nêdé*)	little, not much
nepphán (= *nepphyíŋgá*)	tomorrow
nepphyíŋgá	tomorrow
netté	is deep
nídé	is red
nîdé	is near
nî kabâ	approximately
nu yauʔ	New York
nwâ	bull, ox, cow
nwânòu	milk
nwéi ʔakhá	hot season
nwéi ʔùdù	the hot season
nyà	night
nyábeʔ	right side
nyàgà	last night
nyànéi	afternoon
nyàzá	night meal 'dinner'
nyí	younger brother
nyíʔakóu máunhnama	brothers and sisters
nyímà	younger sister
nyîndé	disputes, disapproves
ŋâ	5
ŋâ	fish
ŋâhîn	fish curry
ŋâmaʔ	1R 4A
ŋâmû	½R, 8A.

ŋayou?	peppers, chilies
ŋâzé	50
ŋédé	is small, little
ŋéŋédôuŋgà	when I was little
ŋéŋégalêi	tiny, very small
ŋóundé	enclose, cover up, shut in (as in the mouth)
ŋwéi	silver, money
ŋwéidai?	treasury
?ódé	cries out, screams
?óðán	the sound of shouting, a shout, a scream
?ôu	pot, jar
?ou? choutté	has charge of, rules, manages
?óudé	is old, aged
?outthou?	hat, cap
pabù shayá	carver, sculptor
pádé	accompanies, is with
padîmbau?	window
pagámbyâ	flat plate, dish
pagánlôun	round bowl, cup
paisshán	money
pají shayá	painter
pají yêidé	paints
palîn	bottle
pân	flower
pânján	flower garden, park
pašû	Malay
pathamà	first
pathamàdân	first class
pátí	party
patté	wraps around
patté	goes around
páumbó	surface of the thigh
páummòun	bread
páun	thigh
pâundé	collects into one, puts on (a turban)
pautté	pierces, is pierced
péi	foot (measure)
pêidé	gives
peitté	is closed, closes
phádé	mends, patches
phalâ	metal cup or bowl
phaleppháun	platform
phán	glass
phana?	shoe
phana? chouθθamâ	shoemaker
phanaccôu	shoe laces
phândé	tries to catch, arrests
pháŋgwe?	drinking glass, tumbler
phatté	reads
pháun	raft
phaussayá	opener

phautté	makes a hole in or through
phayâ	pagoda
phayâbó	upper part of the pagoda
phe?	side
phê	playing cards
pheitté	invites
phêwâin	card game
phòudé	throws into or upon; fills up partially or entirely (as a pit)
phwìndé	opens
phyá	mat
phyâdé	has a fever, is feverish
phya? kùdé	amputates
phyallân	short cut
phyàundé	is straight
phyéidé	loosens, unrolls, unfolds, answers (a question)
phyêidé	is slow, gradual, easy, pleasant, moderate
phyêibyêi (*phyêidé*)	slowly, easily
phyêibyêi hmámhmán	slowly and accurately
phyiphmân	what really happens
phyisséi . . . phyisséi	either . . . or
phyitté	happens
phyi? θwâde	has come to be, has happened
phyoutté	loosens, unties
pîdé	finishes
pímbândé	is tired, fatigued; is tiresome
pímbân khándé	goes to a lot of trouble
pínlé	sea
pò	of course
pódé	appears, comes to light
pôdé	is plentiful, not scarce
pôu	silk
póu cîðâ	is really bigger
póudé	exceeds, is in excess
pòudé	conveys, conducts (to a person or a place)
póun	plan, design, pattern, form
pôun	container
pôundé	hides, conceals oneself
pôu thé	silk cloth
púdé	is hot
pûndé	abrades, bruises, scrapes
pwê	festival
pwêzâ	broker
pyàdé	shows, points out
pyàdai?	exhibition building
pyáimbwê	race, match, contest
pyáindé	engages in rivalry, competes

pyándé returns
pyátá policeman
pyatté is cut
pyâumbû corn
pyâundé changes place, moves
pyautté disappears, is lost
pyéi country
pyéidé loosens, unties, appeases
pyêidé runs
pyèidé is full
pyéiðâ native of a country
pyéi myòu Prome [City of Prome]
pyessîdé is ruined, destroyed
pyetté is ruined, destroyed
pyíndé repair, put in order
pyîndé is violent
pyîndé is bored, lazy
pyínnyá knowledge, art, science
pyínθiʔ French
pyissî object, article, thing
pyissîdéi articles, things
pyitté shoots
pyóbwêzá picnic
pyóbyó šwínšwín happiness, enjoyment
pyódé enjoys oneself, is glad
pyôdé to say, speak
pyôðalóu as you say
pyôðán sound of speech
pyô pyàdé explains
pyóudé is young, in the prime of life
pyôudé plants
pyoutté boils
pyoutté is unloosened by severing of some part
pyoutté is extinct
pyózayá kâundé is fun, 'is good for being happy'

sá a writing, something written
sabâ paddy
sábòuðamâ postman, letter-carrier
sabwê table
sá cìdé studies, compares
sádaiʔ post office
sâdé eats
sàdé starts, begins
sáʔeiʔ envelope
saiʔ káindé plants
saiʔ pyôudé sets out, plants
saitté sets, plants, erects
sakhân station
sáʔouʔ book
sândé tries, feels
satté is hot tasting, pungent
sáun blanket
sàundé waits

sá yêi thâdá	something which has been written and posted
sayîn	list, account, register
sáyweʔ	sheet of paper, form
seʔ	motor, engine
seiʔʔathín	opinion, thought, fancy
seiʔ chàdé	feels comfortable and easy in mind
seiʔʔêi	mental relief
seiʔ kûdé	figures out, plans
séin	diamond
séindé	soaks, steeps
seiʔ ŋédé	is depressed, disspirited, downcast, dejected
seiʔ pádé	is interested
seiʔ shôudé	is angry
seitté	splits, cuts lengthwise
sekkú	paper
sesshí	motor oil
shabín	hair of the head
shabín hnyassháin	barber shop
shabín hnyaθθamâ	barber
shádé	is hungry
sháin	shop, store
sháindé	has jurisdiction
shàin-šín (sháinšín)	proprietor
sháin-yá	jurisdiction
sháin-yá sháin-yá ʔalouʔ	each to his own work
shán	husked rice
shappyá	soap
shâun ʔakhá	the cold season
sháundé	carries, bears, wears
shâun ʔùdù	the cold season
shautté	builds, erects
shayá	teacher, doctor
shayámà	nurse
shayáwún	doctor
shé-	10-
shêi	medicine, tobacco, drug
shêi	tobacco
shêidé	to wash with water
shêileiʔ	cigar
shêi sâdé	takes medicine
shêi thôudé	tattoos
shêiyóun	hospital
shêizá	prescription
sheššín	session
shetté	connects, joins, unites
shí	oil
shín	elephant
shîndé	descends, goes down
shínzwé	ivory
shóu	but you said . . .
shóudá	expression

shóudé	speaks, says
shôundé	comes to an end, is finished; dies
shôun phyatté	decides, settles, adjudicates
shóuðalóu	as the saying goes
shoutté	tears
shù	reward, prize
shùŋwéi	prize money
shwêdé	pulls, draws, hauls
shwéimyôu	relatives
sí	drum, cask, barrel
síbâin	tub
sîdé	wears, rides
sígare?	cigarette
símándé	arranges, orders
síndé	is clean
sìn?ôu	glazed pot or jar
sînzâdé	considers, thinks, deliberates
sipbóu	army officer
sî shîndé	flows down
sisshêidé	examines, investigates
sitta?	army
sitta? sakhân	army encampment
sitté	examines, investigates
siθθâ	soldier
sóundé	is complete
soutté	is torn, rent
sôuyéindé	is concerned, worried
sôzô (sôdé)	early
sutté	puts on, into, through
ša?	shirt
šádé	searches for
šallettóu	short-sleeved shirt
šân lúmyôu	the Shan people
šau? lédé	walks around
šáundé	avoids, shuns
šèi	before, in front of
šéidé	is long
šèidwê	forward car
šèi tèdè	straight ahead
šìdé	exists
šikkâgóu	Chicago
šín	sir (woman speaking)
šódé	washes (clothes, hair)
šôundé	loses
šùdé	see *cì šùdé*
šùmbwe?	mud puddle
šùn	mud
šwéi	gold
šwéi tagóun phayâ	Shwe Dagou Pagoda
šwíndé	rejoices, is joyful
tabáin	1 pie
tabê	1 anna
tabêdán	1 anna denomination
tabyà	1 pice

tachâ other
tacha? 1 of something flat
tachâun 1 of something long and slender
tachîn song
tachîn shóudé sings a song
tachòu some
tadâ bridge
ta?éinzí a hand each
tagabau? door
tagwîn 1 (of circular things)
tai? brick building
taimmìdé hits (by accident, implying inadvertence)
táin post, column
tâindé compares, measures, estimates
táin ka? náyí wall clock
tâin pyéi country
tâin-yînðâ national of one's own country, native
taissí [or *taksí*] taxi
taitté hits, strikes, strikes against, drives against
taitté attack, as a band of dacoits
tai? khaitté fights against, attacks
taja? 1 rupee
takhá taléi sometimes
takhau? once, one time
takhaummà not once
takhù 1 unit
takhùðá only once
takhwe? 1 glass
tamáinlau? about a mile
tándé is fit, sufficient
tanèigà the other day
tanéilôun a whole day
taphe? 1 side
taphyêibyêi slowly, gradually
tareisshán animal
tareisshán-yóun zoo
tashei? a little bit, please
tashìn 1 step, one stage
tatìyà 3rd
tatìyàdân 3rd class
tatté puts in, fixes
ta?û 1 (of respected persons)
táumbó (*táun ?apó*) top of a mountain
táun mountain
táun south
táun chéiyîn foot of the mountain
tâundé asks for, demands
táunðú farmer
táunnabêi side of a mountain
tawe? one half
tayâ law

tayádán sekkú	100 rupee note
tayâ θajî	judge
tayeʔ	one day (24 hrs.)
tayouʔ	Chinese
tazáun	1 of written things
tazeiʔ	mark made by stamping a seal
tazeiʔ gâun	postage stamp
têdé	remains for a while, lodges
tèdè	straight
téindé	is shallow
télíphóun	telephone
télíphóun shetté	makes a telephone call
tê sakhân	rest station
tétté	climbs, ascends, advances, gains on
thâdé	puts, places, leaves
thàdé	arises, gets up
tháindé	sits
thamîn	cooked rice
thamînzáin	restaurant
thândé	carries (on the shoulder)
tháun	1,000
sháundé	sets up, in an upright position
tathé	1 of wearing apparel
thèdé	puts or places in
thí	lottery
thî	umbrella
thìdé	touches
thíndé	thinks
thôbaʔ	butter
thôudé	thrusts at, strikes (as a clock)
thôudé	plays at certain games of chance
thôunzán	custom, manner, way, precedent
thoutté	takes out
thûdé	is different, diverse
thùdé	carves, engraves, sculptures
thúndé	ploughs, harrows
thûzândé	is strange, unusual, odd
thwetté	leaves, departs
tíndé	loads, places upon
tín hmyautté	elects
tín pòudé	exports
tín pyàdé	exhibits, shows
tô	forest, jungle
tódé	is suitable, sufficient
tódé	is clever
tódó	fairly, pretty
tôneʔ	deep or extensive forest or jungle
tóudé	is short
tôywá	country village
tôzaʔ	edge of the jungle

tú	hammer
tûdé	digs
twê	railway car
twêi cautté	ponders, considers (implying doubt or uncertainty)
twêidé	ponders, reflects, considers
twèidé	finds, meets
twetté	calculate, compute
twîn	hole in the ground, pit
θâ	son
θabekkhá	the day after tomorrow
θabô	disposition, nature
θabô càdé	approves, likes, is settled in opinion
θabô thâdé	resolves, determines; considers
θabô túdé	are of one mind, agrees
θabô yàde	is of the opinion, arrives at an opinion
θabyiyyéi	wine
θadì	presence of mind, attention
θadì thâdé	is careful
θadîndau?	newspaper reporter
θadînzá	newspaper
θagáun sayîn	census
θajî	headman of a village
θamâ	one skilled in some work
θámbôun	tin can
θámbyú	tin
θamî	daughter
θamoutdayá	ocean
θán	iron, metal
θana?	gun, rifle
θana? tache?	gunshot signal, one shot
θánjôu yaitté	sends a telegram
θanéjîn	friend
θattù	metals extracted from ore
θâ θamî (*θâðamî*)	sons and daughters, family
θâun	10,000
θautté	drinks, smokes
θauyyéi	drinking water
θayeθθî	mango
θê	sand
θédé	carries from 1 place to another
θei?	very, too
θéidé	dies, is dead
θeillê	too, very much
θêin	100,000
θêinjî zêi	name of a market in Rangoon
θêin thí	The Burma State Lottery
θéi shôundé	dies
θeittò	very much
θéiðéi chájá	definitely, with precision

θeθθádé	is moderate, comfortable; recovers
θìdé	knows
θîmbô	steamer
θîmbôðâ	sailor
θîmbôzei?	steamer dock
θíndé	learns, studies; teaches
θippín	tree
θittá	box
θitté	is new
θittô	forest (timber)
θiθθâ	wood
θiθθî	fruit
θôumma?	12 annas
θôun	3
θôundâun	3,000
θôundé	uses
θôunzáundé	partakes of food (very polite)
θú	he, she, it
θu?	zinc
θúrìyà	name of a newspaper 'The Sun'
θwâ	tooth
θwâdé	goes, went
θwâ kaitté	tooth aches
θwâ néijà lá néijà lân	a road one travels often
θwêi	blood
θwêi sândé	feels the pulse
θwîndé	puts in
?û	sir, uncle
?ùdù	season of the year
wâ	bamboo
wâdô	forest (of bamboo)
wágûn	cotton
wâindé	surrounds, makes a circle
wâ pháun	bamboo raft
wédé	buys
wêidé	is distant
weθθâ	pork
weθθâhîn	pork curry
we??ú	screw
we??úhlè	screwdriver
wín ládé	enters, comes in
wíŋgà	entrance fee
wûn	belly
wúndau?	sub-divisional officer
wûn kaitté	has dysentery
wûn myautté	rejoices, is elated
wûn shádé	is hungry
wûn θádé	rejoices
wutté	wears, dresses
wutthù	story

yá	100
yá	a cultivated piece of ground (not irrigated)
yàdé	gets, obtains
yáŋgóun	Rangoon
yánðú	enemy
yathâ	car, carriage
yatté	stops, stands, bolts, remains
yáðamâ	farmer
yauccâ	man
yaukkhá	time of arrival
yâundé	sells
yautté	arrives
yázawuʔ	criminal case
yázawuʔ tayâ θajî	judge of criminal court
yeʔ	24 hr. day
yéi	water
yéibû	canteen, flask
yéi chôudé	bathes, takes a bath
yéi chôugân	bathroom
yéidaʔ	navy
yéidwîn	well
yeikkhanê	in the way of catching a glimpse of
yéi ŋatté	is thirsty
yêidé	writes
yéidéin	shallow water
yéiʔêi	cold water
yéi kûdé	swims
yéinwêi	warm water
yéi séindé	puts into water to soak, soaks
yéi shwê thâdé	has drawn, painted, sketched
yéi sîdé	current is strong, fast
yéi tagûn	waterfall
yeitté	reaps; mows, shaves
yekkân	weaving
yekkânzín	loom
yetté	weaves
yîzâ	sweetheart
yóbá cuʔ	rubber tube
yôgá	disease
yôudayâ	Thai, Siamese
yóun	booth, shed, building for work or business
yôun	court (-house)
yóundé	believes
yóun cídé	believes implicitly
youššímbwê	movie
youʔ tayeʔ	immediately
yúdé	brings, takes
yúšà	Russian
ywá	village
yweʔ	leaf
ywetthé	canvas, sailcloth

ywettʰéyóun tent
ywêidé selects, chooses
zagâ language, word, speech
zagabyán interpreter
zêi market, price
zûn spoon

Index